STORIES OF
the Children's Songbook

HOW THE PRIMARY SONGS CAME TO BE

PATRICIA KELSEY GRAHAM

Horizon Publishers
An Imprint of Cedar Fort, Inc.
Springville, Utah

To my dear grandchildren,
The messages in the Primary songs are true.
May they help to bring you happiness and harmony.

Love,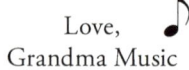
Grandma Music

© 2007, 2015 Patricia Kelsey Graham

All rights reserved.

No part of this book may be reproduced in any form whatsoever, whether by graphic, visual, electronic, film, microfilm, tape recording, or any other means, without prior written permission of the publisher, except in the case of brief passages embodied in critical reviews and articles.

ISBN 13: 978-1-4621-1691-1

Published by Horizon Publishers, an imprint of Cedar Fort, Inc., 2373 W. 700 S., Springville, UT, 84663
Distributed by Cedar Fort, Inc., www.cedarfort.com

The Library of Congress has catalogued the 2007 edition as follows:

Graham, Pat (Patricia Kelsey)
  We shall make music : stories of the Primary songs and how they came to be / Patricia Kelsey Graham.
    p. cm.
  Includes indexes.
  ISBN 978-0-88290-818-2 (alk. paper)
  1. Children's songbook of the Church of Jesus Christ of Latter-day Saints. 2. Church music--Mormon Church. 3. Primary Association (Church of Jesus Christ of Latter-day Saints) 4. Sacred vocal music--Juvenile--Bio-bibliography. I. Title.
  ML3174.G74 2007
  264'.09332023--dc22
                    2006039391

Cover design by Shawnda T. Craig
Cover design © 2015 Lyle Mortimer
Edited by Annaliese B. Cox and Kimiko M. Hammari
Typeset by Jessica B. Ellingson and Emily S. Chambers

Printed in the United States of America

10 9 8 7 6 5 4 3 2 1

Printed on acid-free paper

Contents

Foreword v
Preface vii
Acknowledgments xi
Introduction xiii
Part One: A History of Primary and Children's Music 1
Part Two: The Preparation of the 1989 *Children's Songbook* 21
Part Three: Stories about Primary Songs
    and the People Who Wrote Them 39
    My Heavenly Father 41
    The Savior 65
    The Gospel 99
    Home and Family 152
    Heritage 168
    Nature and Seasons 177
    Fun and Activity 191
    Prelude Music 212
Appendix One: Stories and author/composer information
    about Primary songs that are in the hymnbook but not
    in the *Children's Songbook* 225
Appendix Two: Reviews of the *Children's Songbook* 228

CONTENTS

Appendix Three: *Children's Songbook* activity pages.................. 231
Appendix Four: Author/composer quick reference 235
Appendix Five: Songs published in the *Friend* since
    the 1989 *Children's Songbook* (1988–2006)......................... 253
Index A: Authors, composers, and people of interest................. 258
Index B: Alphabetical song titles 265
Bibliography... 270
About the Author.. 272

Foreword

My earliest recollections of the importance of music in the lives of children came while I was serving as Primary pianist. I had just turned twelve when I received this church calling. At that time, Primary was held in the afternoon on a weekday. For three years, I would hurry home from junior high school and gather my music to be at the chapel with the children.

Music has always been a vital part of Primary. Music calmed the children as they tumbled into the church after school. I saw the smiles on their faces as they sang the fun songs. Rest songs helped get rid of the wiggles. All felt the spirit as the children sang about Heavenly Father and Jesus. I learned then that basic principles of the gospel of Jesus Christ are taught through music.

A special needs child I know was having great difficulty going to sleep at night. His mother asked me for advice. I suggested she play recorded Primary songs softly in the child's room. The spirit of the music touched this boy's heart and he was able to sleep.

When my ninety-six year old mother who was in a care center lost her ability to communicate, she would sit with me and listen as I sang Primary songs to her. Her face would light up, her eyes would sparkle, and she would mouth the words of "Jesus Wants Me for a Sunbeam" and "Little Purple Pansies." Other residents would gather around with smiles on their faces, which were ordinarily sad and unresponsive. Primary music can bring joy at any age and under any circumstance.

I was called as the Primary general president of The Church of Jesus Christ of Latter-day Saints April 5, 1980. This was a historic time for Primary because the consolidated meeting schedule was being implemented, which meant that the children would no longer attend Primary classes during the week but would meet on Sunday. With this change

FOREWORD

came many challenges. New lesson manuals were to be written. Because the Primary time on Sunday was extended, sharing time was added. Resources needed to be developed. Helps were required for weekday activities. One of our responsibilities was to create a new children's songbook which would combine some of the music publications that were currently being used.

Virginia Cannon, first counselor in the Primary General Presidency, was advisor of music. She supervised the project of the new book of children's songs. Pat Graham, a Primary general board member and chairman of the Primary Music Committee, was well prepared for this gigantic assignment. She had already published a book of her own songs. She was creative, visionary, musically skilled, and firm in the faith. She worked tirelessly along with the Primary Board Music Committee and countless other committees and individuals. After five years of diligent labor, the *Children's Songbook* was completed. This masterpiece, with its colorful illustrations and songs for every occasion, blesses the lives of all ages the world over.

Considering Pat's experience as a mother, teacher, composer, Primary leader, and advocate of music, it is appropriate that she now author the book *Stories of the Children's Songbook*. She shares her interactions with composers and authors. We learn of her reverence for music in the Church and particularly for music written specifically for children. This book is a valuable reference because it also contains facts and feelings that were previously published but are no longer in print. The information found in this book will be enlightening to Primary leaders, teachers, parents, and children. Learning the history of music in the Church as outlined by Pat gives greater appreciation for the resources that we have today. Knowing the background of the composers and the songs written will aid in using the selections more appropriately and with more understanding.

I love music and I love children. Our home and our own children have been enriched because of music. I know the value that music plays in reaching the heart and bearing testimony of the truths of the gospel of Jesus Christ. I recommend this book, which will increase understanding and appreciation for children's music and assist in making the music more meaningful for all of us.

Dwan Young

Preface

Aurelia Spencer Rogers, the founder of Primary, believed that children should be "taught everything good and how to behave."[1] That is precisely the purpose of the *Children's Songbook*—to teach children every good thing and how to behave as children of God.

For more than five years, many employees and volunteers worked to prepare the beautiful 1989 *Children's Songbook*. Why should a book of music warrant such an enormous effort? Elder Boyd K. Packer explained that the role of music in the kingdom is to help us feel the words of Christ. "We are able to feel and learn very quickly through music some spiritual things that we would otherwise learn very slowly."[2] It is important for children to learn the gospel, and what better way than through a song?

Previous resources containing the history of Primary and the music of Primary are out of print. This account was written to preserve that history and is intended to serve as a testimony of the effectiveness of music in teaching children the Gospel. It is from the author's perspective and experiences, and was gathered through personal communications with many of the composers and authors.

Important Primary history is contained in the mural, *The First Meeting of the Primary Association*. It was commissioned by the third general Primary president, May Green Hinckley, for the Farmington Rock Chapel in Farmington, Utah. Artist Lynn Fausett, assisted by Gordon Cope, painted the mural on the west wall behind the choir seats in the Farmington, Utah, chapel at 274 North Main. Twenty-one of the thirty-nine figures in the mural portray people who were present. The figures are close to life-size and were painted from photographs.

PREFACE

The First Meeting of the Primary Association: (1) George Rogers, (2) Leone Rogers Stewart, (3) Lucy Rogers Avery, (4) Lucy Robinson Coombs, (5) William Joseph Millard, (6) Amy Leonard, (7) Rose Walker Chaffin, (8) Gertrude Stayner Miller, (9) David Hughes, (10) Clara Leonard, (11) Louisa Leavitt Haight, (12) James Henry Robinson, (13) Amasa Lyman Clark, (14) Bishop John W. Hess, (15) Aurelia Spencer Rogers, (16) Sarah Richards Robinson, (17) Job Welling, (18) Mads Christensen, (19) Helen Mar Cheney Miller, (20) Rhoda Foss Richards, (21) Eliza Roxey Snow.

PREFACE

About the Artists

Lynn Fausett (1894–1977) was the oldest of eight children and was born in Price, Utah. He studied art at Brigham Young University, the University of Utah, and the Art Student's League in New York. For fourteen years, he served as president of that league. He studied fresco painting in France and mosaics in Germany and Italy. His murals adorned important buildings, such as the Nebraska State Capitol and others at the Chicago World's Fair. His mural technique employed gauche and tempera with oil varnishes rather than oil pigment. Many murals were commissioned for the Church, including *The First Meeting of the Primary Association*.

Gordon Nicholson Cope (1906–) was born in Salt Lake City, Utah, and now lives in San Francisco, California. He was a major Utah artist of the Great Depression. He founded the art department at the LDS University, was the director of the Art Barn School (now the Salt Lake Art Center), and taught for the MountainSchool of Art. He is known for his portraits of notorious Utah figures and landscape paintings. In addition to assisting Lynn Fausett with *The First Meeting of the Primary Association*, he worked on the murals for the Utah State Capitol.

The mural was made possible by the contributions of Primary children and leaders. (A duplicate of the mural was on the walls of the Primary general offices when they were located on the twentieth floor of the Church Office Building.) Thirteen of the original members of the first Primary were able to attend the dedication of the mural on August 24, 1941. Elder Charles A. Callis, Primary advisor and member of the Council of the Twelve, gave the dedicatory prayer. He prayed, "Heavenly Father, we thank Thee that Thou did put it in the heart of Thy daughters to instigate this wonderful Primary work. . . . May the memory of those wonderful women live with the organization, and may it stimulate us in every work which is part of heart and hand and soul. . . . We pray Thee to protect us and our children. May none of our children become lost."[3]

David C. Hess, son of Bishop Hess under whose direction Sister Rogers organized the first Primary, gave the invocation. Leone Rogers Stewart, daughter of Sister Rogers, gave the benediction. It was said that she was much like her mother, and in her prayer she said, "We say as she would say, 'Father unto thee we give all the praise and the glory.' Bless those who stand at the head of the wonderful organization, may they continue to receive Thy divine guidance. Bless the children everywhere."[4]

Notes

PREFACE

1 Rogers, *Life Sketches of Orson Spencer and Others, and History of Primary Work*, 207.
2 "The Arts and the Spirit of the Lord," *Ensign*, Aug. 1976, 61.
3 Hess, *My Farmington*, 298.
4 Ibid., 300.

Acknowledgments

Plato said that the best education is that a child should play amongst lovely things.[1] My mother, Mae Feinauer Kelsey, knew that intuitively. She taught me to recite poetry while she curled my hair; she encouraged me to draw and kept scrapbooks of my pictures; and she gave me fifty cents every week to pay for my piano lessons. When I received the assignment to prepare a new songbook, she shared the responsibility with me by tending my young children and loaning her car to me so I could attend meetings. In December 1988, just as the materials were completed and submitted to the printer, Mother had a heart attack. I prayed fervently that she would recover. I desperately wanted her to see the completed songbook, thinking it might somehow be rewarding for her to see what she had helped to bring to pass. I also wanted her to see that her influence had shaped the book through me. The songbook was published in May, and she passed away later that year. She had served twenty-five years in ward and stake Primary callings, and then another nine years with me in my calling. Since I cannot adequately thank her, I will try to be as supportive of my children as she was of me.

I am fortunate to have a husband who has always put "the wind beneath my wings." He built scenery for roadshows, nativity props for Christmas pageants, wooden games that I designed for the East Millcreek Lion's Fourth of July Carnivals, and parade floats for our family and neighbors. He provided the laptop and the new desk that facilitated the completion of this dream. Thank you, Bob, for supporting my creative habits.

Amy Fotheringham Rich, my neighbor and friend, carefully formatted this book. Throughout the project, I have relied on her suggestions and feedback which improved many aspects of the book. It has been a blessing to work with a kindred spirit.

ACKNOWLEDGMENTS

I would like to acknowledge the staff at Cedar Fort, Inc., including Duane Crowther, Heather Holm, Annaliese B. Cox, and Kimiko M. Hammari.

And to my sweet daughter-in-law, Amy Baird Graham; a final thank you for her lovely design suggestions and moral support.

Notes

1. Plato, online, "Quotes by Author," Teachon.com, available from www.teachon.com/zizi/quotes/alphabetical/pages/quotespq.htm.

Introduction

I grew up in the Church on the piano bench. By the time I was fourteen years old, I played either piano or organ everywhere I went. I had never met John Ovard before he gave me my patriarchal blessing, yet he said, "Never lose the virtues of your musical talent, for it will be the means of you doing much good in the Church." I thought I would be an accompanist forever, and I was happy. Years later, those words gave me courage when I felt the weight of my assignment as music chairman for the Primary general board.

The enormous responsibility of preparing a new songbook made me both excited and nervous. I had published a 32-page book of my own songs and became so consumed with the effort that I was overdrawn at the bank, missed voting in an election, and received my first traffic ticket. I wondered what would happen to me as I worked with hundreds of songs! I learned that we are magnified as we make our humble attempt to do what we are asked.

The Lord strengthened me as I worked on this book. I often proofed from eleven at night until three in the morning in order to be prepared for meetings the next day. This was my schedule for many months and I was never sick.

Heavenly Father also protected me. One day it was raining and I was rushing to a meeting at the Church Office Building in Salt Lake City. I had the only copy of the third cycle of the book on the back seat of my car. This was a compilation of all the corrections from four proofreaders who were checking the music type. As I pulled up to a light on 700 East and 2700 South, I had the distinct impression that I should change lanes. I thought to myself, "I am already going to be late. Moving up two car lengths won't make much difference." Then I felt very strongly that I should move, and I did. Just after I pulled into the right lane, a car

INTRODUCTION

skidded into the back of the car where I had been. If I had not moved, the papers would have been strewn on the wet street. Heavenly Father does bless us in natural ways as we serve in the Church.

One of the rewards of the assignment was to have contact with exceptional composers and authors. On a particular day I spoke on the phone with Crawford Gates in Beloit, Wisconsin; Carol Lynn Pearson in Walnut Creek, California; Laurence Lyon in Beaverton, Oregon; and Reid Nibley in Provo, Utah. My admiration for these and other talented Church members increased as I learned how willing gifted writers are to share their talents to strengthen and benefit children.

A little girl said, "You can always tell a Primary song because it makes you feel Heavenly Father-like!" There is a spirit about the *Children's Songbook*. That spirit helps us feel more like our Father in Heaven as we learn the songs that were prepared to strengthen this generation. The preface of the book explains how this can happen:

> As you sing, you may feel warm inside. The Holy Ghost gives you warm feelings to help you understand that the words and messages in the songs are true. You can learn about the gospel in this way, and your testimony will grow as you learn. You will remember more easily what you have learned when you sing about it. The melody of a song helps you remember the words and also brings the feeling of the song to your heart. The illustrations will also help you see what the songs teach. Once you know the songs, they can be with you always (like good friends) to help you make right choices and be happy.[1]

Beautiful art and music open the mind to spiritual feelings, and help condition the heart to recognize truth. The same part of the brain that responds to aesthetic beauty also responds to spiritual experiences. "Good music," said Elder Richard G. Scott, "especially sacred music, makes spiritual things more understandable. It is edifying and conducive to understanding. It prepares emotions for response to promptings of the Holy Spirit."[2]

A testimony is but a collection of whisperings of the Spirit witnessing the correctness of one principle and then another. That is the highest purpose of the songbook—to witness the truth of the gospel as it is sung in a pure and simple form. The last paragraph of the preface addresses this concept for children:

> Someday you will be leaders of the Church and of the world. What you learn from these songs will help you to be faithful and to serve

INTRODUCTION

righteously. The good feelings the songs bring will give you happiness and courage and will help you to remember that you are children of God.[3]

The songs are fulfilling their purpose whether played simply or performed elaborately. Nothing is sweeter than hearing a long-distance grandchild sing Primary songs over the telephone. And it is a divine glimpse of heaven when the Tabernacle Choir and Orchestra at Temple Square perform arrangements that have grown out of these simple songs. Over and over again the songs inspire us whether they are sung at conferences, baptismal services, firesides, and funerals, or enjoyed as organ music in the temple.

I bear testimony that the book is as it was intended to be, for I often saw flashes of it in my mind's eye before it was published. Decisions and choices were often moments of recognition of a design that I had seen before. Because of this sweet opportunity, I know for a surety that it is more wonderful to be an instrument than to play one. As Alma said, "I glory in that which the Lord hath commanded me. I glory not of myself" (Alma 29:9).

May the *Children's Songbook* be a source of inspiration, a thing of beauty, and a joy forever. And from it may we "learn everything good and how to behave."[4]

Notes

1. *Children's Songbook*, preface, iii.
2. Richard G. Scott, "Finding Happiness," *Speeches: Brigham Young University*, 363.
3. *Chidren's Songbook*, preface, iii.
4. Rogers, *Life Sketches of Orson Spencer and Others, and History of Primary Work*, 207.

PART ONE

A History OF Primary and Children's Music

Part One

The following timeline chronicles the development of Primary and music materials for children. The timeline outlines this section and highlights the administration of each general Primary president through the publication of the 1989 *Children's Songbook*.

1835   *A Collection of Sacred Hymns, for the Church of the Latter Day Saints* published
1878   The first Primary organized
1880   *Hymns and Songs* published
1880   *Tune Book for the Primary Associations of the Children of Zion* published
1880   General Primary Association organized with Louis Bouton Felt as president
1904   *Deseret Sunday School Union Music Book* published
1905   *The Primary Song Book* published
1925   May Anderson second general Primary president
1940   *Little Stories in Song* published
1940   May Green Hinckley third general Primary president
1943   Adele Cannon Howells fourth general Primary president
1951   *The Children Sing* published
1951   LaVern Watts Parmley fifth general Primary president
1969   *Sing With Me* published
1974   Naomi Maxfield Shumway sixth general Primary president
1980   Dwan Jacobsen Young seventh general Primary president
1985   *Hymns of The Church of Jesus Christ of Latter-day Saints* published
1988   Michaelene Packer Grassli eighth general Primary president
1989   The *Children's Songbook* published

PART ONE

1835 *A Collection of Sacred Hymns, for the Church of the Latter Day Saints* Published

In 1830, the Prophet Joseph Smith received a revelation instructing his wife, **Emma Hale Smith** (1804–1879), to "make a selection of sacred hymns" (D&C 25:11). This was just three months after the publication of the Book of Mormon and the organization of the Church. The hymns selected by Emma set a worthy standard for subsequent additions. The collection of ninety hymns included thirty-three by the following Mormon authors: twenty-six attributed to W. W. Phelps, three to Parley P. Pratt, one to Thomas P. Marsh and Pratt, and one each to Eliza R. Snow, Edward Partridge, and Philo Dibble. The remaining fifty-seven texts were adapted or rewritten versions of hymns in general use by the Baptists and Campbellites. Phelps was to correct and print the anthology but was delayed because the Book of Commandments was being prepared and printed. Then the Independence printing press was destroyed by a mob, and a new one had to be acquired. Finally, the hymnal was published in August 1835 in Kirtland, Ohio, by F. G. Williams & Company. (In December 2006, one of three known surviving hymnals was sold at auction for $273,600). A replica of *A Collection of Sacred Hymns, for the Church of the Latter-day Saints* was published in 1973 by Herald Heritage Reprint and is available at the Kirtland Temple store and LDS bookstores. The little book measured 3x4½ inches and could fit in a coat pocket. None of the songs were directed specifically to children.

Emma Hale Smith
First General Relief Society President

The brown pocketbook contained texts only, with no music notation. Hymn texts were sung to familiar melodies and often interchanged. A conductor might say, "We will now sing Hymn 86 to the tune of the 'Old Oaken Bucket.'" The same text might be sung to another melody another week by another congregation. This practice continued until music notation was included with hymn texts, and explains the use of more than one melody for some hymns even today.

As an example, a common meter for many songs is 7777. That means the text (such as "Jesus, Once of Humble Birth," Hymn 196) has seven syllables on each of the four lines. The words will fit any other melody that is also described as 7777, such as Hymn 306, "God's Daily Care" (a favorite Primary prayer song selected for the hymnbook). The following Primary melodies are also 7777 and could be interchanged: Thanks to Thee, 6; Heavenly Father, Now I Pray, 19; A Song of Thanks, 20; Thank Thee, Father, 24; We Are Reverent, 27; Little Lambs so White and Fair, 58; Dearest Mother, I Love You, 206; and Rain Is Falling All Around, 241. For more about meters, see page 405 of the 1985 hymnbook.

Music has always been an important part of worshipping God. The Latter-day Saints have sung wherever they gathered, whether at homes, churches, temples, or campfires. They sang songs for rejoicing, for encouragement, and for solace. They sang doctrines of the kingdom, and their songs became prayers unto God.

1878 The First Primary Organized

Bishop John W. Hess had been concerned about the rowdy behavior of the young boys in the Farmington Utah Ward. He called a meeting of the mothers to discuss ways they might help to guide the minds of their children. **Aurelia Spencer Rogers** (1834–1922), one of the mothers, reflected upon the idea and wondered, "Could there not be an organization for little boys wherein they could be taught everything good, and how to behave?"[1] She told **Eliza Roxey Snow** (1804–1887), her friend and the Relief Society general president, about her idea. Eliza suggested the organization be called "Primary." Aurelia thought that they would probably want to have singing in the meetings, and so the girls ought to be included "to make it sound as well as it should."[2] Sister Snow discussed the matter with John Taylor, President of the Council of the Twelve and presiding officer after the death of Brigham Young. He approved and directed Bishop Hess to call Sister Rogers to preside over an organization of the children in Farmington. She was set apart August 11, 1878, with her counselors, **Louisa Leavitt Haight** (grandmother of Apostle David B. Haight) and **Helen Mar Cheney Miller.** Soon after, **Rhoda H. Richards** was chosen as secretary, with her daughter Sarah as assistant, and **Clara A. Leonard** as treasurer.

In the next two weeks, the new presidency visited every home in the ward. They recorded the names and ages of 224 children and invited them to the first Primary meeting. On Sunday, August 25, 1878, Bishop

PART ONE

Hess, Eliza R. Snow, and the new presidency stood before 215 children who had come to the rock chapel for instruction.

Aurelia Spencer Rogers
Founder and First Ward Primary President

There were no manuals, no teachers, and no visual aids. In her life story Aurelia wrote, "We were very weak indeed, but felt to lean upon the Lord in all humility."[3] The women taught lessons on honesty (don't go into orchards and melon patches that are not your own); manners (don't quarrel with your brothers and sisters); and safety (don't hang on to wagons, a practice which is not only wrong, but dangerous). They carried out service projects, such as planting gardens, and also taught the children to sing. Aurelia wrote, "We wish to encourage in our children a love for music, also a love for all things beautiful."[4] Sister Snow's poem, "In Our Lovely Deseret," helped to teach many gospel precepts. It was sung to the tune of a popular Civil War song, "Tramp! Tramp! Tramp!," and became a favorite with the children. The chorus of the same tune was also used as the melody for "Jesus Loves the Little Children."

Sister Snow organized Primaries throughout the territory as she visited in her capacity as general Relief Society president. She felt strongly that "the very best talent in our midst should be employed to preside over the Primary Associations . . . women who loved children and had the faculty of drawing them to them."[5] Her enthusiasm for the work spread throughout the valley.

Aurelia Rogers was the mother of twelve children, five of whom died as infants. She became a beloved role model. She wrote:

> I smile when I hear modern mothers say they can't find time to teach Primary. . . . For sixty years I did my big wash by hand; I kneaded and baked bread sometimes twelve loaves a day; sewed all our clothes with a needle and thread and thimble; swept my floors with a broom made from willows I gathered on the river bank; scrubbed my furniture with sand and rags. I've worked in the fields; I've battled grasshoppers; I supported a large family while my husband was on a mission. I did

have hardships and sorrows, but it was a good life because I loved my husband, my children, my neighbors and my home. Above all, I loved my Heavenly Father.[6]

Sister Rogers served as both Relief Society secretary and Farmington Primary president for fifteen years. She was then called to serve as a Primary general board member, serving twenty-nine years until her death in 1922. As a project for the Jubilee celebration of the Church, the Primary general board sponsored the publication of Aurelia Spencer Rogers' *Life Sketches of Orson Spencer and Others, and History of Primary Work*. Each ward contributed to the effort, which was the first of general Primary projects. In the dedication of her book, Aurelia lovingly wrote: "Our children are our jewels; we have counted well the cost; May their angels ever guard them, and not one child be lost."[7]

1880 *Hymns and Songs: Selected from various authors, for the Primary Associations of the Children of Zion*
Published by Deseret News Printing and Publishing

One-hundred twenty-one pages of songs with words only were in the *Hymns and Songs* publication compiled by Eliza R. Snow. Several songs were given titles, but most were identified only by a number, as were the hymns in Emma's pocketbook. The collection included some of today's favorite hymn texts such as "The Spirit of God," "Joseph Smith's First Prayer," "Do What Is Right," and "O My Father." The remaining pages were children's texts. The following four texts have been included in every songbook since 1880: "All Things Bright and Beautiful," "Dare to Do Right," "I Thank Thee Dear Father," and "I Think When I Read That Sweet Story," formerly entitled "Child's Desire." The suggested melodies, however, did not survive.

1880 **Tune Book for the Primary Associations of the Children of Zion Published**

Eliza R. Snow enlisted **Mrs. Doctor Ferguson** to arrange and notate music for many of the Primary song texts. The result was a forty-page tune book printed in Salt Lake City by the Juvenile Instructor Office. The book included fifty-nine Mormon and non-Mormon hymns with both words and music, which was reissued through the 1890s. Suggestions were included for combining melodies in this collection with other texts in the *Hymns and Songs*.

PART ONE

1880 The General Primary Association Organized with Louie Bouton Felt as President

Before the Farmington Primary was one month old, Eliza Snow had organized another in the Salt Lake City Eleventh Ward. **Louie Bouton Felt** (1850–1928), served as president, and two years later was called as the first general Primary president. When asked to serve, she replied, "I am not worthy and am so ignorant. I could not fill that position. I'm sure I could not." Sister Snow said, "If you thought you could we would not want you."[8] Louie held three positions for the next five years—ward Primary president, stake YLMIA counselor, and general Primary president. She served as general Primary president from the time she was 30 until she was 75 years of age (1880–1925). Her service spanned five prophets—Presidents John Taylor (1877–1887), Wilford Woodruff (1887–1898), Lorenzo Snow (1898–1901), Joseph F. Smith (1901–1918), and Heber J. Grant (1918–1945).

As a young bride, Louie had been called by Brigham Young to go with her husband to settle the Muddy River Mission in Nevada. The hardship of the 300-mile journey had caused a miscarriage, and further complications left her unable to have children. Though childless herself, Louie knew how to influence children for good. She entered their games and danced with them, and was described as "a child among the children, happy in the things she and they loved."[9] She took classes to receive a kindergarten teaching diploma, and moved Primary teaching from rote and drill methods to developmental child-centered teaching, viewing the teacher as a leader rather than a taskmaster. Eventually, Louie encouraged her husband to take two other wives so that he would have posterity. She helped to raise their children, and her generous husband continued to support her Primary work by paying all her travel expenses. She suffered rheumatism but placed duty above discomfort by attending meetings with a slipper on one foot.

Louie Bouton Felt
First General
Primary President

STORIES OF THE CHILDREN'S SONGBOOK

Sister Felt gave her home as collateral for the initial printing of *The Children's Friend*. The magazine was published in 1902 as a resource for teachers and included lessons for each primary grade. Her friend and secretary, May Anderson, helped her wrap the magazines in brown paper, hand address them, tie them with string, and carry them to be mailed. A Primary songbook was printed in 1905, and The Latter-day Saint Children's Convalescent Home and Day Nursery was established in 1922. During her forty-five-year presidency, the Primary general board expanded to twenty-six members, and Primary membership grew to more than 61,000 children.

1904   *Deseret Sunday School Union Music Book* Published

The *Deseret Sunday School Union Music Book* was prepared for the Sunday School, but also served the needs of Primary. The book was reprinted as the *Deseret Sunday School Song Book* and then as *Deseret Sunday School Songs*. Several additional reprints were made into the 1930s. The music collection contained hymns, songs, and voluntaries. At the turn of the century there were very few books written for children, and even fewer songs. Children sang nursery rhymes and game songs or adult folk songs. Preparing a collection of songs for children was very progressive.

1905   *The Primary Song Book* Published by the Primary General Board

The Primary Song Book was prepared with May Andersen directing the selection of songs. The collection updated Eliza Snow's hymnbook and tune book, which had been reissued through the 1890s. *The Primary Song Book* contained ninety-three songs, including marches, voluntaries, and seasonal songs. "Little Johnny Vegetable" and "The Toothbug Song" were two of many favorites. "The Primary Penny Song" motivated children to contribute to the building of the Children's Hospital in Salt Lake City. As they sang "Five pennies make a nickel, two nickels make a dime," boys and girls would drop their coins in a little Primary bank "for the crippled children who cannot walk or run, who have to lie in bed all day and cannot join our fun."[10] The small brown book contained the "Fairies and Elves March" and other pieces with imaginative moods. The level of the music was rather demanding and definitely meant for an adult to play, because there were many left-hand octaves and up to five flats in the key signatures. The collection was updated eight times,

PART ONE

adding holiday songs such as "A Hallowe'en Surprise," "Jolly Old St. Nicholas," and "Up on the Housetop." By 1948 the edition had 131 songs.

1925–1939   May Anderson Second General Primary President

As a young convert to the Church, **May Anderson** (1864–1946), was invited to stay with Louie Felt while Brother Felt went on a business trip. After he returned, Sister Anderson was invited to stay on with them. May's given name was Mary, but there were many other Marys in Louie's circle of family and friends, and so she called her May. The two women enrolled in a kindergarten-training course and opened a school of their own. May was asked to be an instructor at the University of Utah Training School and was counselor to Louie in the Eleventh Ward Primary presidency.

When Louie became general president, she asked May to take notes for her at meetings, and in 1890, May was sustained as general secretary. After fifteen years as secretary, she became first counselor to President Felt. She was the first editor of *The Children's Friend* and directed the publication of *The Primary Song Book*. Following twenty years of service as counselor, Heber J. Grant, who served as the seventh President of the Church (1918–1945), called May to be the next general Primary president. Fourteen years in this calling made a total of forty-nine years' service on the general level.

May Anderson
Second General
Primary President

May Anderson was hesitant when asked to serve as Sister Felt's secretary because she was uncomfortable about speaking in public. Throughout her devoted service she prayed, "Father, put my feet in the path you wish me to tread, and I'll do the best I can."[11] During her presidency, the LDS Children's Convalescent Home and Day Nursery (located on North Temple between Main and West Temple) was financed by children's birthday pennies, and eventually by an annual Penny Parade. The fiftieth Primary "Jubilee" birthday was celebrated in 1928 with parades and

STORIES OF THE CHILDREN'S SONGBOOK

programs, and the first Primary handbook was printed in 1930. Primaries had been organized worldwide under her direction, and enrollment was 100,000 children with 18,000 leaders serving them.

The first two general Primary presidents, though childless themselves, had shaped the first sixty years of the organization. President Felt and President Anderson greatly enriched the lives of the children of the Church.

1940 *Little Stories in Song* **Published by the Deseret Sunday School Union**

A collection of songs for younger children was prepared in 1940. The book included "All Things Bright and Beautiful," "Once Within a Lowly Stable," "Father, We Thank Thee for the Night," and "Little Lambs So White and Fair," which still exist in today's songbook. The major contributors to the book were Moiselle Renstrom (1889-1956) and Frances Kingsbury Thomassen Taylor (1870–1952), two Latter-day Saint early childhood educators and musicians. Sister Renstrom was a teacher who knew the range for children's voices, wrote so that it was easy to play, and taught well with her rhymes. In addition, her work was doctrinally accurate. Her songbooks, *Merrily We Sing*, *Musical Adventures*, and *Rhythm Fun*, have been used by early childhood teachers throughout the world. Sister Taylor received her musical education in piano, organ, harmony, and counterpoint at the University of Utah and Columbia University, and served as secretary of the General Primary Association for eight years. Her songbook, *Kindergarten and Primary Songs*, was used in many Junior Sunday Schools.

1940–1943   May Green Hinckley
Third General Primary President

May Hinckley (1881–1943) had served as a missionary in the Central States Mission, and then became the first manager of the business office at the Salt Lake Medical Clinic. She was stake YWMIA president when she married Bryant S. Hinckley, a widower with thirteen children from two previous wives who had died. Five of the children were still at home, one of them being Gordon Bitner Hinckley. After Bryant and May were married, he was called to serve as president of the Northern States Mission in 1935. She was an effective mission mother, serving as president of the mission's Relief Society, Primary, and YWMIA. She

PART ONE

May Green Hinckley
Third General
Primary President

often closed her correspondence with "Let us love. Let us serve. Let us work together."[12]

Five months after returning from the mission field, President Heber J. Grant (1918–1945) called Sister Hinckley to preside over the Primary. He said, "May, we're going to give you 102,000 children."[13] She expressed her feelings of inadequacy, but her husband encouraged her to try it. During her presidency, an official Primary seal was designed, the scripture theme—"And they shall also teach their children to pray, and to walk uprightly before the Lord" (D&C 68:28)—was adopted and the Primary colors of red, yellow, and blue were selected. Lynn Fausett was commissioned to depict the first Primary meeting, and his mural was dedicated in the rock meetinghouse in Farmington, Utah. The focus of Primary was changed from recreational to scriptural activities. President Hinckley encouraged 18,000 teachers and leaders to "brighten the home, strengthen the hands of parents, and teach the gospel to children during their most impressionable years."[14] Home Primary replaced many Primary meetings in the mission field because of wartime gas rationing, and leadership and conference meetings were eliminated as well as other travel.

May Hinckley suffered acutely from arthritis, and in 1943 entered the hospital for treatment. She insisted that she did not want to go to the hospital, since that was where people go to die. While she was there, she contracted pneumonia. She passed away the day after her sixty-second birthday, just three years after being called to lead the Primary, and eleven years after her marriage. Once childless, she had served thirteen of her husband's children, hundreds of missionaries, and more than 102,000 children of the Church.

1943–1951   Adele Cannon Howells
            Fourth General Primary President

Adele Howells (1886–1951) brought a wealth of experience and vision to her Primary callings. She had traveled the world with her husband,

David, distributing silent movies made in the United States. They had a costume company which provided for many Hollywood productions, and owned many acres of grazing land in northern Utah as well as a ranch in the Uintah Mountains of eastern Utah. David served as the first bishop of the Wilshire Ward in the new Hollywood California Stake, and they were instrumental in obtaining the land for the Los Angeles Temple. When her husband died suddenly of a heart attack, Adele wrote in her diary, "I can't keep my mind off my terrible loss,"[15] and prayed that she would be able to press on. While trying to decide whether to remain in Los Angeles or return to Salt Lake City, she received an answer to her prayer. She was called to serve as a counselor to her friend, May Hinckley. "What a Godsend work is!" she wrote. "I'm so busy I have not time to think about myself and how lonesome I am."[16]

Addie, as her friends called her, was a refined and generous woman. She believed in developing cultural and artistic skills in children as well as in promoting their spiritual education. She had been an English teacher and was appointed editor of *The Children's Friend*. When her service with May was abruptly ended, she wrote, "It poured rain during the night as if nature was weeping for May's death." She generously paid for May's hospital expenses, and wrote in her diary, "I have said good-bye to one of my dearest friends."[17]

Adele Cannon Howells
Fourth General
Primary President

Two months later, President Grant called her to serve as the fourth general Primary president. As counselors, she chose Dessie Grant Boyle (her lifelong friend and the prophet's daughter) and LaVern Watts Parmley. She established new creative sections in *The Children's Friend*, and began a weekly local radio story time in 1946. The program was called *Children's Friend of the Air*, and it was followed in 1948 by a local TV quiz show called *The Junior Council*. Children contributed to the Penny Parade and donated nickels to help erect a "This is the Place" Monument. President Howells donated her own time and money to the building of a new Primary Children's Hospital, and invited children to

PART ONE

give dimes to "buy-a-brick" for the effort. After the war, Primary children in the United States were encouraged to help Primary children in war-torn countries. Children donated clothing and toys to be shipped to Europe.

President Howells believed in the enriching effect of beautiful art and commissioned three murals for the baptismal area of the Idaho Falls Temple. To help children learn scripture stories, she personally paid for a series of Book of Mormon paintings by Arnold Friberg. Prints were published in *The Children's Friend* as part of the fiftieth anniversary of the magazine, and Sister Howells donated the originals to the Church. These unique paintings brought Brother Friberg to the attention of Cecil B. DeMille, who hired him to design sets and costumes for the epoch motion picture, *The Ten Commandments*.

For her community service, Adele Howells was elected to the Salt Lake City Hall of Fame. She always acted on her belief that material blessings were a means to helping others, and taught her three adopted children, "We must not keep everything for our own comfort."[18]

Several days after speaking in the Tabernacle for Primary general conference, she passed away. Her childhood rheumatic fever had weakened her heart, and her friend Dessie said she died "in the harness" as she had always hoped she would.

1951   *The Children Sing* Published

The "blue book" collection of songs for children was prepared by a joint committee from the Sunday School and Primary Association general boards. The songbook contained 199 songs and 13 devotional preludes. The cover had an imprint of three children singing, and the contents were organized into seven categories with a divider page for each section.

This book contained "God Gave Me Dear America," which was sung with energetic actions; a five-page arrangement of the "Crusader's Hymn" (now entitled "Beautiful Savior"); and the original words to the "Handcart Song" (no text credit). Many hymns were included as well as seasonal songs such as "Jolly Old St. Nicholas." The book was for the American Latter-day Saint, and required a high level of piano proficiency.

Author's Note: When I was eleven years old, I was asked to be Primary pianist for the Salt Lake Whittier Ward. I especially loved the classical preludes and postludes in the back of the blue songbook. Primary was on a weekday and I came straight from school to the meeting. I had everything I needed in one book. Although I had been studying piano for four years, many of the songs required a great deal of practice for me to play.

The songs we learn in Primary remain indelible in our minds. How is that possible? At general conference, President Kimball was able to sing the words to every hymn even when he was ill and not able to stand and address us. During the filming of a Primary satellite program, President Ezra Taft Benson sang spontaneously to a group of children seated around him. This was a few months before he died, yet he remembered every word to his favorite Primary song, "I Am a Mormon Boy." How can a song you have not sung for fifty or sixty years remain secure in your memory? Some of us are hard-pressed to remember who spoke in sacrament meeting last week, let alone what they spoke about. Yet, if you were to hear the tune to "Give Said the Little Stream," all of the words would float back into your memory. Advertisers are willing to pay huge sums for catchy commercials because they know we can't get the jingles out of our heads! If you watched TV in the 1950s, you will remember, "You'll wonder where the yellow went when you brush your teeth with _____." That jingle is over fifty years old, yet we can fill in the blank with Pepsodent. Research in connection with Alzheimer patients has shown that words and music memorized together remain after other parts of memory are lost. Knowing this should prompt us to teach the songs as permanent, singable testimonies laminated to children's souls. William Wordsworth (1770–1850), a British poet, expressed the idea by saying, "The music in my heart I bore. Long after it was heard no more."[19]

1951–1974   LaVern Watts Parmley
             Fifth General Primary President

LaVern Parmley (1900–1980) was the mother of three children, an experienced schoolteacher, and a longtime Primary worker. Her youngest child was five years old when she was called to the Primary general board by Sister Hinckley, and she gave continuous service for the next twenty-five years. Sister Parmley served as a counselor to both her predecessors and had seen the Primary enrollment grow to more than 157,000 children. Children often referred to her as "Sister Primary." With two sons of her own, and many brothers in a family of eleven children, she considered boys to be her "specialty." Scouting for the eleven-year-old boys and Cub Scouting were introduced into Primary in 1953. President Parmley became the first woman ever called to a national Scouting committee and the first woman to receive the Silver Buffalo, the highest

PART ONE

LaVern Watts Parmley
Fifth General
Primary President

honor given in Scouting. The Great Salt Lake Council of the BSA said of her, "Probably no other woman has done more to develop and conserve America's most precious resource—Boypower."[20]

The new Primary Children's Hospital on Twelfth Avenue and D Street in Salt Lake City was completed and dedicated in 1952. Years later, after an additional wing had been added, Sister Parmley said, "I think the most rewarding thing I've ever done in my life is to work with the hospital and to see . . . how many children it has helped."[21] At the conclusion of her service in 1974, the Church donated all medical facilities, including her beloved Primary Children's Hospital, to a non-profit organization.

During President Parmley's administration, the Primary general board consisted of seventy capable women who worked hard to perform to her high expectations. They were assigned to visit wards and stakes, and to prepare lesson manuals, training meetings, and general Primary conferences. For the April 1957 General Primary Conference, Sister Parmley asked Naomi W. Randall to write a new song to focus on teaching children the gospel. The introduction of "I Am a Child of God," the result of Sister Randall's words and Mildred T. Pettit's music, was an enduring contribution from her leadership. New Primary music materials were prepared, and *Sing with Me*, the first of three volumes, was published in 1969. Also, under Sister Parmley's administration, *The Children's Friend* magazine simply became known as the *Friend* in 1971. She served with two Church Presidents: David O. McKay (1951–1970) and Joseph Fielding Smith (1970–1972).

1969 *Sing with Me* Published

Judith Wirthlin Parker, Primary music chairman, directed the preparation of *Sing with Me*, which was distinguished by its bright orange cover. Musicians within the Church were asked to write on particular gospel topics to create a volume that would teach the doctrines through music. "The Golden Plates," "Tithing," "Book of Mormon Stories," and many other songs were created that appealed to children and taught principles specific to the Church.

Sing with Me was published in 1969 and contained 217 songs. It was followed by an additional twenty-six songs and thirty-nine poems in *Activity Songs and Verses* in 1977. *More Songs for Children* was completed in 1978 with thirty-four songs, and then finally *Supplement to More Songs for Children* in 1982. The supplement had ten songs, including new class songs and songs from recent Sacrament Meeting presentations. Copyright information was included for the first time in the last supplement. The entire set of "orange" publications had expanded to 297 songs and thirty-nine verses.

Originally, it had been thought that each group of songs would be added to the first hardback spiral book. But in the end, each group was a separate item. That meant the total cost was higher, and it also meant a lot of looking to locate a particular song. The combined cost of the "orange" songbook materials, published from 1969 through 1982 was in excess of $12.

Naomi Maxfield Shumway
Sixth General
Primary President

1974–1980   Naomi Maxfield Shumway
Sixth General Primary President

After serving eleven years on the Primary general board under Sister Parmley, **Naomi Shumway** (1922–2004) became the sixth general Primary president. As a leader, she combined a gentle manner and a giant capacity for dedication. Primary enrollment was 588,000 children and 116,000 leaders. In 1975, the Primary Parade was replaced with the Primary Birthday Pennies which encouraged members to donate to the Children's Medical Center according to their age.

Sister Shumway was active in Scouting and received the Silver Fawn Award. Under her direction, Primaries throughout the world participated in the Primary centennial year with programs, parades, fairs, and tree plantings. She requested the writing of a musical to commemorate the life of Aurelia Spencer Rogers and the beginning

PART ONE

of Primary. *Aurelia* was presented at the Promised Valley Playhouse, and scripts were available for use outside the valley. She said, "The needs of children are still the same as they were a hundred years ago, even though they might be met in different ways."²²

Responding to the worldwide growth of the Church, plans were made to combine the best parts of Junior Sunday School and Primary. New manuals were in process when the consolidated schedule was announced, and Primary was held on Sunday and expanded to one hour and forty minutes.

1980–1988   Dwan Jacobsen Young
              Seventh General Primary President

Dwan Young (1931–) was called to the Primary general board in 1970, the year that her mother completed seventeen years of service on that board. Sister Young is the mother of five children, an accomplished musician, an active Scouter, and the recipient of the Silver Beaver, Silver Antelope, and Silver Buffalo Awards.

When Sister Young became president in 1980, Primary enrollment was 600,000 children and 126,000 leaders worldwide. With the consolidated meeting schedule, Primary was held on Sunday as it was when first organized. The additional block of time in Sunday Primary was named Sharing Time, and leaders were encouraged to actively involve children in teaching each other. Once again, the *Friend* magazine provided appropriate stories and activities that leaders could adapt for Sunday use. During her presidency, new lesson manuals were completed and the Gospel in Action program was implemented.

Dwan Jacobsen Young
Seventh General
Primary President

President Young's board consisted of fourteen women plus the presidency and executive secretary, and stake visits were as invited or assigned by the Priesthood. The wives of Area Authorities received auxiliary training to help with worldwide needs, and the auxiliary offices were moved into the Relief Society Building to unify the work. President Young described Primary by

STORIES OF THE CHILDREN'S SONGBOOK

saying, "Children worldwide are being taught the Gospel of Jesus Christ by loving teachers who are growing as they are serving."[23]

The priesthood advisors to Primary requested that the Primary music resources be consolidated under one cover. This would reduce the cost of music materials. It was also suggested that the songs should be simplified so that more people in the Church could use the book. A survey of the use of Primary songs was made, and the majority of the preparation of the *Children's Songbook* was done under Sister Young's direction.

1985 *Hymns of the Church of Jesus Christ of Latter-day Saints* published

The 1985 hymnbook was published on the 150th anniversary of the first hymnal and is considered part of the scriptural canon of the Church. After issuing a call for submissions, the General Music Committee of the Church evaluated over 6,000 new hymns as well as those contained in the previous hymnal. They carefully sifted out those seldom sung and preserved hymns that represented the finest of former generations. Many of those retained have undergone editing of both text and music. The book contains 341 hymns; seventy-nine are *new* hymns and twenty-six are from Emma's first collection. User-friendly features include seven indexes and a section on how to use the hymnbook. Each hymn includes a tempo marking, introductory brackets, author and composer birth and death dates, and scripture references. For the first time, ten songs written for children were included in the hymnbook.

Michaelene Grassli
Eighth General
Primary President

1988–1994   Michaelene Packer Grassli
Eighth General Primary President

Michaelene Grassli (1940–) became general Primary president in April 1988 after serving five years as a board member with President Shumway and eight years as second counselor to President Young. She had spent many hours driving to meetings in Salt Lake from her home in Pleasant View near Ogden, Utah. Her stewardship included 664,000 children and 134,000 leaders.

PART ONE

Sister Grassli participated in the development of the new songbook and saw the project to its completion in 1989. She said, "I don't think the Church has published anything more lovely than this songbook. It was intended for families to use in their homes as well as for use in Primary. It does what the rest of the world can't do for children, but what we do best—teach the gospel."[24] Her presidency directed the work of translating and recording the songs. She was selected as the 2006 Utah Mother of the Year.

1989   The Children's Songbook Presented to the Church

In April 1989, the completed *Children's Songbook* was presented at a celebration in the Assembly Hall. Authors, composers, and others who had worked on the preparation of the book attended. A children's choir performed, and the following unique features of the book were explained:

1. Beautiful two-page four-color illustrations divide the book into seven sections, with another 150 pieces of small art used to extend the message of the songs.
2. The accompaniments have been simplified and introductory brackets, fingering, and chord symbols are marked.
3. Obbligatos, descants, and ostinatos are provided to challenge older children.
4. Each song has several scripture references, and birth and death dates and maiden names are given for authors and composers.
5. The table of contents lists every song in each section, and there are three indexes—author/composer, topic, and title and first line.
6. A section called "Using the Songbook" provides instructions for teaching, conducting, and accompanying, and includes a chord chart and a dictionary of symbols and terms.
7. Copyright and royalty information is included on the page with each song.
8. The new book is directed to children as well as leaders, and contains 255 songs and thirteen preludes.

There have been many changes since the early music collections. Songs no longer encourage Saints to come to Zion as did the original verses of "The Handcart Song." With the expansion of the Church, generic patriotic songs were needed to meet the needs of all Primary children. The songs in the 1989 *Children's Songbook* were selected to teach gospel principles in a worldwide Church. As its preface reminds us, "Music is a language that everyone can understand. Children all over the world sing these same songs."[25] May the songs build testimony and strength in this generation, so that every child might know how and remember to act like a child of God.

Notes

Line drawings by Beth Maryon Whittaker for my Aug./Sep. 1983 *Friend*, Sharing Time page 34–35 used by permission. Additional drawings of Emma Smith and Michaelene Grassli are the author's.

1. Rogers, *Life Sketches of Orson Spencer and Others, and History of Primary Work*, 207.
2. Ibid., 209.
3. Ibid., 215.
4. Ibid., 229.
5. Madsen and Oman, *Sisters and Little Saints*, 13.
6. Ibid., 27; *Women's Exponent*, 8 Dec. 1879, 110.
7. Rogers, *Life Sketches*, iii.
8. Madsen and Oman, *Sisters and Little Saints*, 29.
9. Ibid.; *Journal History of the Church*, 28 Apr. 1928, 4.
10. *Deseret Sunday School Songs*, 160.
11. Madsen and Oman, *Sisters and Little Saints*, 94.
12. Peterson and Gaunt, *The Children's Friends*, 41.
13. Ibid., 53; "English-Born Leader Guides Destiny of 102,000 Children," *LDS Church News*, 4 Apr. 1964, 20.
14. Madsen and Oman, *Sisters and Little Saints*, 110.
15. Peterson and Gaunt, 67; Adele Howells' diary entries.
16. Ibid.
17. Ibid., 68.
18. Ibid., 75.
19. Graham, *A Children's Songbook Companion*, 8.
20. Peterson and Gaunt, *The Children's Friends*, 95.
21. Ibid., 97.
22. Madsen and Oman, *Sisters and Little Saints*, 190.
23. General Conference Primary Openhouse talk, unpublished.
24. Peterson and Gaunt, *The Children's Friends*, 157.
25. *Children's Songbook*, preface, iii.

PART TWO

The Preparation of the 1989 Children's Songbook

From personal experiences and records of the author

Part Two

"Can anyone doubt that good music is godly or that there can be something of the essence of heaven in great art?"[1]
—President Gordon B. Hinckley

A. Stewardship and Committees

The 1989 *Children's Songbook* was prepared under the leadership of General Primary President **Dwan Jacobsen Young**. First Counselor **Virginia Beesley Cannon** was responsible for music in Primary and was advisor to the Primary Music Committee. I was called as Primary music chairman in October 1983 with **Virginia Byrd Allred** and **Mayre Beth Stevens** as committee members. The songbook project was first explained in January 1984 while I met with Sister Cannon in her office on the twentieth floor of the Church Office Building. As she explained my responsibility, feelings of inadequacy engulfed me, and I was overcome with a desire to disappear through the floor of the room and drop down twenty floors into oblivion. When I realized that that was not an option, a thousand questions overwhelmed me instead. During the following five years, I felt an incredible sense of being lifted up and directed. Many times I experienced a wonderful tingling sensation as the importance of the songbook was confirmed to me. The power of those moments gave me the energy to continue when I was tired, and the faith to search for answers when I didn't know how to do the next step.

The book was to be a compilation and simplification of existing materials rather than a call for new songs as the hymnbook had been. Sister Cannon predicted it might require one year for the preparation of the material. The project, however, grew into five years' work. Authors and composers needed to be located to obtain approval for simplifying music or making word changes as requested by the correlation committee or editing department. There had not been a Church copyright office when the previous book was published, and so arrangements also needed to be made to establish copyrights, permissions, and royalty agreements for each song.

A small office space was located in the basement of the Relief Society Building (corner of North Temple and Main Street) where we could

PART TWO

begin to work. We inherited an old copy machine—the kind in which the top slowly moved over and back across the page. Since we weren't sure how to proceed, I guess it didn't matter that we started in slow motion. We copied everything that was to be considered, and then assigned about fifteen songs at a time to a batch. These batches were reviewed and circulated through four committees: the General Primary Presidency, the General Primary Music Committee, the General Music Committee, and an Ad Hoc Committee that represented the opinion of the leaders in "the field."

I served as General Primary Music Committee chairman. Board members **Virginia Byrd Allred**, **Mayre Beth Stevens**, **Susan Clark Kenney**, **Suzanne Sessions Moesinger**, **Laurel Parker Rohlfing**, and **Ann Aylett Wood** served on the committee, two or three at a time, over a period of five years. This music committee reviewed and selected songs; tracked the progress of the work on each song; located maiden names, addresses, and birthdates of authors and composers; planned the organization of the book; approved art and graphic design; and proofed scriptures, words, notation, fingering, and metronome markings.

The Primary Ad Hoc Committee members and assignments were **Grietje Terburg Rowley** (simplifying, transposing, proofing of typeset) and **Mary Curtis Gourley**, **Trudy Swenson Shipp**, and **Linda Call Stewart** (review and selection of songs, topical index, selection of scripture references, picture suggestions). This committee was also assigned to compile, write, and edit lesson plans for each of the songs in the book. This was to be printed as a music guide in conjunction with the songbook. Due to the growth of the Church, a decision was made to publish only material that could be translated. The rote teaching method was integral to the lesson plans and used statements such as "Listen for the word on the highest note in the song." After translating the words of a song, the answer would be a different word in every language, and so the lesson plan would have to be rewritten in every language. Even though the project had been completed and submitted to correlation, it was not printed by the Church. With approval, the book was eventually published commercially. The Primary stewardship elements were removed, and the book was entitled *A Children's Songbook Companion,* 1995 Aspen Books; revised 2005 Cedar Fort/Horizon Publishers.

Michael Finlinson Moody, chairman of the General Music Committee and the 1985 Hymnbook Committee, assisted the Primary in every way. He met with our committee once a week in the beginning and with me daily in the end. He was both optimistic and practical, and equally as talented in writing music as in bringing out the best from everyone he worked with. It was a privilege to learn from him. Other General Music Committee members were **Darwin Wolford** (music editing and typeset proofing, selection and simplification of prelude music); **Vanja Yorgason Watkins** and **Ruth Muir Gardner** (revision suggestions); **Jerolde Harris, Dan Carter** (typeset proofing); **Jenny Runswick Bennett** (fingering and chording); and **Elaine Rich Anderson** (guitar chording and proofing). When possible, the original composer was asked to determine metronome markings for their songs. Otherwise, I would decide a mood and tempo marking, and Sister Bennett and Sister Anderson would check and give their opinion.

I had been writing the monthly Sharing Time Page for the *Friend* since it began in 1981, and had the usual travel assignments, region visits, conference open house preparations, and so on. With the increasing demands of the songbook deadlines, I was struggling to keep up with my assignments. In January 1988, I made an appointment to meet with Sister Young after our Thursday board meeting and intended to discuss how I should handle the load. In the meeting that morning, she announced that her husband, Tom, had been called as a mission president to Calgary, Canada, and that our board would be released. That changed all the dynamics. I was relieved of my overload, but then worried how I could ever explain the process to someone else if I were released from the project.

At the 1988 April General Conference, our presidency and board were released. **Michaelene Packer Grassli**, former second counselor, became president with **Betty Jo Nelson Jepson** and **Ruth Broadbent Wright**, former board members, as counselors. I was asked to finish the songbook project. I had not had to ask for help, and was able to focus on the songbook full-time through the end of the year to see that it was ready for the printer by January 1989.

A four-color illustrated hardbound quality book is expensive to produce. A comparable commercial product would sell, in 1989, for $45 or more. The original low price of the book was a result of church service volunteered by many capable people, plus the fact that 500,000 copies were run on the first printing. Among the valuable employees who contributed were **Diane Kirk**, our kind and conscientious editor; **Stan Thurman**, art and graphics coordinator; and **Randy Nicola**, who

PART TWO

devised the computer typeset. Numerous production personnel combined their best efforts to make a unique book.

In "Our Children's Songs," Virginia Cannon wrote, "The great desire of all who have been involved in the preparation and publication of the *Children's Songbook* is that children's lives will be enriched and blessed through the songs of the gospel—that they will be given strength to resist temptations and have a commitment to live the commandments of the Lord."[2]

B. Selection and Revision of Songs

Evaluation of FAVORITE Primary Songs. In 1983, a survey was taken throughout the United States and several countries of 350 children's songs in Church resources. Primary presidencies and music leaders rated songs in three categories: (1) frequency, (2) familiarity, and (3) favorite. The resulting rank order showed which songs were not being used in the field. The following list shows the results in the "favorite" category. (Interestingly, the top three favorite songs merely changed places for "frequent" [I Am a Child of God] and "familiar" [Book of Mormon Stories] lists.)

1983 Survey Results

1. Popcorn Popping
2. I Am a Child of God
3. Book of Mormon Stories
4. The Golden Plates
5. Smiles
6. Families Can Be Together Forever
7. Do As I'm Doing
8. Jesus Wants Me for a Sunbeam
9. I Hope They Call Me on a Mission
10. The Chapel Doors
11. Give Said the Little Stream
12. Once There Was a Snowman
13. A Happy Family
14. Reverently, Quietly
15. Kindness Begins with Me
16. Daddy's Homecoming
17. Happy, Happy Birthday
18. We Wish You a Merry Christmas

19. I Love to See the Temple
20. The Wise Man and the Foolish Man
21. Saturday
22. Jesus Said Love Every One
23. When We're Helping
24. Hinges
25. Go the Second Mile
26. In the Leafy Tree Tops
27. Away in a Manger
28. I Have Two Little Hands
29. When Grandpa Comes
30. Our Primary Colors
31. Oh, What Do You Do in the Summertime?
32. Hello Song
33. I Feel My Savior's Love
34. Away in a Manger
35. Where Love Is
36. My Heavenly Father Loves Me
37. Your Happy Birthday
38. Quickly I'll Obey
39. Jesus Once Was a Little Child
40. Tell Me the Stories of Jesus
41. Teach Me to Walk in the Light

Compare these results with a 2003 survey, taken by visitors of the exhibit "Primary Makes Me Happy" who were given the opportunity to vote on their three favorite Primary songs.

2003 Survey Results

1. I Am a Child of God
2. I Love to See the Temple
3. A Child's Prayer
4. We'll Bring the World His Truth
5. Book of Mormon Stories
6. Popcorn Popping
7. I Belong to the Church of Jesus Christ of Latter-day Saints
8. Jesus Wants Me for a Sunbeam
9. Love One Another
10. Latter-day Prophets

PART TWO

11. When I Am Baptized
12. "Give" Said the Little Stream
13. Nephi's Courage
14. Families Can Be Together Forever
15. Follow the Prophet
16. I Hope They Call Me on a Mission
17. Scripture Power
18. Love is Spoken Here
19. Once There Was a Snowman
20. Teach Me to Walk in the Light
21. I Feel My Savior's Love
22. I'm Trying to Be Like Jesus
23. My Heavenly Father Loves Me
24. Called to Serve
25. Little Purple Pansies
26. The Wise Man and the Foolish Man
27. Search, Ponder, and Pray
28. Jesus Once Was a Little Child
29. Our Primary Colors
30. Do As I'm Doing

Voting. The Primary General Presidency, the Primary Music Committee, the General Music Committee, and the Primary Ad Hoc Committee of one stake and two ward music leaders met as separate committees to consider each song and give it a rating. Each song was analyzed and critiqued with suggestions such as key change, simplification, extended use with alternate words, etc., written on a tracking sheet. Each of the eleven people voted 3 (yes), 2 (maybe), or 1 (no) for each song, and the points were combined to help decide which songs to keep. Some songs actually received a perfect score of 33, while others received single digits. As it was a decision based on the input of the entire group plus the survey status, it was not possible for one person to keep or cut a song. Sometimes the General Music Committee would give a song a low rating because it was poorly constructed, and then the Ad Hoc Committee would give it a high rating, saying that the children loved to sing that song. The book now consists of songs that appeal to children, written with melodies and accompaniments that fine musicians would approve, containing doctrinally accurate messages that are grammatically correct. It is quite a compliment to have something in the book. It means the song has survived

STORIES OF THE CHILDREN'S SONGBOOK

correlation, editing, the music committee, and the vote of music leaders throughout the Church on behalf of the children they teach.

Topics. The number of songs on a given topic was considered as well as whether the songs were for older or younger children. Junior Sunday School had been for children eight years old or younger, and so the greater proportion of songs had been for younger children. With the consolidated meeting schedule, there was a need for material to challenge older children. There were no songs on special needs, which justified requesting new songs. Because the sacrament was not passed in Primary, only two songs were kept on that topic for teaching purposes.

Word Changes. Changes in the song texts were made sparingly for the following reasons:

1. **Clarifying doctrine.** In order for the prayer song, "Lord We Thank Thee," to be more clearly addressed to Heavenly Father, the words and title have been revised to "Thank Thee Father." The world at large considers "God" and "Lord" as interchangeable titles. Correlation explained that "God" generally means "Heavenly Father," and "Lord" means "Jesus." So it would be more accurate to address the prayer to "God" than to the "Lord." All suggested changes but one were made —"Tell Me Dear Lord" could not be adjusted. Correlation still approved it, as it was a preferred recommendation, not an absolute necessity.

2. **Avoiding words with inappropriate connotations.** The word *gay* has been revised in the songs, "Autumn Day," "My Mother Dear," "When Grandpa Comes," and "Pioneer Children." These changes were requested in numerous letters from music leaders in the field.

3. **Adjusting for word and music accents.** An unimportant word can feel awkward when it receives emphasis by falling on an important musical accent, such as the first beat of a measure. In the second verse of "The Golden Plates," the original phrase "a godly man" gave musical emphasis to "a" which is not an important word. "Written in days of old" matches the natural accent of "written" with the musical accent of the first beat, and also describes the golden plates rather than Nephi.

4. **At the request of the author or composer.** A low pitch skipping to a higher note can cause children to sing in their chest voice, whereas beginning high in the head voice enables a child to use their singing voice and continue that way. Vanja Watkins

PART TWO

suggested several pitch changes for this reason. For example, page 228, "Whenever I hear the song of a bird," now begins high b flat rather than b flat below middle c.

As part of the final proofing, each tracking sheet was reread to see if every suggestion had been acted upon. Only one item (out of at least one million) had not been handled. It was intended that "A Young Man Prepared" be transposed one step lower, and it simply was overlooked.

Songs in both Hymns and the Children's Songbook. The following seven songs are in both the 1985 Hymnbook and the *Children's Songbook:* "I Am a Child of God," "I Know My Father Lives," "Families Can be Together Forever," "Keep the Commandments," "Love One Another," "Called to Serve," and "Teach Me to Walk in the Light." Each song received a new treatment for the Primary collection in order to justify being printed in more than one Church resource.

Children's songs in *Hymns* but not in the *Children's Songbook* are "God's Daily Care," "In Our Lovely Deseret," and "The Light Divine." Information about these three Primary songs is included in Appendix One of this book.

C. Design and Binding

I could not imagine a book of children's material without pictures. All of my training and experience as a music teacher and educator had convinced me that valuable learning occurs through feelings. And both music and art create lasting impressions. It was my dream that children might be able to feel the beauty of the gospel through the beauty of the new songbook. I hoped that as little ones would see the pictures and hum the melodies on each lovely page, the feeling of the songs would be indelibly imprinted in their hearts.

Having the songbook illustrated was "a good seed that grew." I talked about it with my committee and with our presidency. Soon, President Young was talking about how wonderful it would be when the book had illustrations. Eventually our advisors were saying that we could have the book illustrated if it didn't raise the cost of the book over the previous materials. We were told as late as August 1988 that including the artwork hinged on the results of the bid price. We all rejoiced when the cost was projected to be $5.60 per book! Of course, printing 500,000 copies on the first run had a great deal to do with the economics, as well as the fact that so much of the labor had been donated. It would have been a grave error not to have had the pictures which extended the teaching visually, and which made it a book for children.

Double-page Illustrations. Initially, we had been advised against the use of two-page pictures. The printing process was not always satisfactory because of the difficulty with alignment and color matching. We were told not to plan for it in our design. We entertained other options, such as an oval on each page with a drawing in one and the section title in the other. The art was lovely, but it did not feel right. I had trouble sleeping for two nights and kept seeing double-page pictures when I closed my eyes. At first, I supposed I had been looking at too many beautiful Caldecott books and was being unrealistic about what we could have. When I told President Young that I couldn't let go of the idea of the two-page pictures, she personally discussed the issue with our Priesthood advisor, Hugh Pinnock. He reported that the new web press that the Church was installing at the printing center would have the capability of successfully handling double-page pictures, and we could go ahead with our dreams. The web press was installed in December of 1988. Our project went to press the next month. I am grateful I followed the promptings.

Small Art. After the order of the songs was determined, a "dummy" was made showing where each song would be placed. Small pictures were planned wherever there was space. The Ad Hoc Committee had made a list of pictures that were not available in library materials—pictures that would be helpful in explaining the meaning of certain songs. Using that list and juggling songs to create space in the right places, specific drawings could be requested. The artist assigned would make a small sketch of the request, and it would be reviewed to see if it solved the need. The intent was to have the art help explain the message of the song. This kind of illustrating is very different from decorating blank spaces. Different cultures were represented in the drawings, and Church Correlation checked the pictures to make sure that clothing and furniture were accurate for the country.

Border Color. At first the committee talked about having a border for each song that might relate to the content—perhaps even one border for each section. It became complicated and cluttered, and yet a simple line around each page seemed too plain. I remembered a school curriculum in which each chapter was printed on a different color. The color made it easy to find your place. Suddenly it was clear—why not have one

PART TWO

color *in* the border for each section? The color could help you locate the song. The idea has proven itself.

Binding. The first printing was bound with a "perfect binding," like the hymnbook. As the book was opened and pressed at many places, the book would eventually lay open on a piano. An additional binding was made with a soft cover and a small spiral. This was not as durable, but laid open easily on the piano. After several years, the orders for spiral outnumbered the perfect binding. Eventually, a combination hardback spiral edition was made, which raised the cost substantially.

I was given the very first book printed with the original binding. It lays open, and it looks beautiful and has no pages torn next to the spiral. I prefer the perfect binding, and it is my opinion that if people had tried the book they would have found it to be satisfactory and more durable. In addition, the pictures are not spoiled with the large spiral. Often, my piano students have pages tear away from the spiral as they turn pages during practice. Even so, it is a magnificent book that is accomplishing the end for which it was created.

D. Illustrators

The artwork of Caldecott Award Winners Tasha Tudor and Brinton Turkle was suggested as a model for those who were asked to submit sample illustrations. We hoped for a gentle, timeless art. Three freelance artists, whose work was compatible, were selected to prepare the 150 illustrations, the cover, and eight double-page section pictures. A fourth artist helped to meet the deadlines.

Phyllis Luch drew the cover, all double-page section pictures, and the small art in sections I, II, and III. Sister Luch is well-known for her silhouettes and drawings for Church magazines. She said that her grandchildren were her inspiration, and that she prayed a lot. Her last name is hiding on the first and second section double-page pictures. She also wrote the poem that became the song "I Often Go Walking."

Beth Maryon Whittaker prepared the entire Heritage section and small art in sections I, II, and III. Her finished work is impeccable, and she is in demand for Church magazines and other projects. Two children were born to her while she prepared art for the book. One day after the book had been printed, I asked Heather Back what Primary song she wanted to study for her piano lesson. She turned to my song "I Am Like a Star" and said she wanted to learn it because she had been the model for the picture. She was a neighbor to Sister Whittaker. I was quite amazed that the drawing of a piano student of mine was used on the same page as my song!

Virginia Sargent created the Nature and Seasons small art. She had previously been on the art staff of the *Friend* magazine, and an illustrator for Mattel Toys. During this time, she suffered a broken hip and was unable to continue work on the last sections of the book.

Richard Hull, a member of the Brigham Young University art faculty, completed the thirty-five drawings needed for Home and Family, Fun and Activity, and the Prelude sections. His style captures movement and appears in many Church magazines. Stan Thurman, the graphic designer, contracted with Brother Hull, and he was able to meet the deadlines.

After the publication of the songbook, a small pre-school daughter of one of my piano students came with her mother to her piano lesson. As she walked in the door, she said, "Can I look at your pretty book?" I got her seated on the couch and then laid the *Children's Songbook* on her lap. During her mother's lesson, I heard her humming as she carefully turned the pages until she recognized a picture she could "sing." I thought how well the illustrations were accomplishing their purpose. I secretly wished that every child could grow up with this glorious book.

E. Title and Cover

The previous song collections were directed to leaders. Throughout the project the book was referred to as the *Primary Songbook*. However, as the artwork was being prepared and the preface was approved, the title evolved into the *Children's Songbook*, because this book *was* for the children of the Church.

Four preliminary thumbnail sketches were offered as possible designs for the cover. One design was a match to the hymnbook with a small picture of children in place of the organ logo. The other three ideas were various printing styles for the book title and different groupings of children. I felt very strongly about one of the sketches, as though I was recognizing something I had seen in my mind's eye. The selection was narrowed to two, and I asked if we could have them drawn to scale and then decide.

I was out of town and could not attend the next meeting. I wondered if I should have been more verbal about my preference. When I returned, Brother Moody showed me the artboard of the design that had been selected. As he pulled it from a large envelope, he said, "I think you will

PART TWO

like what I have to show you." It was the drawing of the picture I had hoped for. When it was drawn to the actual size, everyone preferred it. I realized once again that it was not a matter of casting votes, but that when it was correct we would all agree.

The following letter, written by Kathy Futrell of Las Vegas, Nevada, describes what the cover has meant to her son:

> Our son Troy was born with multiple handicaps. Throughout his life, he has had many struggles. He has always been positive and has had a sweet spirit. He is truly a blessing in our home everyday as he constantly reminds us of who we are and what we are aiming for in our lives.
>
> The artwork on the cover of the *Children's Songbook* has brought Troy much joy in his life. From his very earliest years, Troy has taken the songbook wherever he has gone. We have gone through multiple copies because he has worn them out. He can stare at the picture for what seems like hours! Every time he sees it, it seems like the first time because he lights up all over again. He will search high and low throughout the house if it is missing. He cannot sleep peacefully without his picture close by.

F. Preface

As chairman, it was my responsibility to initiate and finalize assignments. Working "in committee" means many points of view and many evaluations will be written on top of the original. You need to have thick skin to work in committee.

The preface was the last item to be written. I was to make a rough draft and present it to the entire committee for their suggestions. To prepare myself, I read every music book preface I could find. I interviewed Brother Moody as well as several music educators. With a prayer in my heart, I sat at the typewriter and wrote with fervor on the importance of music in a child's life and the effectiveness of teaching the gospel through music. It was a wonderful thesis for parents and leaders.

First Draft of Ideas about *Children's Songbook* Preface July 21, 1988

Purpose of music in the Church:

> Music is a language of emotion and communicates feelings. Each time we sing a song, we stir the memory of our past experiences with it, and

our hearts are touched again For example, you may cry every time you hear "O My Father" if the song was sung at your father's funeral.

Music can move our souls and refine our response to things of the spirit. Often it is through beautiful music that a reverent atmosphere is created which allows the spirit to be felt. It is possible to feel personal promptings as we are touched through the message and mood of a song. Small children can respond to reverent moods in music long before they can understand the meaning of words. (Five-year-old describing prelude music—makes me feel Heavenly Father-like).

Music reaches our deepest feelings, and brings the Spirit of the Lord into our homes and our meetings (temple dedication, bishop, choir). There is unity through music in the Church. Everyone can participate and we are brought closer together as we sing together. Our whole perception of humanity is enriched as we share in the universal language of music, and we can experience great joy as we sing about the gospel. (I like our Primary songs—they make me feel good).

Teaching songs to children is a very efficient way for them to learn the principles of the gospel. The melody helps to retain the words, and if words and music are memorized together, they can be remembered indefinitely.

Familiar songs with gospel messages give impressions of righteousness and goodness that will become reservoirs of spiritual strength. Our testimonies can be reinforced as the Spirit witnesses truth through warm feelings experienced while singing.

As I began to reread, I knew it was not what was needed. The ideas were accurate and true, but it felt like a sermon. Suddenly I had the most exhilarating idea. Why not write to the children—why not address this message to the boys and girls the songs were written for? I took a clean paper and typed quickly, saying the same things but speaking as I would to a child. In the middle, I paused to phone Brother Moody and ask him what he thought of my proposal. He said to finish writing and then submit it to the committee.

I finished and braced myself for the inevitable changes and red pencil marks from the committee. Having my last effort on this enormous project come back intact was a sweet conclusion. The editor tightened it up—I use too many words to explain myself—but the ideas as explained to little ones survived scrutiny. I felt that I had been an instrument in directing the book to the children.

PART TWO

G. Table of Contents and Order of Songs

There are 255 songs in the *Children's Songbook*, plus thirteen simplified preludes. Seventeen of the songs were considered "new" since all others were in previous Church resources. These songs were selected or written because of a topical need. They are as follows: I Lived in Heaven, 4; I Pray in Faith, 14; This Is My Beloved Son, 76; The Church of Jesus Christ, 77; On a Golden Springtime, 88; When I Am Baptized, 103; Follow the Prophet, 110; I'll Walk with You, 140; Every Star Is Different, 142; The Word of Wisdom, 154; How Dear to God Are Little Children, 180; How Will They Know? 182; Grandmother, 200; Little Seeds Lie Fast Asleep, 243; Fun To Do, 253; We Are Different, 263; and You've Had a Birthday, 285.

If you had 268 songs to put in a collection, how would you organize them? Would you put the preludes first because you use them first in Primary, or would you put the songs about the principles of the Gospel at the beginning because they remind us of things we should do? It was decided to tell a story with the order of the songs. The story begins at our beginning in Heaven with the most often sung Primary song, "I Am a Child of God."

The entire table of contents was planned to fit on two facing pages to make it possible to see the complete collection at once. It shows the order of the songs within eight sections. Each section has a different color in the border which serves as one more way to help locate a song. Remembering page numbers can be a challenge, but remembering the color of the border of a song is easy. Flipping through the pages in the yellow section for a song which is on the left side near the front can be easier for a "visual person" than remembering the correct title and finding the page number in the Index.

H. Format matched the Hymnbook, with the addition of Fingering and Chording

The format of the hymnbook was followed to include:

1. **Maiden Names and Birth and Death Dates.** Locating this information became a genealogy project for the one hundred ninety-nine authors and composers that needed to be researched. Two of the living composers did not want to have the date of their birth printed.

2. **Scripture References.** The Ad Hoc Committee recommended

scriptures that gave credibility to the message of the song. A successful formula for impromptu speaking could be to (1) select a favorite song, (2) read the scriptures, and (3) bear testimony of the message. Some songs in "Nature and Seasons" and "Fun and Activity" were not matched to a reference.

3. **Introduction Brackets.** Brackets above the treble staff indicate a possible introduction. The purposes for playing an introduction are to remind the singers of the melody and rhythm, to establish the key of the song, and to give the beginning pitch. Generally, an introduction includes the first phrase and the last phrase of the song. Some other possibilities have been indicated that can occur in the middle of the song or the end only. The brackets can be highlighted to make them easier to find when playing.

4. **Metronome Tempos.** The two numbers indicate the slowest to the fastest appropriate speeds. Where possible, the composer was asked to make these suggestions. If a metronome is not available, you can use a second hand to measure ♩ = 60 and estimate from there.

5. **Credit Lines.** As new information was discovered, credit lines were revised. Options were given to composers and authors for the control of royalties for any commercial use of their song. Some writers contribute their royalties to the Church, while others depend on the income as part of their livelihood. There are 199 names credited for the 268 songs included in the *Children's Songbook*. Fifty-eight are the work of non-LDS writers and composers, and 141 were written by members of The Church of Jesus Christ of Latter-day Saints. In this book, their names are followed by LDS. Many times a song was requested to fill a particular need, and the request was usually given to someone currently on the Primary general board, General Music Committee, or other proven writers. Other times, a song was submitted to the Church Music Department Contest or to the *Friend* magazine after having been successful in a local setting. Brother Moody often advised aspiring authors and composers to write for their stewardship and "the cream will rise."

6. **Typeset.** As we began receiving the first cycle of music typeset, I would place it on my piano and have students read and play to proof it. The computer font was the same as the hymnbook

PART TWO

notation, and I noticed children leaning forward to read it. Of course, piano method books have "big notes" in the early levels, but it was an indication that perhaps the notes needed to be larger. This concern was discussed, and we were informed that notes could be no larger with the font we were using. There was concern about slender noteheads for young pianists, as well as those who wear bifocals to play. I visited the office of **Randy Nicola,** who had devised the computer music notation program for the Church, to discuss the concern. He explained that we could not add more height to the notes or the size of the lines and spaces would be affected, which would affect the entire book and require more room for music, expand the number of pages, increase the cost, and so on. As we talked, he got an idea and asked me to wait. He experimented for about fifteen minutes, and returned with what we called "the *fat* note." He enlarged the width of the note, which gave it a bigger appearance, and did not cause any of the other problems. I learned that if something doesn't seem right, there will be a solution if you keep talking about it.

7. **Fingering.** Piano students are accustomed to fingering helps, and the suggestions given are to guide beginning accompanists. The fingering was planned for a small hand and is noted sparingly.

8. **Chording.** Chord names were given at essential harmonic changes. When chord progressions occurred on every count, we simplified to the basics. Soon after the publication of the book, we received a thank you note from a Primary pianist in California. She explained that she played "by ear" and could pick out the melody of a song but struggled with reading the left hand. Normally, she would spend a lot of time figuring the chords for Church music and writing the symbols above the melody, like a "lead sheet." She was so happy to see the chords printed in the book and was grateful for the hours of work we had done for her.

I. Translating

The songbook was printed first in English, and then work began to prepare translated copies. Some printing would be done in church printing centers outside of the United States to avoid huge shipping costs. It was prudent to prepare a "short list" version of the book for translation and to use less color. Work is still being done to prepare translations so that books are available in every language where there are Primaries.

It is important to have translating done by someone excellent in the original and the second language, and someone who is a poet and a musician. Some early translations were uncomfortable to sing because (1) the message was distorted, (2) musical accents and word accents did not match, or (3) many extra syllables required additional melody notes. When visiting Quebec, Canada, on a Primary assignment, a music leader confided to me that she simply did not use some of the songs because she felt the translations were not of high quality. I am grateful to say that problem no longer exists.

Notes

1 Gordon B. Hinckley, "Ten Gifts from the Lord," *Ensign*, Nov. 1985, 89.
2 Cannon, *Our Children's Songs*, 3.

PART THREE
Stories about Primary Songs and the People Who Wrote Them

Song entries include author and composer bios, how the song came to be, inspirational stories about the song, and a cross-reference to other songs by the same person.

Part Three

"I thank the Lord with all my soul, and bless my teachers, that I was taught these gospel songs in my youth. All through the years they have been flowing through my mind. I have hummed and sung them as I have ridden over interminable miles. . . . By their messages I have been inspired to reach heavenward."[1]
—Apostle Marion G. Romney

Sections

My Heavenly Father

The Savior

The Gospel

Home and Family

Heritage

Nature and Seasons

Fun and Activity

Prelude Music

PART THREE

My Heavenly Father

> "The principal virtue of music is a means of communication with God."[2]
> —Igor Stravinsky (1882–1971)
> Russian-born U.S. composer

It is important for children to understand their relationship to their Heavenly Father. That is the focus of the inspirational songs in this section. Apostle J. Reuben Clark said, "We get nearer to the Lord through music than perhaps any other thing except prayer."[3] Songs on prayer, thankfulness, and reverence have been grouped together. Phyllis Luch originally sketched the beautiful two-page artwork as a possible design for the "Nature and Seasons" section. Even in the early pencil drawing, there was an obvious feeling that the child in the picture knew she was a daughter of God, which made it perfect for the first divider page.

I AM A CHILD OF GOD, 2

Words: Naomi Ward Randall (1908–2001) LDS
Music: Mildred Tanner Pettit (1895–1977) LDS
Arranged: Darwin Wolford (1936–) LDS

In 1957, **Naomi Randall** was to make arrangements for a new song to be written for a Primary conference. She called **Mildred Pettit,** a former Primary general board member who had written songs and operettas for children, and asked if she would help with the music. Sister Randall said she would write the words for the song and then send them to Sister Pettit. Before retiring that night, Sister Randall prayed for help in finding the right words for the song. Some hours later she awakened, got out of bed, and wrote the words for three verses. Then she thanked Heavenly Father for helping her. The next day, she mailed the lyrics to Sister Pettit in California.

Sister Pettit also wanted to have the music the way the Lord wanted it. She felt that she knew how the melody was supposed to go, but she worked on the closing phrase over and over and had her children sing it many times until she was finally satisfied that it was right. The two women worked on the chorus together, and within another week the song was completed.

After hearing the song sung at a stake conference, Elder Spencer W. Kimball suggested that "Teach me all that I must *know*" be changed to "I must *do*." He said, "To know isn't enough . . . we have to do something."[4] Pres. Kimball often said, with a twinkle in his eye, that he helped Sister Randall write this wonderful song.

Sister Randall believes that "we can learn the gospel through songs," and that "the truths that are sung into our hearts will help us at critical times in our lives."[5] The author added a fourth verse in 1978.[6] In 1981, I sat for the first time with the Primary general board on the stand in the Tabernacle for the Women's Conference. I heard Sister Camilla Kimball refer to this song in her talk as "the gospel in a nutshell."

Even without a survey to tell us, we know that this is the most often sung Primary song. For years, it only had three verses—even in the 1985 hymnbook arrangement. We were pleased to include the fourth verse, which added the word "celestial" to the vocabulary of the songbook. Because this song is also in the hymnbook, the key was changed from D to C, and a descant for voice or instrument was written by **Darwin Wolford**. Brother Wolford was integral to the quality of the music in the book as he edited and refined every piece in the collection.

A nice way to enhance this song is to sing three verses from the songbook and conclude with the hymnbook. In other words, three verses sung in the key of C (sing the descant with verse three), and the fourth verse in the key of D (have a violin or flute transpose the descant up one step).

When we were determining the style for the illustrations in the book, Beth Whittaker submitted the drawing on this page. We loved the timeless look of the little girl and assigned it to this song.

I have heard many inspirational stories about "I Am a Child of God." Here are two—one of conversion and one of comfort:

> When Akiko Hirano first visited a Mormon Church meeting in Japan, she heard some missionaries sing "I Am a Child of God." The spirit whispered to her that she, too, was a child of God. She agreed to have the discussions and soon was baptized. When I met her, she was preparing to serve a mission. She said, "I am very happy to be Mormon and to live in gospel. I want to play piano and sing songs with family all around." I felt fortunate to have Akiko come to my home and tell me how this song helped her recognize the gospel.[7]

PART THREE

Sister Daryl Van Dam Hoole shared her tender experience with this song in the following letter:

The very premature birth of our twin baby girls, Janet and Jean, on January 18, 1958, caught Hank and me totally by surprise. Then the subsequent death of little Janet six days later found us even more unprepared. We were advised against a graveside service, saying it would be much better to hold a short funeral so our family and friends could be protected from the wintry elements and so music and the spoken word could be heard without the sound of the wind and passing traffic.

Mother suggested some special music. She told of a beautiful, new children's song that had been introduced at a recent Primary general conference and offered to contact the young nine-year-old girl who had sung the song in the Tabernacle in hopes she would do so again for Janet. Little did we know then that the inspired song would become one of the most beloved and frequently sung of any hymn throughout the entire Church. I never hear it sung here at home or as we visit other countries, without thinking of Janet.[8]

See also **Randall**: I Want to Live the Gospel, 148 (words).

See also **Pettit**: Beauty Everywhere, 232 (music); Father I will Reverent Be, 29 (words and music); Mother Dear, 206 (music); *Hymns*, The Light Divine, 305 (music).

See also **Wolford**: Beautiful Savior, 62 (arrangement); Had I Been a Child, 80 (music); I Have a Family Tree, 199 (music); In Quietude, 291 (music); Keep the Commandments, 146 (arrangement); Mary's Lullaby, 44 (arrangement); Our Chapel Is a Sacred Place, 30 (music); Stars Were Gleaming, 37 (arrangement); Supplication, 297 (music); Teach Me to Walk in the Light, 177 (obbligato); Thanks to Thee, 6 (music); The Lord Gave Me a Temple, 153 (music); *Hymns*, Sons of Michael, He Approaches, 51 (music); We Listen to a Prophet's Voice, 22 (music).

I LIVED IN HEAVEN, 4

Words and music: Janeen Jacobs Brady (1934–) LDS

Janeen Jacobs Brady was asked to write a song about heaven that would explain Heavenly Father's plan for His spirit children. Interestingly, she had an unpublished idea on the topic that she had already worked on. When the song was completed, she described it as a ballad—a story song—and said that it is a *true* story. Janeen had been a mentor to me when I first began composing, and I was especially happy to have her work included in the book. She and her husband, Ted, founded BRITE Music Company to publish her work. Her memorable songs teach positive values as well as school curriculum. She is a vocal performer as well as an accompanist and composer, and is the mother of nine children, one of whom is handicapped and has been the inspiration for messages in some of her songs.

Sister Brady believes happy songs are like ammunition to fight evil. She said, "If we can fill our minds with good music and thoughts, we won't have room for evil thoughts. And when evil thoughts try to come in, we can sing the happy songs we know, and they will go away."[9]

I KNOW MY FATHER LIVES, 5

Words and music: Reid N. Nibley (1923–2008) LDS

Reid Nibley, a concert pianist and Brigham Young University faculty member, was asked to write a song about testimony for the *Sing With Me* collection. He said he wrote quickly because as he started thinking of how a child would express a testimony, the words and music came at the same time. The song was very short and simple. Brother Nibley is a very knowledgeable musician, so he began adding notes. It became more and more complicated. He said, "Thank goodness I had a big eraser!" He erased all the unnecessary notes, and when he finished the song was just as he had written it the first time!ized[10]

Because the song is also in the hymnbook, Brother Nibley was asked to do something different with it. He was in the process of writing piano teaching materials, and he chose to write a duet accompaniment for this version of his song. This is one of the few songs in the book that does not have the melody in the accompaniment. You can use the hymnbook while the children are learning the melody, and then play the accompaniment from the songbook when they are secure. Or use two people and follow the instructions for making a duet.

See also **Nibley**: I'll Walk With You, 140 (music); *Hymns,* I Know My Father Lives, 302 (words and music—melody in accompaniment).

THANKS TO THEE, 6

Words: Mary R. Jack (1896–1985) LDS
Music: Darwin Wolford (1936–) LDS

Mary R. Jack, the author, served on the Primary general board for nineteen years under the first two general presidents. She was an editor for *The Children's Friend* and a member and secretary of the Tabernacle

PART THREE

Choir. **Darwin Wolford**, the composer of 12 songs in this collection, combined her sweet text with music for this childlike prayer song. Brother Wolford skillfully simplified most of the songs in this collection so that they are musically accurate yet accessible to the average pianist. He has a PhD in organ and composition, taught at Brigham Young University–Idaho, and served on the 1985 Hymnbook Committee.

When I first met with Brother Moody, General Music chairman, to discuss how we would work together on the project, I asked if Brother Wolford would be available to help us. I knew of his expertise and hoped he could be a resource. Brother Moody said he didn't think we should plan on him because he had had major involvement in the Hymnbook Committee and probably needed a rest. So we didn't ask him. After the songs had been chosen and we knew what work needed to be done with each of them, I inquired again. Brother Moody said he would call and "feel him out." Later, Brother Wolford told me what had happened prior to that call.

One night, after family prayer, Darwin's wife, Julie, said that she thought he would be involved in the work on the Primary materials. Darwin said that he hadn't been asked, and dismissed the idea. When Michael phoned him, it was like he had been prepared to say yes. I have always been grateful to Julie for telling about her impression. Darwin's hand on things raised the musical standard of the book. Because he lives in Idaho, we did a great deal over the phone, and I appreciated his sense of humor, which lightened the load, as well as his music editing skills.

See also **Wolford**: Beautiful Savior, 62 (arrangement); Had I Been a Child, 80 (music); I Have a Family Tree, 199 (music); I Am a Child of God, 2 (arrangement); In Quietude, 291 (music); Keep the Commandments, 146 (arrangement); Mary's Lullaby, 44 (arrangement); Our Chapel Is a Sacred Place, 30 (music); Stars Were Gleaming, 37 (arrangement); Supplication, 297 (music); Teach Me to Walk in the Light, 177 (obbligato); The Lord Gave Me a Temple, 153 (music); *Hymns*, Sons of Michael, He Approaches, 51 (music); We Listen to a Prophet's Voice, 22 (music).

I THANK THEE, DEAR FATHER, 7

Words: anonymous
Music: George Careless (1839–1932) LDS

The composer, **George Edward Percy Careless**, was sent to the Royal Academy of London to study violin, piano, conducting, voice, and theory when he was a young boy. After joining the Church, he directed Latter-day Saint choirs in London. He immigrated to Salt Lake City, Utah, and composed "The Morning Breaks" while on the boat that brought him to America. He directed the Salt Lake Theater Orchestra and helped produce full-scale productions of Gilbert and Sullivan operettas. He conducted the first performance of Handel's *Messiah* in the Rocky Mountains, and in 1869 became the conductor of the Tabernacle Choir. Nine of his hymn tunes are included in the 1985 *Hymns*. In 1905, this song was included in the *Primary Songbook*.

Conducting four beats to a measure makes this song feel "heavy," and so the time signature was changed to two beats per measure, resulting in a lighter lilt.

See also **Careless**: *Hymns*, Again We Meet Around the Board, 186 (music); Arise, O Glorious Zion, 40 (music); Behold the Great Redeemer Die, 191 (music); He Died! The Great Redeemer Died, 192 (music); O Lord of Hosts, 178 (music); O Thou Kind and Gracious Father, 150 (music); Prayer Is the Soul's Sincere Desire, 145 (music); The Morning Breaks, 1 (music); Though Deepening Trials, 122 (music).

FATHER WE THANK THEE FOR THE NIGHT, 8

Words: Rebecca Weston (1835–1895)
Music: Grietje Terburg Rowley (1927–) LDS

The poem by **Rebecca Weston** was printed in *My Little Book of Prayers and Graces*, London, 1964. The words had been set to several other melodies for earlier songbooks, but, according to the survey, the song was not being used. A new melody was created which seems to enhance the words successfully.

The composer, **Grietje** (GREE-chuh) **Terburg Rowley**, is of Dutch descent, and taught school in Hawaii where she joined the Church. When she is working on a song, she always prays that it will be the way Heavenly Father would want it to be. She tries to make the music sound pretty, to make it easy to sing and to play and, above all, easy to remember. She was a Primary pianist for most of her life and believes that music can calm and inspire. She served on the Ad Hoc Committee for the *Children's Songbook*, contributing her talents in simplifying, arranging, composing, and proofreading. She often encouraged us by saying that this book was important for the children of the Church and Heavenly Father would help us to make it the way it should be.

The artwork on this page was the sample Phyllis Luch submitted when we were deciding the style of the pictures. She drew the cover, the large double-page section divider pictures, and many small pictures in the first three sections. She said that her grandchildren were her inspiration for many of the drawings, and that she prayed a lot.

See also **Rowley**: A Smile is Like the Sunshine, 267 (music); Distant Bells, 299 (music); Each Sunday Morning, 290 (music); I Want to Be a Missionary Now, 168 (words and music); Roll Your Hands, 274 (arrangement); Samuel Tells of the Baby Jesus, 36 (music); *Hymns,* Be Thou Humble, 130 (words and music).

CAN A LITTLE CHILD LIKE ME? 9

Words: Mary Mapes Dodge (1831–1905)
Music: W. K. Bassford (1839–1902)

Mary Dodge, the author, grew up in a wealthy family, educated by tutors, and in the company of literary and scientific people. After seven years of marriage, her husband died and she began writing to support her two sons. She is best known for her children's story, *Hans Brinker or the Silver Skates,* which was inspired by stories she had heard from Dutch emigrants. She founded a children's magazine, *St. Nicolas,* and was the editor for thirty-two years.

William Kipp Bassford, the composer, was born in New York City, New York. He gave piano concerts, composed songs and piano pieces, and was a Church organist. This song first appeared in the *Primary Songbook* in 1920.

THANK THEE FOR EVERYTHING, 10

Words: Vanja Y. Watkins (1938–) LDS
Music: Wilford A. Beesley, Jr. (1927–) LDS

The original title for this gentle prayer song was "Thanks for our World," but was changed to a line from the text for the 1989 *Children's Songbook.* **Vanja** (VON-yuh) **Yorgason Watkins** wrote the lovely poem. She contributed words, music, or both for fourteen other songs in this collection, plus the music for the Thirteen Articles of Faith. Her contribution over the years has shaped Primary music. Vanja was a music television teacher and a music specialist in Salt Lake City Schools. She was called to the Primary general board by LaVern Parmley, and was a member of the General Church Music Committee and the 1985 Hymnbook Committee. For many years, she taught at the Brigham Young University Church Music Workshop and on the faculty at Brigham

Young University.[11] As songs were being evaluated for the *Children's Songbook* collection, her suggestions were invaluable.

Wilford (Bill) Beesley carries on the music legacy of his grandfather, Ebenezer Beesley, composer and director for the Tabernacle Choir. He composes songs for special occasions, and enjoys playing the piano and singing with his family. He and Vanja Watkins lived in the same ward, and she remembered how well he played and improvised at the piano. When members were invited to create songs for *Sing With Me*, Bill wanted to offer something and asked Vanja to put words to one of his lovely melodies. Their collaboration was selected for the 1969 songbook. He also collaborated on a stake musical with Jay Heslop. Besides his musical skills, Brother Beesley served a mission to Denmark, and is now an attorney and an excellent skier and golfer.

See also **Watkins**: Easter Hosanna, 68 (words and music); Families Can Be Together Forever, 188 (music); For Thy Bounteous Blessings, 21 (arrangement); I Want to Be Reverent, 28 (music); I Will Be Valiant, 162 (words and music); I Will Follow God's Plan, 164 (words and music); It's Autumntime, 246 (arrangement); Latter-day Prophets, 134 (music); Thank Thee for Everything, 10 (words); The Articles of Faith, 122–132 (music); The Sacrament, 72 (words and music); The Things I Do, 170 (music); This Is My Beloved Son, 76 (music); To Be a Pioneer, 218 (arrangement); Truth from Elijah, 90 (words and music); *Hymns*, Families Can Be Together Forever, 300 (music); Press Forward Saints, 81 (music).

I'M THANKFUL TO BE ME, 11

Words: Joy Saunders Lundberg (1936–) LDS
Music: Janice Kapp Perry (1938–) LDS

Joy Saunders Lundberg is an artist as well as a poet, and has collaborated on many projects with her cousin, Janice Kapp Perry. When Sister Lundberg was a little girl, she used to lie on the floor by the stove in the family farmhouse and draw pictures and write poems while she listened to music on the radio. After attending Brigham Young University and a private art school, she served as a writer for the Church Curriculum Department. She became chairman of a committee writing Primary lessons. Joy and Janice have written cantatas, songs and songbooks, and a Latter-day Saint musical, *It's a Miracle*. Sometimes they get their ideas while they walk together.

Originally, line three said, "I see my friends and teachers, too, and all my family." Other songs mention family, so it was suggested that this one say "and others who love me" to include others who might be caring for Primary children.

Janice Kapp Perry is one of the most prolific musicians in the Church. She often said that writing music was her mission until she and her husband could serve a mission together. She sang in the Tabernacle Choir and then served a mission to Chile with her husband. Now she is focusing on composing songs for Spanish-speaking members of the Church.

See also **Perry**: A Child's Prayer, 12 (words and music); I Love to See the Temple, 95 (words and music); I Pray in Faith, 14 (words and music); I'm Trying to Be Like Jesus, 78 (words and music); Love Is Spoken Here, 190 (words and music); Mother, Tell Me the Story, 204 (words and music); The Church of Jesus Christ, 77 (words and music); The Word of Wisdom, 154 (words and music); We'll Bring the World His Truth, 172 (words and music); *Hymns*, As Sisters in Zion, 309 (music).

A CHILD'S PRAYER, 12

Words and music: Janice Kapp Perry (1938–) LDS

Janice Kapp Perry, the author/composer, said, "We are all human and occasionally wonder, in difficult times, if the Lord is really there to hear and answer our prayers." Concerning the loss of the use of her left hand, she continued, "During one of my times of frustration over a seemingly unanswered prayer, I wrote a song called 'Lord, Are You There?' and later decided to write a children's version, which I entitled 'A Child's Prayer.'"[12] The struggle resulted in a heart-felt plea and reassurance that speaks to children and adults.

The Correlation Committee expressed some concern about the lack of prayer language in the text of the song. As we discussed options, we found "Thee" and "Thou" seemed too formal and not at all childlike (Heavenly Father, art thou really there? And dost Thou hear and answer ev'ry child's prayer?). Sister Perry had a strong feeling that the words were as a child would express them, and that the song was more about a small child praying than about teaching prayer language. The decision was made to leave it as it was.

In her book *Songs from my Heart*, Sister Perry relates a time when the words of the song calmed her spirit. She and her husband were involved in a serious car accident in which the front of her throat was badly ruptured and bleeding internally. To assess the damage, the doctor told her to lie absolutely still for thirty minutes for a CAT scan. Janice could barely breathe or swallow and searched for something to calm herself. She closed her eyes and repeated these words over and over for the duration of the test: "Pray, He is there; speak, He is listening. You are His child, His love now surrounds you." With surgery and rest she was eventually healed. At a critical time, she received comfort through her own song. When the Tabernacle Choir recorded the song, Sister Perry was asked to write additional lines for the beginning and the end.

See also **Perry**: I Love to See the Temple, 95 (words and music); I Pray in Faith, 14 (words and music); I'm Thankful to Be Me, 11 (music); I'm Trying to Be Like Jesus, 78 (words and music); Love Is Spoken Here, 190 (words and music); Mother, Tell Me the Story, 204 (words and music); The Church of Jesus Christ, 77 (words and music); The Word of Wisdom, 154 (words and music); We'll Bring the World His Truth, 172 (words and music); *Hymns*, As Sisters in Zion, 309 (music).

I PRAY IN FAITH, 14

Words and music: Janice Kapp Perry (1938–) LDS

The previous children's songbooks had been used in both Primary (ages 3–11), and Junior Sunday School (ages 3–7). As a result, there were more songs for younger children. **Janice Kapp Perry's** song "Love Is Spoken Here" had given children the experience of singing harmony, and we thought that others like it might provide a challenge for older children. Sister Perry was asked to write another two-part song that would teach the parts of prayer. When she mailed the new song, she included a note that said, "Make any changes that you personally feel would improve the piece." Everyone wanted the book to be the best it could be.

See also **Perry**: A Child's Prayer, 12 (words and music); I Love to See the Temple, 95 (words and music); I'm Thankful to Be Me, 11 (music); I'm Trying to Be Like Jesus, 78 (words and music); Love Is Spoken Here, 190 (words and music); Mother, Tell Me the Story, 204 (words and music); The Church of Jesus Christ, 77 (words and music); The Word of Wisdom, 154 (words and music); We'll Bring the World His Truth, 172 (words and music); *Hymns*, As Sisters in Zion, 309 (music).

IF WITH ALL YOUR HEARTS, 15

Words: Julius Schubring (1806–1889)
Music: from *Elijah* by Felix Mendelssohn (1809–1847)

PART THREE

After the success of Felix Mendelssohn's first oratorio, *St. Paul,* friends suggested he consider writing a second. Felix asked **Julius Schubring** to try a libretto based on Elijah. Schubring was a tutor, theologian, pastor, and philologist, and served as rector of St. George's Church in Dessau, Germany. After several years the project was shelved. In 1845, William Bartholomew was asked by Felix to translate the Schubring libretto for a music festival scheduled in Birmingham for the summer of 1846. Felix wrote his brother early in July: "I foresee completing my Elijah in ten to twelve days; the larger part of the second half is already in England, and the choruses are starting to learn it. A few weeks ago I was quite worried . . . but now am slowly beginning to look forward."[13]

Felix Mendelssohn is considered to be one of the greatest German pianists, composers, and conductors. He grew up in a refined and cultured family with choir and orchestral concerts in their home. At the age of nine he began performing with his older sister, Fanny. Soon he was conducting his own works in Germany and England, including his oratorio, *Elijah*. In 1847, at the young age of thirty-eight, the composer died. We can only imagine how many more beautiful melodic pieces he might have created.

Even though greatly simplified by Vanja Watkins, with suggestions by Darwin Wolford, the beloved melody still retains the dignity and impact of a great classic. Children prefer only what they are familiar with, and this sweeping melody gives them a lovely taste of one of the finest religious oratorios ever composed. It can also be enjoyed as a prelude.

See also **Mendelssohn**: O Rest in the Lord, 295 (music); *Hymns*, Cast Thy Burden upon the Lord, 110 (music); Hark! The Herald Angels Sing, 209 (music); O God, the Eternal Father, 175 (music).

CHILDREN ALL OVER THE WORLD, 16

Words: Peggy Hill Ryskamp (1949–) LDS
Music: Beth Groberg Stratton (1944–) LDS

Peggy Hill Ryskamp served a mission to France and was a high school language teacher. She wrote a poem to teach children that Heavenly Father hears and understands the prayers of all children, no matter what language they are spoken in. She said, "I know that when the children in Primary try their hardest to sing, our Father in heaven really is proud of them."[14] **Beth Groberg Stratton** is a private piano teacher and composer of the music. She received a BA in music from Brigham Young University and a certification from the American College of Musicians.

The words for "thank you" are given in seven different languages in this song. Previously, the phonetic pronunciations were given at the bottom of the page of the song to help people pronounce the words correctly. If you've ever conducted this song, you will know why we chose to print the pronunciations *where they occur!*

The introduction is a little bit of the beginning and a little bit in the middle. The pianist would play the complete first line (inside the brackets) and then jump down to the third line and play inside the brackets over the words "own special way." It is helpful to mark the brackets in red so you can easily find them.

I NEED MY HEAVENLY FATHER, 18

Words and music: Judith Wirthlin Parker (1919–2000) LDS

Judith Wirthlin Parker wrote "My Heavenly Father Wants Me to Be Happy" for the 1968 Primary Reverence Program to help teach children that living righteously brings happiness. For this publication, the title was changed to the first line. Sister Parker was a music research scholar and believed that "music opens doors to other lands and cultures."[15] She served as the music chairman for the Primary general board when *Sing With Me* was prepared. She said that one day she was working with her committee in her living room. They were finalizing the pages for the printer. A car slid on the ice on her street and crashed into her front window. The papers were scattered all over and glass and ice were everywhere. She felt that someone was trying to prevent a good thing from happening! Fortunately, no one was hurt and the papers were rescued and put in order, and then published. Sister Parker is a sister to Apostle Joseph B. Wirthlin.

HEAVENLY FATHER, NOW I PRAY, 19

Words and music: Alvin A. Beesley (1873–1940) LDS

Alvin Beesley is the son of pioneer musician Ebenezer Beesley. He wrote the words and music for this Primary song, as well as many others included in earlier children's songbooks. The original title was "Jesus, Unto Thee I Pray" when first published in the 1905 Primary songbook. The change to "Heavenly Father, Now I Pray" distinguishes the Latter-day Saint understanding of praying to Heavenly Father in the name of Jesus Christ.

PART THREE

Brother Beesley was a twenty-five-year veteran Boy Scouter and a member of the Executive Council of the Boy Scouts of America. When he led the singing in his ward, he would walk up and down the aisles and sing in a vibrant tone to encourage everyone to sing. He was president and general manager of the Beesley Music Company in Salt Lake City, and often took his orchestra to the Utah State Prison to hold services for the inmates.

A SONG OF THANKS, 20

Words: anonymous
Music: J. Battishill (1738–1801)

Jonathan Battishill was one of the finest organists in London in the late 1700s. He also was a principal tenor soloist for many of England's churches. He played the harpsichord for Covent Garden Theater, taught organ, and was organist at St. Clement's Cathedral. Unfortunately, he was an alcoholic, which kept him from reaching greater success. He is buried in St. Paul's Cathedral. We do not know who wrote the poem for this song, so it remains anonymous.

Originally the music was in the key of G. It was lowered one step to the key of F so that D rather than E, would be the highest note of the melody.

THANKS TO OUR FATHER, 20

Words: Robert Louis Stevenson (1850–1894)
Music: Franz Joseph Haydn (1732–1809)

Two very famous people wrote this song. However, **Franz Joseph Haydn**, the great Viennese Classical composer, died before the author was born. It is not known if Stevenson wrote his poem to fit Haydn's music, or if someone else put the poem to the music. **Robert Louis Stevenson** was born in Scotland and suffered poor health. He eventually sought relief in Samoa, where he lived until his death. He wrote *Treasure Island*, *Kidnapped*, and *Dr. Jekyll and Mr. Hyde*, which are classics in literature. *A Child's Garden of Verses* contains this and other prayer verses for children.

Haydn was one of twelve children. His father was a wheelwright, and his mother worked in a kitchen. Franz became a choirboy when he was eight years old, and as a teenager he taught himself to play the harpsichord. At age seventeen, he became music director to a noble family in Austria. Eventually, he was appointed deputy music director for Prince

Esterhazy. For twenty-nine years he composed and performed all the music needed in his palace. Haydn invented the string quartet and improved the symphonic form. He composed over one hundred symphonies and twenty operas, popular concertos, choral works, and superb string quartets.

Originally this melody was in the key of G, but was lowered one step to the key of F. Children can easily sing C and D if they use their head voice rather than their chest, or speaking, voice. It is often the music leader who feels the song is "too high." You can help children find their "singing voice" by encouraging a light tone in their head. Singers who "belt" in their speaking voice often damage their vocal cords.

FOR HEALTH AND STRENGTH, 21

Words and music: anonymous

Originally, only the melody and words were printed. For this collection, we added chords and a simple left hand. When sung as a round, children can experience hearing harmony while singing a melody.

FOR THY BOUNTEOUS BLESSINGS, 21

Words: Lester Bucher
Music: traditional melody
Arrangement: Vanja Y. Watkins (1938–) LDS

This is the only prayer song in the *Children's Songbook* that is in a minor key. Previously, both the words and music were not credited. **Lester Bucher** was "found" as the author, but without any information about him.

Vanja (VON-yuh) **Yorgason Watkins** was asked to write an arrangement for this anonymous melody. She didn't use a piano, but wrote by "ear." She found that by being obedient to the rules of theory, she could be successful. She said she liked what she heard when it was completed, and it was a good lesson as well. Her teacher at BYU, Lou Groesbeck, began giving her other projects to work on, and eventually she was called to serve on the Primary general board. She realized later that Sister Groesbeck had been "grooming" her. She became Primary general board music chairman and then served as a member of the General Church Music Committee. She has credit lines for arrangements, words, music, and words and music—fourteen songs plus the thirteen Articles of Faith, making a total of twenty-seven entries.[16]

The round can be sung with two to four groups, using the numbers

PART THREE

to show starting places. Children can take turns strumming an autoharp accompaniment using just two chords—F and C7. It is also possible to play chimes or tone bells giving one note in each chord to seven children. Use F, A, C (I Chord) and C, E, G, B flat (V7 chord). Direct the children to play as you show pointer finger for the I-chord notes, and all five fingers for the V7 chord.

See also **Watkins:** Easter Hosanna, 68 (words and music); Families Can Be Together Forever, 188 (music); I Want to Be Reverent, 28 (music); I Will Be Valiant, 162 (words and music); I Will Follow God's Plan, 164 (words and music); It's Autumntime, 246 (arrangement); Latter-day Prophets, 134 (music); Thank Thee for Everything, 10 (words); The Articles of Faith, 122–132 (music); The Sacrament, 72 (words and music); The Things I Do, 170 (music); This Is My Beloved Son, 76 (music); To Be a Pioneer, 218 (arrangement); Truth from Elijah, 90 (words and music); *Hymns*, Families Can Be Together Forever, 300 (music); Press Forward Saints, 81 (music).

A PRAYER SONG, 22

Words and music: Robert P. Manookin (1918–1997) LDS

Robert Manookin simplified his song by changing from the key of B flat to G major. In a letter he said, "I have taken out the dissonant spots and made it flow, I think, a bit better. Thank you for the privilege of adding my little bit to the children's worship and learning through music."[17] Then he left for another mission to the Manila Philippines Temple. He had previously served a mission in Germany, and missions with his wife in the Sydney Australia and New Zealand Temples. He composed the New Zealand Temple Pageant music and the dedicatory music for the Orson Hyde Memorial Gardens in Jerusalem. Dr. Manookin served on the General Church Music Committee and contributed six hymns to the 1985 LDS Hymns.

Brother Manookin studied with many of the great Church musicians: organ with Frank W. Asper, Alexander Schreiner, and J. J. Keeler; conducting with J. Spencer Cornwall; and composition with B. Cecil Gates and Crawford Gates. After teaching and serving in administrative positions, he was named Professor Emeritus of Music at Brigham Young University.

See also **Manookin:** Our Bishop, 135 (words and music); Repentance, 98 (music); *Hymns*, Like Ten Thousand Legions Marching, 253 (music); Rise, Ye Saints, and Temples Enter, 287 (music); Saints of

STORIES OF THE CHILDREN'S SONGBOOK

Zion, 39 (music); See the Mighty Priesthood Gathered, 325 (music); Thy Will, O Lord, Be Done, 188 (music); We Have Partaken of Thy Love, 155 (music).

A PRAYER, 22

Words and music: Moiselle Renstrom (1889–1956) LDS

Moiselle Renstrom was a teacher who had the gift of becoming as a little child. She thrilled to new ideas and discoveries with her students and shared their enjoyment of learning. Her songbooks, *Merrily We Sing*, *Musical Adventures*, and *Rhythm Fun*, have been used by early childhood teachers throughout the world. She wrote both words and music to thirteen songs included in this collection. Most were written the year before her death in response to a request from the General Church Music Committee.

During the evaluation of songs for the *Children's Songbook*, it was noticed that Sister Renstrom's work required no changes. She knew the range for children's voices, wrote so that it was easy to play, taught well with her rhymes, and was doctrinally accurate. A favorite picture shows her seated at an upright piano, with beautiful finger-waves in her white hair, and little children happily singing all around her.

See also **Renstrom**: A Happy Family, 198 (words and music); A Happy Helper, 197 (words and music); I Am Glad for Many Things, 151 (words and music); I Love to Pray, 25 (words and music); Jesus Loved the Little Children, 59 (words and music); Jesus Said Love Everyone, 61 (words and music); Little Seeds Lie Fast Asleep, 243 (words and music); Once There Was a Snowman, 249 (words and music); Rain Is Falling All Around, 241 (words and music); The World Is So Lovely, 233 (words and music); To Get Quiet, 275 (words and music); Two Little Eyes, 268 (words and music).

FATHER UP ABOVE, 23

Words: Mabel Jones Gabbott (1910–2004) LDS
Music: Gladys Ericksen Seely (1899–1985) LDS

Mabel Jones Gabbott, the author, has worked on the staffs of the Church magazines and as a member of the YWMIA General Board and the General Church Music Committee. She chaired the Hymnbook Text Committee for the 1985 hymnbook. She was a very small lady with a very large talent for writing. She has written the words for sixteen

PART THREE

Primary songs and four hymns. Sister Gabbott lived in Bountiful, Utah, grew roses and cherries, and said, "I love to hear children sing."[18]

Gladys Ericksen Seely's mother had prayed for a daughter who could play the piano, and her ninth child answered that prayer. Gladys showed a natural musical talent at a young age, and could play any music she heard in any key. She played for silent movies in the theater and for dancing schools in Mt. Pleasant, Utah. She also expressed her testimony through her music. She was a piano teacher and accompanist, and created a charming melody for the poem "Father Up Above."

See also **Gabbott**: Baptism, 100 (words); Before I Take the Sacrament, 73 (words); Did Jesus Really Live Again?, 64 (words); Had I Been a Child, 80 (words); Have a Very Happy Birthday!, 284 (words); Have a Very Merry Christmas!, 51 (words); He Sent His Son, 34 (words); My Country, 224 (words); Samuel Tells of the Baby Jesus, 36 (words); Sleep, Little Jesus, 47 (words); The Family, 194 (words); There Was Starlight on the Hillside, 40 (words); To Think about Jesus, 71 (words); We Are Reverent, 27 (words); Who Is the Child, 46 (words); *Hymns*, In Humility, Our Savior, 172 (words); Lord, Accept Into Thy Kingdom, 236 (words); Rejoice, Ye Saints of Latter Days, 290 (words); We Have Partaken of Thy Love, 155 (words).

See also **Seely**: Before I Take the Sacrament, 73 (music).

HEAVENLY FATHER, WHILE I PRAY, 23

Words and music: Becky-Lee Hill Reynolds (1944–) LDS

The original title for the song was "My Prayer." The change to the first line was debated because there is another prayer song entitled "Heavenly Father, Now I Pray." However, the first line seemed to more clearly identify the song. The author/composer, **Becky-Lee Reynolds**, served a mission to France. Her grandmother, Maryhale Woolsey, was also an author and wrote the Utah favorite, "Springtime in the Rockies," as well as several Primary songs in previous collections.

See also **Reynolds**: My Mother Dear, 203 (words and music).

THANK THEE, FATHER, 24

Words: Alice Cushing Donaldson Riley (1867–1955)
Music: F. Remsen

An American poet, **Mrs. Alice Riley**, who lived in Illinois and California, wrote the poem for this song. She studied at Park Institute in Chicago and abroad. Her works for children were published in books and periodicals and included plays, pageants, poems, and song verses.

The song was first printed in *The Primary Song Book* in 1920. Originally the title was "Lord, We Thank Thee" and verse two said, "Help us Lord." In the Old Testament and in the world at large, "Lord" and "God" are used interchangeably. In the LDS Church today, "God" usually refers to Heavenly Father and "Lord" to the Savior. So the title and words were revised to more clearly address Heavenly Father. This also was the case with several other prayer songs that were adjusted. Only "Tell Me, Dear Lord" could not satisfactorily be changed, and became the exception.

The composer, **F. Remsen**, deserves to be complimented on the charming music, but there is no information about him available.

WE BOW OUR HEADS, 25

Words: Anna Johnson (1892–1979) LDS
Music: Alexander Schreiner (1901–1987) LDS

Anna Johnson was a special feature writer for the *Deseret News* and the author of "Hopscotch Valley," a children's column. Many books of her poetry were published, and **Dr. Alexander Schreiner**, tabernacle organist, wrote tunes for over a hundred of them. She also worked in the office of the YWMIA. One of Sister Johnson's hobbies was collecting foreign dolls. To her, the dolls represented children everywhere in whom she was interested. The collection was given to the Primary Children's Hospital in Salt Lake City, Utah.

Brother Schreiner was born in Germany and played the piano at the age of five. At age eight, he became a Church organist. He also studied the violin. He came to Salt Lake City at the age of eleven and played his first recital in the Tabernacle while in his teens. Soon after, he was appointed Tabernacle organist, a position he held for fifty-three years. He excelled as organist, composer, arranger, writer, and concert artist. Millions of people heard his organ broadcasts from the Tabernacle. Dr. Schreiner earned the first PhD given in music at the University of Utah. His tune for "We Bow Our Heads" was also used for the words "An Angel Came to Joseph Smith." He composed the music for nine hymns in the 1985 LDS hymnbook.[19]

See also **Johnson**: A Smile Is Like the Sunshine, 267 (words); An Angel Came to Joseph Smith, 86 (words); I Think the World Is Glorious,

PART THREE

230 (words); Jesus Is Our Loving Friend, 58 (words) My Flag, My Flag, 225 (words).

See also **Schreiner**: I Think the World Is Glorious, 230 (music); Jesus Is Our Loving Friend, 58 (music); My Flag, My Flag, 225 (music); *Hymns*, Behold Thy Sons and Daughters, Lord, 238 (music); God Loved Us, So He Sent His Son, 187 (music); Holy Temples on Mount Zion, 289 (music); In Memory of the Crucified, 190 (music); Lead Me into Life Eternal, 45 (music); Lord, Accept into Thy Kingdom, 236 (music); Thy Spirit, Lord, Has Stirred Our Souls, 157 (music); Truth Eternal, 4 (music); While of These Emblems We Partake, 174 (music).

I LOVE TO PRAY, 25

Words and music: Moiselle Renstrom (1889–1956) LDS

K. Moiselle Renstrom was a teacher who had the gift of becoming as a little child. She was thrilled by new ideas and discoveries with her students and shared their enjoyment of learning. Her songbooks, *Merrily We Sing, Musical Adventures,* and *Rhythm Fun*, have been used by early childhood teachers throughout the world. She wrote both words and music to thirteen songs included in this collection. Most were written the year before her death in response to a request from the General Church Music Committee.

During the evaluation of songs for the *Children's Songbook*, it was noticed that Sister Renstrom's work required no changes. She knew the range for children's voices, wrote so that it was easy to play, taught well with her rhymes, and was doctrinally accurate. Both words and music to thirteen of her songs are included in this collection. Many of her songs for little children encourage them to pretend and move with the music (i.e., "Once There Was a Snowman"). A favorite picture shows her seated at an upright piano, with beautiful finger waves in her white hair, and little children happily singing all around her.

See also **Renstrom**: A Happy Family, 198 (words and music); A Happy Helper, 197 (words and music); A Prayer, 22 (words and music); I Am Glad for Many Things, 151 (words and music); Jesus Loved the Little Children, 59 (words and music); Jesus Said Love Everyone, 61 (words and music); Little Seeds Lie Fast Asleep, 243 (words and music); Once There Was a Snowman, 249 (words and music); Rain Is Falling All Around, 241 (words and music); The World Is So Lovely, 233 (words and music); To Get Quiet, 275 (words and music); Two Little Eyes, 268 (words and music).

REVERENTLY, QUIETLY, 26

Words and music: Clara Watkins McMaster (1901–1997) LDS

While serving on the Primary general board, **Clara McMaster** was asked to write a song for the first reverence program. She worked hard and prayed that she would be prompted to write what would be best for the children. As she was looking out the window and pondering her assignment, an idea came to her. She went to the piano and quickly wrote it down. The new song was "Reverently, Quietly." "I felt very humble," she said. "If you prepare and do all that you can do, then Heavenly Father will help you."[20]

Sister McMaster was the eleventh child in her family, and she learned to love music at an early age. She sang and accompanied others on the piano while she grew up in Brigham City, Utah. For twenty-two years she was a member of the Tabernacle Choir. She said, "Music is a rich gift of God, and it is in the world to make the lives of His children happier and better."[21] Sister McMaster served on the Primary general board for fourteen years, and was on the music committee for some of that time. She and her husband, J. Stuart McMaster, received the 1978 Franklin S. Harris Fine Arts Award from Brigham Young University for their musical contributions to the Church and community. They also presided over the Missouri Independence Mission.

See also **McMaster**: Choose the Right Way, 160 (words and music); Kindness Begins with Me, 145 (words and music); My Heavenly Father Loves Me, 228 (words and music); Remember the Sabbath Day, 155 (words and music); Teach Me to Walk in the Light, 177 (words and music); *Hymns*, Teach Me to Walk in the Light, 304 (words and music).

REVERENCE, 27

Words: Ruth H. Chadwick (1900–1973) LDS
Music: Leah Ashton Lloyd (1894–1965)

Ruth Chadwick was a talented writer and was involved in the National League of American Pen Women and the Utah Poetry Society. For ten years she served on the Primary general board. **Leah Lloyd** became Primary organist at age fourteen, and then choir organist. She taught piano lessons and had music classes for children at the Primary Children's Hospital. She was a member of the Primary general board for twenty years and was instrumental in the preparation of *The Children Sing*.

PART THREE

See also **Lloyd**: I Think When I Read That Sweet Story, 56 (music).

WE ARE REVERENT, 27

Words: Mabel Jones Gabbott (1910–2004) LDS
Music: A. Laurence Lyon (1934–2006) LDS

Mabel Jones Gabbott, the author, worked on the staffs of all the Church magazines, and was a member of the YWMIA General Board and the General Church Music Committee. She chaired the 1985 Hymnbook Text Committee. She was a very small lady with a very large talent for writing. Her poems were used as texts for sixteen Primary songs and four hymns. Sister Gabbott lived in Bountiful, Utah, and grew roses and cherries. She said, "I love to hear children sing."[22]

Laurence Lyon, the composer, was born in Holland while his father, T. Edgar Lyon, was mission president. He later served a mission to Holland as a young man. He received a doctorate in composition from Eastman School of Music, and has more than one hundred published compositions, many performed by the Tabernacle Choir. He served on the Sunday School General Board and the General Church Music Committee.

Brother Lyon said, "There need to be more quiet moments in life, moments to reflect and meditate about the important things of life, such as the life of the Savior." This song uses "a contemplation of the quiet things in nature as an example," he said.[23]

Originally the song was entitled "Quiet Song," but was changed to emphasize the message of reverence. Because being reverent is more about what we do than what we know, verse one, line two, was changed. "As we *learn to do* right" now says "As we *do what is* right." This follows the logic taught by President Kimball with the word change he suggested in "I Am a Child of God"—teach me all that I must *do*, rather than the original word *know*.

See also **Gabbott**: Baptism, 100 (words); Before I Take the Sacrament, 73 (words); Did Jesus Really Live Again?, 64 (words); Father Up Above, 23 (words); Had I Been a Child, 80 (words); Have a Very Happy Birthday!, 284 (words); Have a Very Merry Christmas!, 51 (words); He Sent His Son, 34 (words); My Country, 224 (words); Samuel Tells of the Baby Jesus, 36 (words); Sleep, Little Jesus, 47 (words); The Family, 194 (words); There Was Starlight on the Hillside, 40 (words); To Think about Jesus, 71 (words); Who Is the Child?, 46 (words); *Hymns*, In Humility, Our Savior, 172 (words); Lord, Accept Into Thy Kingdom,

236 (words); Rejoice, Ye Saints of Latter Days, 290 (words); We Have Partaken of Thy Love, 155 (words).

See also **Lyon**: An Angel Came to Joseph Smith, 86 (music); Christmas Bells, 54 (words and music); How Will They Know?, 182 (arrangement); I Have Two Ears, 269 (music); Little Pioneer Children, 216 (words and music); We Are Reverent, 27 (music); Whenever I Think about Pioneers, 222 (music); *Hymns*, Each Life That Touches Ours for Good, 293 (music); Saints, Behold How Great Jehovah, 28 (music).

I WANT TO BE REVERENT, 28

Words: Primary Committee
Music: Vanja Y. Watkins (1938–) LDS

Vanja (VON-yuh) **Yorgason Watkins** was asked by Mayre Beth Nielsen, a member of the Children's Sacrament Meeting Committee, to write music for a short poem the committee wanted as a song. Initially the second line began "I'll be quiet and listen." Vanja suggested, "I will quietly listen," and the committee approved the literary improvement, her melody, and accompaniment as well. Sister Watkins served seven years on the Primary general board, and her doctor-husband arranged office hours to help care for their small children while she fulfilled her responsibilities. She said, "The tender mercies of the Lord allowed it all to work out."[24] Sister Watkins served another twelve years as a member of the General Church Music Committee, often taking her youngest daughter to meetings and tucking her under the table. Her motive for writing is her love of children, her love of music, and her love of the gospel. She is glad she can write a little song to serve.

See also **Watkins**: Easter Hosanna, 68 (words and music); Families Can Be Together Forever, 188 (music); For Thy Bounteous Blessings, 21 (arrangement); I Want to Be Reverent, 28 (music); I Will Be Valiant, 162 (words and music); I Will Follow God's Plan, 164 (words and music); It's Autumntime, 246 (arrangement); Latter-day Prophets, 134 (music); Thank Thee for Everything, 10 (words); The Articles of Faith, 122–132 (music); The Sacrament, 72 (words and music); The Things I Do, 170 (music); This Is My Beloved Son, 76 (music); To Be a Pioneer, 218 (arrangement); Truth from Elijah, 90 (words and music); *Hymns*, Families Can Be Together Forever, 300 (music); Press Forward Saints, 81 (music).

PART THREE

I WILL TRY TO BE REVERENT, 28

Words and music: Wilma Boyle Bunker (1910–1992) LDS

Wilma Bunker was a high school teacher and taught piano lessons for sixty-three years. She served on the Primary general board for eight years, was a national president of the League of American Pen Women, and in 1962 received a Distinguished Service Award from the Brigham Young University Alumni Association.

See also **Bunker**: Hello, Friends!, 254 (words and music).

FATHER, I WILL REVERENT BE, 29

Words and music: Mildred Tanner Pettit (1895–1977) LDS

Mildred Pettit studied piano, pipe organ, and composition at the McCune School of Music in Salt Lake City. She served for thirty-five years in the Primary, with four of those years on the Primary general board. Collaborating with Matilda Watts Cahoon, she wrote many programs and songs for children.

Originally, "Father, I Will Reverent Be," had a second verse. Many other prayer songs had only one verse, and because this was a longer song it was decided not to include both verses. There was also discussion about deleting the last line, which repeats the first and is like a coda–an additional ending. The decision was made to include the fifth phrase.

See also **Pettit**: Beauty Everywhere, 232 (music); I Am a Child of God, 2 (music); Mother Dear, 206 (music); *Hymns*, The Light Divine, 305 (music).

THIS IS GOD'S HOUSE, 30

Words: Louise M. Oglevee (Abt.1866–1954)

Music: William G. Oglevee (1865–1939)

Louise Oglevee was a talented girl and a perfect match for her husband, **William**, a Presbyterian preacher. When she could find no suitable materials for young children, she developed her own. This included writing songs for nursery school and Sunday School. William's music was published in many volumes. They lived in Oklahoma, Iowa, and Illinois, where he served as pastor.

A granddaughter, Mary Louise Oglevee Rack, corrected the previous spelling of the name Ogelvee to Oglevee. The left-hand accompaniment was thinned for this arrangement.

STORIES OF THE CHILDREN'S SONGBOOK

OUR CHAPEL IS A SACRED PLACE, 30

Words: adapted, Polly Bourgeous (1937–)
Music: Darwin Wolford (1936–) LDS

Eva Pauline Bourgeous joined The Church of Jesus Christ of Latter-day Saints at the age of nineteen. She has served in all of the auxiliaries, mainly with her musical talents. She earned a degree from New Mexico State University and is a piano teacher living in California with her husband. They are the parents of five children.

The melody originally was equal quarter notes for the first two measures of each line. The words *place* and *pray* now have a dotted quarter to allow for a breath.

Darwin Wolford was a music professor at BYU–Idaho and holds a PhD in organ and composition. He is widely published, and his works have been performed by the Mormon Tabernacle Choir and the Utah Symphony. He served on the General Church Music Committee and the 1985 Hymnbook Executive Committee. We are very much indebted to him for his expertise in simplifying and refining the songs for the 1989 *Children's Songbook*. It was a monumental time commitment with no recognition, yet he gave cheerful service on the project. Batches of songs would be mailed to him with suggestions, and he was always able to fill the need. The high musical standard of the book can be credited to his careful scrutiny and advice.

See also **Wolford**: Beautiful Savior, 62 (arrangement); Had I Been a Child, 80 (music); I Am a Child of God, 2 (arrangement); I Have a Family Tree, 199 (music); In Quietude, 191 (music); Keep the Commandments, 146 (arrangement); Mary's Lullaby, 44 (arrangement); Stars Were Gleaming, 37 (arrangement); Supplication, 297 (music); Teach Me to Walk in the Light, 177(obbligato); Thanks to Thee, 6 (music); The Lord Gave Me a Temple, 153 (music); *Hymns*, Sons of Michael, He Approaches, 51 (music); We Listen to a Prophet's Voice, 22 (music).

REVERENCE IS LOVE, 31

Words and music: Maggie Olauson (1949–) LDS

The author, **Margaret Louise Olauson**, has an interior design degree from Brigham Young University, and teaches piano in her home. She is married to a Navy chaplain, and they are the parents of three sons and three daughters. The song was first published in 1986 in the *Friend*, and was simplified for the *Children's Songbook*.

PART THREE

The Savior

"The greatest thing that ever happened on earth was accompanied by music."
—Anonymous

The songs about the Savior are in chronological order beginning with the prophecy of the Savior's birth, the Christmas songs, Jesus' childhood and ministry, songs of Easter, resurrection and the sacrament, why we want to be like Him, and songs of His Second Coming.

The beautiful picture of the Nativity on the first lavender page depicts children presenting a Christmas pageant. Look carefully on the curtain in the lower right hand corner, and you will see LUCH, the artist's last name. The committee worked very closely with the artists to arrive at the best possible way to picture the correct message. The original sketch of the Nativity divider had a wise man on each side of the manger. It was suggested that the shepherds came first and it might be a teaching point to show them closest to the baby. So Sister Luch changed the crowns for cloths, added shepherd's staves, and put the wise men to the right.

"He Sent His Son" is a transition between the first two sections of the book, Heavenly Father and The Savior. It is a Christmas song, an Easter song, and a song about the Savior's mission.

HE SENT HIS SON, 34

Words: Mabel Jones Gabbott (1910–2004) LDS
Music: Michael Finlinson Moody (1941–) LDS

Mabel Gabbott said the poem for "He Sent His Son" was written "when I was wondering about our Father in Heaven sending His spirit children to earth to be tested. How could He teach them the way to return to Him? The answer: He sent His Son."[25] Sister Gabbott worked on the staffs of the Church magazines and was a member of the YWMIA General Board and the General Church Music Committee. She chaired the 1985 Hymnbook Text Committee. She was a very small lady with a very large talent for writing. Her poems have been used as texts for sixteen Primary songs and four hymns. Sister Gabbott lived in Bountiful, Utah, grew roses and cherries, and said, "I love to hear children sing."[26]

The composer, **Michael Moody**, believes that "music is a tool for building families. It can bring a sweet spirit into the home. My family sings before scripture reading, before meals, and when we're traveling in our car."[27] Brother Moody was chairman of the General Church Music Committee for twenty-five years and Haiti Mission president. He is now serving with his wife, Maria, on a music mission at the Brigham Young University Jerusalem Center.

Every year Brother Moody writes a Christmas song for his family and friends. For his Christmas song in 1981 he wrote a musical phrase to emphasize each question and answer in Sister Gabbott's poem, "He Sent His Son." It was published in the *Friend* magazine, December 1984. Several melody notes were mistakenly changed in the first typesetting of the music. Brother Moody said maybe it was better that way, and left the change. The optional notes in the last three measures were added for a children's choir in the tabernacle in 1985.

See also **Gabbott**: Baptism, 100 (words); Before I Take the Sacrament, 73 (words); Did Jesus Really Live Again?, 64 (words); Father Up Above, 23 (words); Had I Been a Child, 80 (words); Have a Very Happy Birthday!, 284 (words); Have a Very Merry Christmas!, 51 (words); My Country, 224 (words); Samuel Tells of the Baby Jesus, 36 (words); Sleep, Little Jesus, 47 (words); The Family, 194 (words); There Was Starlight on the Hillside, 40 (words); To Think about Jesus, 71 (words); We Are Reverent, 27 (words); Who Is the Child, 46 (words); *Hymns*, In Humility, Our Savior, 172 (words); Lord, Accept Into Thy Kingdom, 236 (words); Rejoice, Ye Saints of Latter Days, 290 (words); We Have Partaken of Thy Love, 155 (words).

See also **Moody**: Faith, 96 (music); Have a Very Happy Birthday!, 284 (music); Have a Very Merry Christmas!, 51 (music); Sleep, Little Jesus, 47 (music); Teacher, Do You Love Me?, 178 (words and music); There Was Starlight on the Hillside, 40 (music); Who Is the Child?, 46 (music); *Hymns*, Testimony, 137 (music).

SAMUEL TELLS OF THE BABY JESUS, 36

Words: Mabel Jones Gabbott (1910–2004) LDS
Music: Grietje Terburg Rowley (1927–) LDS

When the song first appeared in the *Friend* (Dec. 1985, 29), it was entitled "Christmas in Zarahemla." The title was changed to help emphasize the message of the song.

Mabel Jones Gabbott was one of nine children and received her

PART THREE

education at the University of Idaho and the University of Utah. She served a mission to the Northwestern States, and then became secretary to Elder LeGrand Richards. Sister Gabbott worked on the staffs of the Church magazines and as a member of the YWMIA General Board and the General Church Music Committee. She chaired the Hymnbook Text Committee for the 1985 hymnbook.

Sister Gabbott was a very small lady and wore her hair swept up on top of her head. She had, however, a very large talent for writing and has sixteen entries in the Author and Composer Index. Her poems have also been used for the text's four hymns. She lived in Bountiful, Utah, and grew roses and cherries. She said, "I love to hear children sing."[28]

The composer, **Grietje** (GREE-chuh) **Terburg Rowley**, is of Dutch descent, and taught school in Hawaii where she joined the Church. About this song she said, "Every Christmas our family reads the Christmas story from the New Testament. We also read in the Book of Mormon about the first Christmas in America. We try to imagine how the people felt about Jesus' birth. I tried to make the music sound a little like both Jewish and Indian music."[29] Sister Rowley had worked on words of her own and felt they were too complicated. When she used Sister Gabbott's poem, she couldn't get the musical ideas down fast enough—they flowed naturally When she is working on a song, she always prays that it will be the way Heavenly Father would want it to be. She tries to make her songs easy to sing, easy to play, and easy to remember.

Sister Rowley served on the Ad Hoc Committee for the *Children's Songbook* contributing her talents in simplifying, arranging, composing, and proofreading. She often encouraged us by saying that this book was important for the children of the Church and Heavenly Father would help us to make it the way it should be.

See also **Gabbott**: Baptism, 100 (words); Before I Take the Sacrament, 73 (words); Did Jesus Really Live Again?, 64 (words); Father Up Above, 23 (words); Had I Been a Child, 80 (words); Have a Very Happy Birthday!, 284 (words); Have a Very Merry Christmas!, 51 (words); He Sent His Son, 34 (words); My Country, 224 (words); Sleep, Little Jesus, 47 (words); The Family, 194 (words); There Was Starlight on the Hillside, 40 (words); To Think about Jesus, 71 (words); We Are Reverent, 27 (words); Who Is the Child, 46 (words); *Hymns*, In Humility, Our Savior, 172 (words); Lord, Accept Into Thy Kingdom, 236 (words); Rejoice, Ye Saints of Latter Days, 290 (words); We Have Partaken of Thy Love, 155 (words).

STORIES OF THE CHILDREN'S SONGBOOK

See also **Rowley**: A Smile is Like the Sunshine, 267 (music); Distant Bells, 299 (music); Each Sunday Morning, 290 (music); I Want to Be a Missionary Now, 168 (words and music); Roll Your Hands, 274 (arrangement); *Hymns*, Be Thou Humble, 130 (words and music).

STARS WERE GLEAMING, 37

Words: Nancy Byrd Turner (1880–1971)
Music: Polish Carol
Arrangement: Darwin Wolford (1936–) LDS

At the suggestion of the correlation committee, a significant word change was made in the first verse. The text had been "Stars were gleaming, shepherds dreaming; *winter* night was dark and chill." Because we believe that it was in the spring of the year when the Savior was born, *winter* was changed to *and the*. The notation was returned to the form used in *The Children Sing*, beginning on beat 3 (pickup) rather than beat 1 (downbeat) as in *Sing With Me*. Try it both ways and you will feel why it was changed.

Nancy Byrd Turner was the daughter of an Episcopalian pastor, and became a writer, editor, and lecturer. She wrote for magazines in both America and England, and for many years was the editor of the children's page of the *Youth Companion*. She also authored several children's books.

Darwin Wolford received his doctorate in composition at Utah State University. He studied organ with Alexander Schreiner and Robert Cundick, and composition with Leroy Robertson, Ned Rorem, and John LaMontaine. His works for organ, piano, orchestra, and chorus are published widely, and he was director of organ studies at BYU–Idaho. Brother Wolford served on the General Music Committee of the Church and the 1985 Hymnbook Committee. His expertise was invaluable as he revised and simplified Primary songs for the *Children's Songbook*. The musical standard of the book is due to his careful scrutiny and advice. We are very much in his debt.

See also **Wolford**: Beautiful Savior, 62 (arrangement); Had I Been a Child, 80 (music); I Am a Child of God, 2 (arrangement); I Have a Family Tree, 199 (music); In Quietude, 191 (music); Keep the Commandments, 146 (arrangement); Mary's Lullaby, 44 (arrangement); Our Chapel Is a Sacred Place, 30 (music); Supplication, 297 (music); Teach Me to Walk in the Light, 177(obbligato); Thanks to Thee, 6 (music); The Lord Gave

PART THREE

Me a Temple, 153 (music); *Hymns*, Sons of Michael, He Approaches, 51 (music); We Listen to a Prophet's Voice, 22 (music).

WHEN JOSEPH WENT TO BETHLEHEM, 38

Words: Bessie Saunders Spencer (1898–1989)
Music: L. Reed Payne (1930–) LDS

Bessie Spencer was a Methodist and a freelance poet and writer. She contributed to many religious and popular magazines and anthologies, and received awards in local and national poetry contests. She affiliated with the Poetry Society of Colorado, the National League of American Pen Women, American Poetry League, and Daughters of American Colonists.

When her poem was originally published in December 1960, the Reed Payne family cut it out of *The Children's Friend*. Over the years, their children learned to recite it. Eventually, Brother Payne set it to music. He said, "In an hour's time the music was written. The poem seemed to call for a simple, flowing melody to match the beautiful and sacred words of that first Christmas . . . 'When Joseph Went to Bethlehem' is a song that helps us picture the events surrounding the birth of Jesus more clearly from a father's perspective. Joseph was not just an observer or an onlooker, but very involved as a new father and guardian of baby Jesus. We can easily imagine Joseph's . . . practical effort and spiritual awe as he assisted Mary in this most wondrous of all births."[30]

Dr. Reed Payne played for dance bands as a young man, and now taught psychology at Brigham Young University, including a class on the psychology of music. He states, "Music carries the message of a song, stirs our feelings, and strengthens our testimony. Music helps us worship with meaning and expression."[31]

LITTLE JESUS, 39

Words: Marilyn Curtis White (1941–) LDS
Music: Mark Newell (1961–) LDS; and Charlene Anderson Newell (1938–) LDS

Marilyn White is a mother of eight, and a freelance writer. She earned degrees in journalism and American history at Brigham Young University, and was editor for *Asia Pacific Defense Forum*. She is a chairperson for the American Association of Women. Originally the last phrase of her sweet poem said, "Happy Birthday, Christmas Day." Correlation asked that it be changed because of our belief that the Savior was actually born in the spring, and that the celebration of His birth was originally held in conjunction with other winter festivities. It now says, "Praise we sing on Christmas Day!"

Mark Newell was Primary age when he wrote the tune for this poem—just ten years old! Brother Newell is a carpenter and mechanic, and plays drums, piano, and trumpet. He says, "Music is an eternal gift and is enjoyed at home, church, and work. Melodies and lyrics that make you feel good are constructive to the soul."[32] He is the oldest of twelve children, and his mother, **Charlene Newell**, is also a composer. Her music has been published in the *Friend,* and she won the 1977 Relief Society song contest. Her music has been performed in the Tabernacle and at the dedication of the Nauvoo Monument to Women. She is an outstanding pianist and has taught private voice and organ lessons and music in Utah's Granite School District.

See also **Newell**, Charlene: He Died That We Might Live Again, 65 (music); The Commandments, 112 (music); Your Happy Birthday, 283 (words and music); *Hymns*, A Key Was Turned in Latter Days, 310 (music).

THERE WAS STARLIGHT ON THE HILLSIDE, 40

Words: Mabel Jones Gabbott (1910–2004) LDS
Music: Michael Finlinson Moody (1941–) LDS

Mabel Jones Gabbott was one of nine children. She received her education at the University of Idaho and the University of Utah. She served a Northwestern States mission and then was secretary to Elder LeGrand Richards. Sister Gabbott worked on the staffs of the Church magazines and as a member of the YWMIA General Board and the General Church Music Committee. She chaired the 1985 Hymnbook Text Committee. At Christmastime, she and Brother Moody often collaborated on a Christmas greeting. Many of their songs were printed in the *Friend*, and six of them are in the *Children's Songbook*. Sister Gabbott lived in Bountiful, Utah, grew roses and cherries, and said, "I love to hear children sing."[33]

Michael Moody believes that "music is a tool for building families. It can bring a sweet spirit into the home. My family sings before scripture reading, before meals, and when we're traveling in our car."[34] Brother Moody served a mission in France and France East, and earned a doctorate in church music from the University of Southern California. He was director of the music division of the Church for twenty-five years and

PART THREE

chairman of the 1985 Hymnbook Executive Committee. He also served as the Haiti Mission president, and with his wife, Maria, on a music mission at the BYU Jerusalem Center.

See also **Gabbott**: Baptism, 100 (words); Before I Take the Sacrament, 73 (words); Did Jesus Really Live Again?, 64 (words); Father Up Above, 23 (words); Had I Been a Child, 80 (words); Have a Very Happy Birthday!, 284 (words); Have a Very Merry Christmas!, 51 (words); He Sent His Son, 34 (words); My Country, 224 (words); Samuel Tells of the Baby Jesus, 36 (words); Sleep, Little Jesus, 47 (words); The Family, 194 (words); To Think about Jesus, 71 (words); We Are Reverent, 27 (words); Who Is the Child, 46 (words); *Hymns*, In Humility, Our Savior, 172 (words); Lord, Accept Into Thy Kingdom, 236 (words); Rejoice, Ye Saints of Latter Days, 290 (words); We Have Partaken of Thy Love, 155 (words).

See also **Moody**: Faith, 96 (music); Have a Very Happy Birthday!, 284 (music); Have a Very Merry Christmas!, 51 (music); He Sent His Son, 34 (music); Sleep, Little Jesus, 47 (music); Teacher, Do You Love Me?, 178 (words and music); Who Is the Child?, 46 (music); *Hymns*, Testimony, 137 (music).

THE SHEPHERD'S CAROL, 40

Words and music: Daniel Lyman Carter (1955–) LDS

This charming round was published in the December 1981 *Friend*, with one verse and a melody line only. We requested an additional verse and accompaniment for the *Children's Songbook*.

As a young boy in Idaho, **Dan Carter** often cried when he listened to the Tabernacle Choir at conference time because of the beautiful music. He said, "I always yearned to be able to share my testimony and feelings of the gospel through music."[35] He fulfilled his desire by earning a degree in musical composition from Brigham Young University and composing many choral and keyboard pieces. He served as a member of the General Church Music Committee, and is employed in the Church Music Editing and Publishing Division. He has been responsible for the translation of the Primary songs.

Compositions by Brother Carter include numerous published choral pieces as well as a beautiful sacrament hymn.

See also **Carter**: A Young Man Prepared, 166 (words and music); *Hymns*, As Now We Take the Sacrament, 169 (music).

ONCE WITHIN A LOWLY STABLE, 41

Words and music: Patty Smith Hill (1868–1946) and Mildred Hill (1859–1916)

Author's Note: The Committee had not been able to find any information about **Patty Hill***, the author of this song—only that she had also written "Happy Birthday to You." While proofing the songbook late one night, I noticed an article in a newspaper that had been left on the table. Although I had not read a newspaper for months, the headline "'Happy Birthday' Not Expected to Go for a Song" caught my eye. The article told about the sale of the copyright. As I read with excitement, I found Patty's complete name, birth date, and the fact that she had been a kindergarten teacher in Louisville, Kentucky, around the turn of the century. We were able to contact the new copyright holder for verification and give credit to Patty and Mildred, her sister, rather than to "words anon." I am sure I did not "find" this information, but was led to it. The word "and" was added on verse two, measure five, to give the two verses the same number of syllables (strophic.)*

Patty Hill grew up in an educational environment. Her father, the Reverend William Wallace Hill, was president of a college for young women. She and her sister, Mildred, wrote a book called *Song Stories for the Sunday School*, published in 1893. Patty became the director of a model kindergarten visited by educators from around the country. She was joint author of *Kindergarten and Song Stories for the Kindergarten*, and later the director of the department of primary education at Columbia Teacher's College. She wrote the words and Mildred wrote the music for "Good Morning to You," which then became "Happy Birthday to You." The *Guinness Book of World Records* cites this song as the most often sung song in the world. We had intended to use this famous song in our collection, but the royalty fee was very high, so it was pulled from the layout. See "You've Had a Birthday," 285, for the resulting little miracle.

AWAY IN A MANGER, 42

Words: anonymous, ca. 1883, Philadelphia
Music: anonymous

Popular myths claim that this is the cradlesong Martin Luther authored and sang to his children in the fifteenth century. Unfortunately, there is no documentation to that effect. The words first appeared in the United States in the 1880s and have been sung to many melodies. Some versions use "wee" rather than "sweet head," and "take us to" rather than

PART THREE

"fit us for heaven." The verses in the songbook were edited to match the hymnbook words. The "Asleep, asleep" chorus is especially childlike.

The 1985 hymnbook uses a melody by William Kirkpatrick, but the composer of the tune in this collection remains unknown.

MARY'S LULLABY, 44

Words: Jan Underwood Pinborough (1954–) LDS
Music: German folk tune; arranged by Darwin Wolford (1936–) LDS

Originally, the words to this song were a German translation of the poem "Mary's Lullaby to the Infant King." The copyright holders were asking $2000 royalty for the use of the song, payable every ten years rather than for the life of the book. That seemed extremely high when negotiations for most other commercial copyrights were about $40. We didn't feel the words were all that meaningful, and it was the melody that made the song wonderful. The music was in public domain, meaning that it could be used without a fee. A wonderful solution occurred to us—why not write a new text that the Church could copyright?

Jan Pinborough, an editor for Church magazines with an MA in linguistics, was asked to read the original German and write two verses that would teach about the divinity of the Savior. Her poem tells of the Savior's divine father and Joseph, who cares for him on earth. Sister Underwood has served on Church writing committees preparing the *Family Home Evening Resource Book* and writing Relief Society lessons.

Darwin Wolford masterfully wove the melody into the accompaniment and supported the descant with the left hand. It was suggested that we contact the copyright holders to see if they would like to buy the new arrangement for $2000! But of course, we didn't.

Brother Wolford is a music professor at BYU–Idaho and holds a PhD in organ and composition. He is widely published, and his works have been performed by the Mormon Tabernacle Choir and the Utah Symphony. He served on the General Church Music Committee and the 1985 Hymnbook Executive Committee. We are very much indebted to him for his expertise in simplifying and refining the songs for the 1989 *Children's Songbook*. It was a monumental time commitment, with no recognition, yet he gave cheerful service on the project. Batches of songs would be mailed to him with suggestions, and he was always able to fill the need. The high musical standard of the book is due to his careful scrutiny and advice.

See also **Wolford**: Beautiful Savior, 62 (arrangement); Had I Been a Child, 80 (music); I Am a Child of God, 2 (arrangement); I Have a Family Tree, 199 (music); In Quietude, 191 (music); Keep the Commandments, 146 (arrangement); Our Chapel Is a Sacred Place, 30 (music); Stars Were Gleaming, 37 (arrangement); Supplication, 297 (music); Teach Me to Walk in the Light, 177(obbligato); Thanks to Thee, 6 (music); The Lord Gave Me a Temple, 153 (music); *Hymns*, Sons of Michael, He Approaches, 51 (music); We Listen to a Prophet's Voice, 22 (music).

See also **Pinborough**: *Hymns*, A Key Was Turned in Latter Days, 310 (words).

WHO IS THE CHILD? 46

Words: Mabel Jones Gabbott (1910–2004) LDS
Music: Michael Finlinson Moody (1941–) LDS

Mabel Jones Gabbott was one of nine children. She received her education at the University of Idaho and the University of Utah. She served in the Northwestern States mission, and then became secretary to Elder LeGrand Richards. Sister Gabbott worked on the staffs of all of the Church magazines. She served as a member of the YWMIA General Board, the General Church Music Committee, and chairman of the 1985 Hymnbook Text Committee. She contributed texts to sixteen songs in the *Children's Songbook*. This is another of the beautiful texts **Michael Finlinson Moody** set to music as a Christmas greeting. When we were evaluating songs for inclusion in the songbook, Brother Moody would always write on his songs, "Not needed. Use other's works for variety." But the messages and the music were unique and needed.

The composer, **Michael Moody**, believes that "music is a tool for building families. It can bring a sweet spirit into the home. My family sings before scripture reading, before meals, and when we're traveling in our car."[36] Brother Moody was director of the music division of the Church for twenty-five years and chairman of the 1985 Hymnbook Executive Committee. He served a mission to France and France East, was the Haiti Mission president, and is now serving with his wife, Maria, on a music mission at the BYU Jerusalem Center.[37]

See also **Gabbott**: Baptism, 100 (words); Before I Take the Sacrament, 73 (words); Did Jesus Really Live Again?, 64 (words); Father Up Above, 23 (words); Had I Been a Child, 80 (words); Have a Very Happy Birthday!, 284 (words); Have a Very Merry Christmas!, 51 (words); He Sent His Son, 34 (words); My Country, 224 (words); Samuel

PART THREE

Tells of the Baby Jesus, 36 (words); Sleep, Little Jesus, 47 (words); The Family, 194 (words); There Was Starlight on the Hillside, 40 (words); To Think about Jesus, 71 (words); We Are Reverent, 27 (words); *Hymns*, In Humility, Our Savior, 172 (words); Lord, Accept Into Thy Kingdom, 236 (words); Rejoice, Ye Saints of Latter Days, 290 (words); We Have Partaken of Thy Love, 155 (words).

See also **Moody**: Faith, 96 (music); Have a Very Happy Birthday!, 284 (music); Have a Very Merry Christmas!, 51 (music); He Sent His Son, 34 (music); Sleep, Little Jesus, 47 (music); Teacher, Do You Love Me?, 178 (words and music); There Was Starlight on the Hillside, 40 (music); *Hymns*, Testimony, 137 (music).

SLEEP, LITTLE JESUS, 47

Words: Mabel Jones Gabbott (1910–2004) LDS
Music: Michael Finlinson Moody (1941–) LDS

Mabel Jones Gabbott was a very small lady who wore her hair swept up on top of her head. She had a very large talent for writing and has written the words for sixteen Primary songs and four hymns. She said, "I love to hear children sing."[38] She lived in Bountiful, Utah, and grew roses and cherries. She worked on the staffs of the Church magazines and as a member of the YWMIA General Board and the General Church Music Committee. She chaired the Hymnbook Text Committee for the 1985 hymnbook.

The composer, **Michael Moody**, also lived in Bountiful, Utah. He often used Sister Gabbott's poems for his annual musical greeting. Invariably, people who received the greeting would submit the song to the *Friend* magazine. Brother Moody believes that "music is a tool for building families. It can bring a sweet spirit into the home. My family sings before scripture reading, before meals, and when we're traveling in our car."[39] Brother Moody was director of the music division of the Church for twenty-five years and chairman of the 1985 Hymnbook Executive Committee. He served a mission to France and Switzerland, was the Haiti Mission president, and is now serving with his wife, Maria, on a music mission at the BYU Jerusalem Center.

See also **Gabbott**: Baptism, 100 (words); Before I Take the Sacrament, 73 (words); Did Jesus Really Live Again?, 64 (words); Father Up Above, 23 (words); Had I Been a Child, 80 (words); Have a Very Happy Birthday!, 284 (words); Have a Very Merry Christmas!, 51 (words); He Sent His Son, 34 (words); My Country, 224 (words); Samuel

Tells of the Baby Jesus, 36 (words); The Family, 194 (words); There Was Starlight on the Hillside, 40 (words); To Think about Jesus, 71 (words); We Are Reverent, 27 (words) Who Is the Child, 46 (words); *Hymns*, In Humility, Our Savior, 172 (words); Lord, Accept Into Thy Kingdom, 236 (words); Rejoice, Ye Saints of Latter Days, 290 (words); We Have Partaken of Thy Love, 155 (words).

See also **Moody**: Faith, 96 (music); Have a Very Happy Birthday!, 284 (music); Have a Very Merry Christmas!, 51 (music); He Sent His Son, 34 (music); Teacher, Do You Love Me?, 178 (words and music); There Was Starlight on the Hillside, 40 (music); Who Is the Child?, 46 (music); *Hymns*, Testimony, 137 (music).

OH, HUSH THEE, MY BABY, 48

Words and music: Joseph Ballantyne (1868–1944) LDS
Ostinato: Patricia Haglund Nielsen (1936–2009) LDS

Joseph Ballantyne was born in Ogden Valley, Utah. He is the son of Richard Ballantyne, the founder of the Sunday School of the Church. He studied music in New York and with musicians from Chicago, New York, London, and Paris. He directed the Ogden Tabernacle Choir, and then chaired the music committee for the Deseret Sunday School Board. During this time, he wrote many children's songs, including this one which was originally entitled "Christmas Cradle Song." In 1905, it was first printed in *The Primary Song Book* and the *Deseret Sunday School Songbook*.

When Brother Ballantyne moved to Long Beach, California, he directed the Los Angeles Stake choir and the choir at St. Anthony's Church. He also taught private voice lessons.

For many years, **Pat Nielsen** taught at the Brigham Young University Church Music Workshops, sharing her expertise as a music educator. She received her MA in music education at Teachers College, Columbia University. We asked her to create several ostinatos (a repeated pattern) to challenge older children, and she wrote words and music to this one and also "Quickly, I'll Obey."

See also **Ballantyne**: Jesus Once Was a Little Child, 55 (music); Little Purple Pansies, 244 (music); Shine On, 144 (words and music); Stand for the Right, 159 (words and music);

See also **Nielsen**: Quickly, I'll Obey, 197 (ostinato).

PART THREE

PICTURE A CHRISTMAS, 50

Words and music: Patricia Kelsey Graham (1940–) LDS

Pat Graham illustrated her poems and homework, wrote school assemblies, learned to play the organ, and fell in love with teaching children. She was an elementary school teacher, a piano teacher, and Junior Sunday School coordinator. When Sister Graham was called to serve on the Primary general board, she was asked to create the Sharing Time page for the *Friend*. She wrote the page from 1980–1988. "Picture a Christmas" was used for one of the December pages.

Author's Note: In 1977, I wrote a ward Christmas program and song. In order to make it personal, several people were invited to share their own true Christmas experiences—a picture of Christmas that they treasured in their memory. While each story was told, a scene was posed in a wood panel frame with an oval cut out. A song relating to the story was selected, and then the song "Picture a Christmas" tied it all together. Some years later, I received a letter from Sandy Fugal who, while teaching school at a United States Military Installation in West Germany, used the song as the basis of a Christmas program. I was warmed to know that my little song could help someone so far away get the same idea I had when it was first written.

The original words were:

> Picture a Christmas without children,
> Picture a snowstorm without snow.
> And could you see a Christmas tree with not one gift below?
> There is no Christmas without children,
> It's a child's birth we celebrate.
> Sing praise to Him; remember Him,
> As you picture Christmas this year.

For the Sharing Time page (*Friend*, Dec. 1983, 28, 33–34), the words were revised to focus on the Savior's birth. The accompanying activity was a picture frame with cutouts of the stable, star, angel, and the baby Jesus to be added to the frame as the song was sung.

Jill Thomasen of Syracuse, Utah, said that during a difficult Christmas while her brother was very ill, the song had been a comfort to them and had helped their family focus on the Savior. I am glad that I wrote the verses with that focus and that the song proved useful to others.

See also **Graham**: I Am Like a Star, 163 (words and music); The

STORIES OF THE CHILDREN'S SONGBOOK

Hearts of the Children, 92 (words and music); The Nativity Song, 52 (words and music); We Are Different, 263 (words and music).

HAVE A VERY MERRY CHRISTMAS!, 51

Words: Mabel Jones Gabbott (1910–2004) LDS
Music: Michael Finlinson Moody (1941–) LDS

Mabel Gabbott said that the words to this poem were inspired by the happy experiences in her home and with her own children at Christmastime. She was a very small lady with a very large talent for writing. Her poems have been used as the words for sixteen Primary songs and four hymns. She served as chairman of 1985 Hymnbook Text Committee.

Michael Moody wrote the music, which is adapted from the music he composed for the twin song, "Have a Very Happy Birthday!" The meter is slightly different, and so this song begins on the downbeat (first count of the measure) and the birthday message, which has more syllables, begins on the upbeat. Brother Moody earned a doctorate in church music from the University of Southern California, and was employed as executive secretary of the General Church Music Committee for five years. He became the chairman of the music division of the Church in 1977 and directed the preparation of the 1985 hymnbook. He wisely coached us through the preparation of the 1989 *Children's Songbook* and helped us realize more than we had even hoped was possible aesthetically. He served as a mission president in Haiti soon after and is now serving with his wife, Maria, on a music mission at the BYU Jerusalem Center.

See also **Gabbott**: Baptism, 100 (words); Before I Take the Sacrament, 73 (words); Did Jesus Really Live Again?, 64 (words); Father Up Above, 23 (words); Had I Been a Child, 80 (words); Have a Very Happy Birthday!, 284 (words); He Sent His Song, 34 (words); My Country, 224 (words); Samuel Tells of the Baby Jesus, 36 (words); Sleep, Little Jesus, 47 (words); The Family, 194 (words); There Was Starlight on the Hillside, 40 (words); To Think about Jesus, 71 (words); We Are Reverent, 27 (words); Who Is the Child, 46 (words); *Hymns*, In Humility, Our Savior, 172 (words); Lord, Accept Into Thy Kingdom, 236 (words); Rejoice, Ye Saints of Latter Days, 290 (words); We Have Partaken of Thy Love, 155 (words).

See also **Moody**: Faith, 96 (music); Have a Very Happy Birthday!, 284 (music); He Sent His Son, 34 (music); Sleep, Little Jesus, 47 (music); Teacher, Do You Love Me?, 178 (words and music); There Was Starlight on the Hillside, 40 (music); Who Is the Child?, 46 (music); *Hymns, Testimony*, 137 (music).

THE NATIVITY SONG, 52

Words and music: Patricia Kelsey Graham (1940–) LDS

Pat Graham, the composer, served as the chairman of the General Primary Music Committee, which prepared the 1989 *Children's Songbook*, and also originated and wrote the Sharing Time page for the *Friend* for seven years. She co-authored *A Children's Songbook Companion*, a collection of lesson plans for all the songs in the *Children's Songbook*. She has a master's in education and has taught elementary school and private piano and organ lessons, and loves to accompany singers and musicians.

Author's Note: When I write a song, I usually write the message as a poem, and then set the poem to music. "The Nativity Song" was an exception for me. I wrote the music first for an assignment in a composition class at the University of Utah. I felt pleased with what I had composed and was even happier when I earned an A+ on my paper. I had read a charming poem that described each of the figures in the Nativity story, and I wondered if I could make a song with that format. I thought the song could be sung while the Nativity figures were put into a scene. As I thought about the idea, I kept humming the melody from my class assignment and pretty soon I had a new work that had spring-boarded from the poem. The song was used for our 1979 ward Christmas program. I drew posterboard-sized figures for the children to hold. Fortunately, I laminated the figures and we still use them today with our grandchildren. Sometimes we dress the children in costumes and form the Nativity scene. I hope the song can help families as they retell the true story of the Savior's birth.

See also **Graham**: I Am Like a Star, 163 (words and music); Picture a Christmas, 50 (words and music); The Hearts of the Children, 92 (words and music); We Are Different, 263 (words and music).

CHRISTMAS BELLS, 54

Words and music: Laurence Lyon (1934–2006) LDS

Laurence Lyon, the composer, was born in Holland while his father, T. Edgar Lyon, was mission president. He later served a mission to Holland as a young man. He received a doctorate in composition from Eastman School of Music, and has more than one hundred published compositions, many performed by the Tabernacle Choir. He served on the Sunday School General Board and the General Church Music Committee.

When Brother Lyon was a graduate student, he was working on a complicated orchestral piece. He said, "In the midst of doing this complex writing, this little tune just popped out of my head and onto the piano, accompaniment, words and all. . . . Then, before I could continue on to my viola concerto, another melody, which seemed to fit the first melody, also seemed to want to be written down. I sang the second melody with the first, and they fit."[40] This was the first children's song he had composed.

See also **Lyon**: An Angel Came to Joseph Smith, 86 (music); How Will They Know? 182 (arrangement); I Have Two Ears, 269 (music); Little Pioneer Children, 216 (words and music); We Are Reverent, 27 (music); Whenever I Think about Pioneers, 222 (music); *Hymns,* Each Life That Touches Ours for Good, 293 (music); Saints, Behold How Great Jehovah, 28 (music).

JESUS ONCE WAS A LITTLE CHILD, 55

Words: James R. Murray (1841–1905)
Music: Joseph Ballantyne (1868–1944) LDS

James R. Murray, the son of Scottish immigrants, studied with fine musicians in the Eastern United States. After serving as a Union soldier in the Civil War, he taught music in the public schools and worked for music publishing houses. He composed many Sunday School and gospel songs and anthems, and compiled and edited many collections. He headed the John Church Company publishing department and edited the monthly magazine, the *Musical Visitor.*

Joseph Ballantyne was born in Ogden Valley, Utah, and is the son of Richard Ballantyne, the founder of the Sunday School of The Church of Jesus Christ of Latter-day Saints. He studied music in New York and with musicians from Chicago, New York, London, and Paris. He directed the Ogden Tabernacle choir, and then chaired the music committee for the Deseret Sunday School Board. During this time, he wrote many children's songs, including "Jesus Once Was a Little Child," which was printed in 1905 in *The Primary Song Book* and the *Deseret Sunday School Songbook.*

When he moved to Long Beach, California, he directed the Los Angeles Stake choir and the choir at St. Anthony's Church. He also taught private voice lessons.

PART THREE

See also **Ballantyne:** Little Purple Pansies, 244 (music); Oh, Hush Thee, My Baby, 48 (words and music); Shine On, 144 (words and music); Stand for the Right, 159 (words and music).

I THINK WHEN I READ THAT SWEET STORY, 56

Words: Jemima Luke (1813–1906)
Music: Leah Ashton Lloyd (1894–1965) LDS

Jemima Luke contributed to *Poems for the Children's Hour* and *Sunday At Home*, a family magazine published by Piccadilly in England. She also wrote hymns. Her poem with the same words as used in the current song first appeared in 1874 under the title "That Sweet Story." In 1905, the poem was printed in *The Primary Song Book* with the title "Child's Desire." In 1939, it was re-titled "I Think When I Read That Sweet Story" and given a new melody and accompaniment by Leah Lloyd.

Leah Ashton Lloyd taught piano lessons, and had music classes for children at the Primary Children's Hospital. She was a member of the Primary general board for twenty years and was instrumental in the preparation of *The Children Sing,* published in 1951.

See also **Lloyd**: Reverence, 27 (music).

TELL ME THE STORIES OF JESUS, 57

Words: W. H. Parker (1845–1929)
Music: F. A. Challinor (1866–1952)

William Henry Parker apprenticed in machine-construction in a lace-making plant, and was later head of an insurance company. In 1885, he wrote a text with six stanzas for the anniversary of the Chelsea Street Baptist Church in Nottingham, England. As an active member, he wrote many hymns for Sunday School anniversaries. Fifteen of his hymns appear in the National Sunday School Union's *Sunday School Hymnary,* 1905.

In 1903, **Frederic A. Challinor** composed music for the six stanzas of W. H. Parker, and the song was the prize-winning tune in a competition sponsored by the National Sunday School Union, London. Challinor had labored in a brickyard and worked as a coal miner and in a china factory prior to earning degrees from the Royal College of Music and an English university. He published over 1,000 compositions and wrote his own verses to many hymns and songs. Some of his work is published in a Methodist hymnal and in the *Sunday School Hymnary,* 1905.

STORIES OF THE CHILDREN'S SONGBOOK

LITTLE LAMBS SO WHITE AND FAIR, 58

Words and music: anonymous

Many authors and composers might wish to have written such a perfect little piece. The verse approaches scripture, and ends with a commitment. The music reminds us of the beauty of simplicity—two measures with a first ending, and the same two measures with a satisfying conclusion. It resembles Moiselle Renstrom's work.

JESUS IS OUR LOVING FRIEND, 58

Words: Anna Johnson (1892–1979) LDS
Music: Alexander Schreiner (1901–1987) LDS

Anna Johnson was a special feature writer for the *Deseret News* and the author of "Hopscotch Valley," a children's column. Many of her poems were published as books, and Dr. Schreiner, Tabernacle organist, wrote tunes for over a hundred of them. She also worked in the office of the YWMIA. One of Sister Johnson's hobbies was collecting foreign dolls. To her, the dolls represented children everywhere in whom she was interested. The collection was given to the Primary Children's Hospital in Salt Lake City, Utah.

Brother **Alexander Schreiner** was born in Germany and played the piano at the age of five. At age eight, he became a Church organist. He also studied the violin. He came to Salt Lake City at the age of eleven and played his first recital in the Tabernacle while in his teens and soon after was appointed Tabernacle organist, a position he held for 53 years. He excelled as organist, composer, arranger, writer, and concert artist, and millions of people heard his organ broadcasts from the Tabernacle. Dr. Schreiner earned the first PhD given in music at the University of Utah. His tune for "We Bow Our Heads" was also used for the words "An Angel Came to Joseph Smith." He composed the music for nine hymns in the 1985 LDS hymnbook.[41]

See also: **Johnson**: A Smile Is Like the Sunshine, 267 (words); An Angel Came to Joseph Smith, 86 (words); My Flag, My Flag, 225 (words); I Think the World Is Glorious, 230 (words); We Bow Our Heads, 25 (words).

See also **Schreiner**: I Think the World Is Glorious, 230 (music); My Flag, My Flag, 225 (music); We Bow Our Heads, 25 (music); *Hymns*, Behold Thy Sons and Daughters, Lord, 238 (music); God Loved Us, So He Sent His Son, 187 (music); Holy Temples on Mount Zion, 289

PART THREE

(music); In Memory of the Crucified, 190 (music); Lead Me into Life Eternal, 45 (music); Lord, Accept into Thy Kingdom, 236 (music); Thy Spirit, Lord, Has Stirred Our Souls, 157 (music); Truth Eternal, 4 (music); While of These Emblems We Partake, 174 (music).

JESUS LOVED THE LITTLE CHILDREN, 59

Words and music: Moiselle Renstrom (1889–1956) LDS

K. **Moiselle Renstrom** wrote both words and music to thirteen songs included in this collection. She was a gifted teacher, and her volumes for little children encourage them to pretend and move with the music, as in "Once There Was a Snowman." As we were evaluating songs, we noticed that her work required no changes. She knew the range of children's voices, wrote so that it was easy to play, taught well with her rhymes, and was doctrinally accurate. Her songbooks, *Merrily We Sing*, *Musical Adventures*, and *Rhythm Fun*, have been used by early childhood teachers everywhere.

See also **Renstrom**: A Happy Family, 198 (words and music); A Happy Helper, 197 (words and music); A Prayer, 22 (words and music); I Am Glad for Many Things, 151 (words and music); I Love to Pray, 25 (words and music); Jesus Said Love Everyone, 61 (words and music); Little Seeds Lie Fast Asleep, 243 (words and music); Once There Was a Snowman, 249 (words and music); Rain Is Falling All Around, 241 (words and music); The World Is So Lovely, 233 (words and music); To Get Quiet, 275 (words and music); Two Little Eyes, 268 (words and music).

JESUS WANTS ME FOR A SUNBEAM, 60

Words: Nellie Talbot (1874–?)
Music: Edwin O. Excell (1851–1921)

Unfortunately, there is no information available on **Nellie Talbot**, the author. The composer, **Edwin Othello Excell**, was an excellent singer and wrote music for gospel songs. He was the son of a German Reformed Church minister in Pennsylvania. Mr. Excell worked on the West Coast as a brick mason, but studied piano in his spare time. He organized singing schools, was recognized as a great song-leader, and became involved in revival work.

"Jesus Wants Me for a Sunbeam" was first entitled "I'll Be a Sunbeam," and was first printed in *The Primary Song Book* in 1927. The song was number six on the 1983 survey of favorite Primary songs. Two of Edwin Excell's hymn melodies are also favorites in the 1985 hymnbook.

See also **Excell**: *Hymns*, Count Your Blessings, 240 (words); Scatter Sunshine, 230 (words).

JESUS SAID LOVE EVERYONE, 61

Words and music: Moiselle Renstrom (1889–1956) LDS

K. Moiselle Renstrom was a teacher who had the gift of "becoming as a little child." She thrilled to new ideas and discoveries with her students and shared their enjoyment of learning. Her songbooks, *Merrily We Sing*, *Musical Adventures*, and *Rhythm Fun*, have been used by early childhood teachers everywhere.

Sister Renstrom wrote both words and music to thirteen songs included in this collection. Many of her songs for little children encourage them to pretend and move with the music, as in *Once There Was a Snowman*. As we were evaluating songs, we noticed that her work required no changes. She knew the range for children's voices, wrote so that it was easy to play, taught well with her rhymes, and was doctrinally accurate.

See also **Renstrom**: A Happy Family, 198 (words and music); A Happy Helper, 197 (words and music); A Prayer, 22 (words and music); I Am Glad for Many Things, 151 (words and music); I Love to Pray, 25 (words and music); Jesus Loved the Little Children, 59 (words and music); Little Seeds Lie Fast Asleep, 243 (words and music); Rain Is Falling All Around, 241 (words and music); The World Is So Lovely, 233 (words and music); To Get Quiet, 275 (words and music); Two Little Eyes, 268 (words and music).

BEAUTIFUL SAVIOR, 62

Words: anonymous, twelfth century
Music: Silesian folk song, arranged by Darwin Wolford (1938–) LDS

Lorin Wheelwright financed his education with his piano and organ abilities and received a doctorate degree from Columbia University. He became music supervisor for the Salt Lake City schools in 1937. Brother Wheelwright served as a member of the Sunday School General Board and Associate Editor of the *Instructor* magazine. He was president of Pioneer Music Press, which printed the work of many LDS composers. He was dean of the College of Fine Arts and Communication at Brigham Young University and an assistant to President Dallin H. Oaks.

PART THREE

Author's Note: I remember the thrill of singing in a huge songfest for elementary schools held in the Salt Lake Tabernacle. One of the songs we sang was "The Crusader's Hymn," which Brother Wheelwright had arranged for The Children Sing *songbook. Each verse had a different accompaniment and grew to a huge finale. Unfortunately, the score filled five pages, required a high G for the soprano, and needed a skilled pianist to perform the large chords and octaves.*

To reduce the number of pages needed for this and other songs, words were put in the piano stave rather than on a separate melody line; this alone saved three or four lines per page. "Beautiful Savior" was condensed from its former five pages to just two by putting the words in the piano stave and giving instructions to sing verse one in unison and verse two with the alto. This simplified strophic approach makes use of an optional descant for voice or instrument with verse 3 and still achieves the dignity of the earlier version. The words to this tune date back to the 12th century—that is proof of the appeal of the song.

Darwin Wolford was a music professor at BYU–Idaho and holds a PhD in organ and composition. He is widely published, and his works have been performed by the Mormon Tabernacle Choir and the Utah Symphony. He served on the General Church Music Committee and the 1985 Hymnbook Executive Committee. We are very much indebted to him for his expertise in simplifying and refining the songs for the 1989 *Children's Songbook*. It was a monumental time commitment with no recognition, yet he gave cheerful service on the project. Batches of songs would be mailed to him with suggestions, and he was always able to fill the need. The high musical standard of the book can be credited to his careful scrutiny and advice.

See also **Wolford**: Had I Been a Child, 80 (music); I Am a Child of God, 2 (arrangement); I Have a Family Tree, 199 (music); In Quietude, 191 (music); Keep the Commandments, 146 (arrangement); Mary's Lullaby, 44 (arrangement); Our Chapel Is a Sacred Place, 30 (music); Stars Were Gleaming, 37 (arrangement); Supplication, 297 (music); Teach Me to Walk in the Light, 177(obbligato); Thanks to Thee, 6 (music); The Lord Gave Me a Temple, 153 (music); *Hymns*, Sons of Michael, He Approaches, 51 (music); We Listen to a Prophet's Voice, 22 (music).

DID JESUS REALLY LIVE AGAIN?, 64

Words: Mabel Jones Gabbott (1910–2004) LDS

STORIES OF THE CHILDREN'S SONGBOOK

Music: Royce Campbell Twitchell (1939–2011) LDS

Mabel Jones Gabbott was one of nine children. She received her education at the University of Idaho and the University of Utah. Although she was a very small lady who wore her hair swept up on top of her head, she had a very large talent for writing. Her poems have been used as words for sixteen Primary songs and four hymns. She served a Northwestern States mission and then became Elder LeGrand Richards's secretary. Sister Gabbott worked on the staffs of the Church magazines and as a member of the YWMIA General Board and the General Church Music Committee. She chaired the 1985 Hymnbook Text Committee. "I love to hear children sing,"[42] she said. She lived in Bountiful, Utah, and grew roses and cherries.

Royce Campbell Twitchell is a very capable accompanist married to Noel, an outstanding bass soloist. They were both members of Brigham Young University Opera Workshop when I was accompanist, and over the years I have enjoyed Noel's performance in "Amahl and the Night Visitors" as well as the two of them on concert series performances. He has done work on Broadway, and Royce accompanies. When Royce was eleven years old, she decided that she wanted to be a professional accompanist, so she took every opportunity to use her musical skills. She was Primary pianist while she was Primary age and went on to accompany for the Circus, Valley Music Hall, Brigham Young University Opera Workshop, Utah Opera Company, Utah Oratorio Society, Promised Valley Playhouse and Triad Theatre. The following excerpt from a letter explains a sweet purpose this song has filled:

> "Did Jesus Really Live Again?" was truly a blessing to our family after the passing of my grandmother. My three-year-old daughter was very troubled by the death and could not be comforted. She would plead every night with her Father in Heaven that He would bring her grandma back to her. It broke my heart to see her that way.
>
> Finally, one day as we talked about the Savior together, she and I sang Sister Gabbott's beautiful song and the Spirit touched her heart. She truly received a testimony of the resurrection when she was only barely four. Never again has she been troubled by death. Now her prayers contain a request that Heavenly Father will watch over Grandma until she can see her again.[43]

See also **Gabbott**: Baptism, 100 (words); Before I Take the Sacrament, 73 (words); Father Up Above, 23 (words); Had I Been a

PART THREE

Child, 80 (words); Have a Very Happy Birthday!, 284 (words); Have a Very Merry Christmas!, 51 (words); He Sent His Son, 34 (words); My Country, 224 (words); Samuel Tells of the Baby Jesus, 36 (words); Sleep, Little Jesus, 47 (words); The Family, 194 (words); There Was Starlight on the Hillside, 40 (words); To Think about Jesus, 71 (words); We Are Reverent, 27 (words); Who Is the Child, 46 (words); *Hymns*, In Humility, Our Savior, 172 (words); Lord, Accept Into Thy Kingdom, 236 (words); Rejoice, Ye Saints of Latter Days, 290 (words); We Have Partaken of Thy Love, 155 (words).

HE DIED THAT WE MIGHT LIVE AGAIN, 65

Words: Thelma McKinnon Anderson (1913–1997) LDS
Music: Charlene Anderson Newell (1938–) LDS

Thelma McKinnon Anderson graduated from Brigham Young University and taught school in Price, Utah. She directed many musical programs in the school district, and has written many poems. Her daughter, **Charlene Anderson Newell**, composed the music for many of her mother's poems. When first published in 1976, the title of the song was "Easter Song." To more specifically identify the message of the song, "Rejoice and Sing" was suggested, but finally the first line seemed best.

Charlene Newell's music has been published in the *Friend,* and she won the 1977 Relief Society song contest. Her music has been performed in the Tabernacle and at the dedication of the Nauvoo Monument to Women. She is an outstanding pianist and has taught private voice and organ lessons as well as music in Utah's Granite School District.

See also **Newell**, Charlene: Little Jesus, 39 (music); The Commandments, 112 (music); Your Happy Birthday, 283 (words and music); *Hymns*, A Key Was Turned in Latter Days, 310 (music).

HOSANNA, 66

Words: Rita S. Robinson (1920–2011) LDS
Music: Rita S. Robinson (1920–2011) LDS
Arrangement: Chester W. Hill (1912–1997) LDS

Rita S. Robinson's father died when she was three years old. Although her mother was not a member of The Church of Jesus Christ of Latter-day Saints, she sent Rita to meetings because it had been important to her father. After graduating with honors from the University of Utah, she taught school and later worked as a master welder for the Navy during World War II. She published twenty-seven songs for children in a collection called *I Like to Sing*. After her husband's death, she served a mission in California.

For this collection, two verses of this song were combined into one so it could be used for Christmas or Easter. The fermatas were deleted, and the echo was written in rhythm with an extended descant ending. This made the second part more integral to the song and hopefully would be another opportunity for part-singing with older children.

Chester W. Hill played piano for priesthood meeting when he was ten years old. Brother Hill composed in his early teens, and after studying music at Brigham Young University, Juilliard School of Music, and Columbia Teacher's College, he taught at Ricks College (BYU–Idaho) and Brigham Young University. He served as director of concerts at the Washington, DC chapel. He prepared the original arrangement of Sister Robinson's words and melody.

See also **Robinson**: Saturday, 196 (words and music).

EASTER HOSANNA, 68

Words and music: Vanja Y. Watkins (1938–) LDS

There was a need for a Book of Mormon Easter song, and **Vanja** (VON-yuh) **Yorgason Watkins** was asked to write and submit an idea to Lucile Reading, editor of the *Friend*. The words were edited several times, and the resulting song about Christ's appearance to the Nephites was published in the *Friend*, Apr. 1982, 44. Sister Watkins has the ability and temperament to incorporate suggestions and find more than one way to solve a musical need.

From the time she began her music studies at Brigham Young University, Vanja was developing skills for revising and refining children's music. Lou Groesbeck, a teacher she adored, was a faculty member and Primary general board member. She would ask her opinion on songs and then invite Vanja to "fix" the musical problem. This was a preparation for her call to the Primary general board where she served for seven years. After her release, she served as stake Primary president and then was called as a member of the General Church Music Committee, serving for another twelve years. During this time, she was raising five children. Her doctor husband arranged his office hours so that he could help care for their little ones when she had meetings. She remembers taking their youngest daughter to music meetings and "tucking" her under the table while the committee met. Her children often went with her to the BYU Church Music Workshops where she taught every summer. The children

PART THREE

didn't feel deprived because of her calling but enjoyed it with her. The index of authors and composers shows her to have credit lines on twenty-seven songs.[44]

See also **Watkins:** Families Can Be Together Forever, 188 (music); For Thy Bounteous Blessings, 21 (arrangement); I Want to Be Reverent, 28 (music); I Will Be Valiant, 162 (words and music); I Will Follow God's Plan, 164 (words and music); It's Autumntime, 246 (arrangement); Latter-day Prophets, 134 (music); Thank Thee for Everything, 10 (words); The Articles of Faith, 122–132 (music); The Sacrament, 72 (words and music); The Things I Do, 170 (music); This Is My Beloved Son, 76 (music); To Be a Pioneer, 218 (arrangement); Truth from Elijah, 90 (words and music); *Hymns*, Families Can Be Together Forever, 300 (music); Press Forward Saints, 81 (music).

JESUS HAS RISEN, 70

Words and music: Thelma Johnson Ryser (1898–1984) LDS

Thelma Johnson Ryser was a member of the Primary general board for ten years. "Jesus Has Risen" was originally published in *The Children's Friend* in March of 1959. The introduction had been composed as 4/4, but was changed to help establish the 3/4-meter. The last note of the introduction had been C but was moved to A, which gives the pitch. Sister Ryser was a member of the Utah Federation of Music Clubs, Mu Phi Epsilon, Opera Appreciation Club, and the Art Barn. She played the organ for Larkin Mortuary for over forty years.

TO THINK ABOUT JESUS, 71

Words: Mabel Jones Gabbott (1910–2004) LDS
Music: Robert Cundick (1926–) LDS

Mabel Jones Gabbott, the author, said, "After much prayer and study, I said to myself, 'It shouldn't be hard to write about Jesus and reverence.' The words gave me my first line, and the ideas and words followed quickly."[45] The words "though I am small" can be changed to "when I've grown tall" for older children. Sister Gabbott has worked on the staffs of the Church magazines and as a member of the YWMIA General Board and the General Church Music Committee. She chaired the Hymnbook Text Committee for the 1985 hymnbook.

Robert Cundick, the composer said, "The music is reminiscent of music written many years ago in modal harmony (begins in the Key of C minor and ends with a C major chord). It is written in the style of a folk song."[46] Dr. Cundick was the first noted Mormon musician to receive his entire musical training from the University of Utah. He played jazz piano in dance bands, taught at Brigham Young University, served as organist for the Hyde Park Chapel in London and the Brigham Young University Jerusalem Center, and was Tabernacle Organist for more than twenty-five years. He holds associate and fellowship certificates from the American Guild of Organists.

Author's Note: I was very fortunate to have studied piano with Brother Cundick at Brigham Young University, and I value the penciled suggestions that he wrote on my pieces.

See also **Gabbott**: Baptism, 100 (words); Before I Take the Sacrament, 73 (words); Did Jesus Really Live Again?, 64 (words); Father Up Above, 23 (words); Had I Been a Child, 80 (words); Have a Very Happy Birthday!, 284 (words); Have a Very Merry Christmas!, 51 (words); He Sent His Son, 34 (words); My Country, 224 (words); Samuel Tells of the Baby Jesus, 36 (words); Sleep, Little Jesus, 47 (words); The Family, 194 (words); There Was Starlight on the Hillside, 40 (words); We Are Reverent, 27 (words); Who Is the Child, 46 (words); *Hymns*, In Humility, Our Savior, 172 (words); Lord, Accept Into Thy Kingdom, 236 (words); Rejoice, Ye Saints of Latter Days, 290 (words); We Have Partaken of Thy Love, 155 (words).

See also **Cundick**: *Hymns*, That Easter Morn, 198 (music); Thy Holy Word, 279 (music).

THE SACRAMENT, 72

Words and music: Vanja Y. Watkins (1938–) LDS

Vanja (VON-yuh) **Yorgason Watkins** knew that singing a scripture would make it memorable. She used the words of the Savior, "This do in remembrance of me," in the first verse of the song, and then wrote a second verse with a personal commitment, "I will remember him." She wrote "thinking time" while the piano plays alone in the middle of the "commitment" as though the singer is reflecting on the meaning. She gives credit to Mabel Gabbott for giving her suggestions that led to this successful formula.[47]

Sister Watkins served as Primary General Board music chairman and then as a member of the General Church Music Committee. The index of authors and composers shows her to be the greatest contributor to the songbook. She has credit lines for arrangements, words, music, and words and music—fourteen songs plus the thirteen articles of faith,

PART THREE

making a total of twenty-seven entries. Many are favorites according to the survey, and all are of high quality musicianship.

See also **Watkins**: Easter Hosanna, 68 (words and music); Families Can Be Together Forever, 188 (music); For Thy Bounteous Blessings, 21 (arrangement); I Want to Be Reverent, 28 (music); I Will Be Valiant, 162 (words and music); I Will Follow God's Plan, 164 (words and music); It's Autumntime, 246 (arrangement); Latter-day Prophets, 134 (music); Thank Thee for Everything, 10 (words); The Articles of Faith, 122–132 (music); The Sacrament, 72 (words and music); The Things I Do, 170 (music); This Is My Beloved Son, 76 (music); To Be a Pioneer, 218 (arrangement); Truth from Elijah, 90 (words and music); *Hymns*, Families Can Be Together Forever, 300 (music); Press Forward Saints, 81 (music).

BEFORE I TAKE THE SACRAMENT, 73

Words: Mabel Jones Gabbott (1910–2004) LDS
Music: Gladys Ericksen Seeley (1899–1985) LDS

Mabel Jones Gabbott was one of nine children and received her education at the University of Idaho and the University of Utah. She served a mission to the Northwestern States and then became secretary to Elder LeGrand Richards. Sister Gabbott worked on the staffs of the Church magazines and was a member of the YWMIA General Board and the General Church Music Committee. She chaired the 1985 Hymnbook Text Committee. Her poems have been used for the texts of sixteen Primary songs and four hymns. Sister Gabbott lived in Bountiful, Utah, where she grew roses and cherries. She said, "I love to hear children sing."[48]

Gladys Ericksen Seely's mother had prayed for a daughter who could play the piano, and her ninth child answered that prayer. Gladys showed a natural musical talent at a young age and could play any music she heard in any key. She played for silent movies in the theater and for dancing schools in Mt. Pleasant, Utah. She also expressed her testimony through her music.

See also **Gabbott**: Baptism, 100 (words); Did Jesus Really Live Again?, 64 (words); Father Up Above, 23 (words); Had I Been a Child, 80 (words); Have a Very Happy Birthday!, 284 (words); Have a Very Merry Christmas!, 51 (words); He Sent His Son, 34 (words); My Country, 224 (words); Samuel Tells of the Baby Jesus, 36 (words); Sleep, Little Jesus, 47 (words); The Family, 194 (words); There Was Starlight on the Hillside,

40 (words); To Think about Jesus, 71 (words); We Are Reverent, 27 (words); Who Is the Child, 46 (words); *Hymns*, In Humility, Our Savior, 172 (words); Lord, Accept Into Thy Kingdom, 236 (words); Rejoice, Ye Saints of Latter Days, 290 (words); We Have Partaken of Thy Love, 155 (words).

See also **Seely**: Father Up Above, 23 (music).

HELP US, O GOD, TO UNDERSTAND, 73

Words and music: D. Evan Davis (1923–1979) LDS

D. Evan Davis earned his Doctorate in music education from the University of Oregon, and eventually became head of the Brigham Young University Music Education Department. When he served on the Sunday School General Board, he wrote for the *Era* magazine and also a monthly column for the *Instructor* entitled "Our Worshipful Hymn Practice."

The original title of his song was "Our Savior's Love." It was changed to the first line because of the hymn with that title in the 1985 hymnbook. When the song was published in *Sing With Me*, a bad xerox copy did not show the left hand "f" at the end of the first line. The family requested that we put the missing note in its place. It is a much nicer voice leading.

I FEEL MY SAVIOR'S LOVE, 74

Words: Ralph Rodgers, Jr. (1936–1990) LDS
Words: Laurie Huffman (1948–) LDS
Words and Music: K. Newell Dayley (1939–) LDS

The pageant *III Nephi* was presented at the Marriott Center on the University of Utah campus in 1979. This song was written for the scene portraying the Savior as He appeared to the Nephites.

Author's Note: My daughter was in the cast and sang and walked with all the children meeting Jesus. She was holding a small child, and Jesus took them both in his arms. She said, "Oh, Mother, it seemed so real!" I see the picture of that sweet embrace whenever I hear this beautiful song.

For many years, **Ralph Rodgers** entertained professionally with Pat Davis. He had an amazing tenor voice and played the comic. They had met while directing roadshows in their wards. Eventually they served on the Cultural Arts Committee of the Church and at the Promised Valley Playhouse, where they starred in and directed plays and musicals. Brother Rodgers also served as director of the Polynesian Cultural

PART THREE

Center, mission president in Samoa, and regional representative before his untimely death. He said, "I believe that God gave us talents to be used in his service and not just for our own enjoyment. As long as we use those talents in that way, he will continue to bless and magnify those talents."[49] The Rodgers Memorial Theater in Bountiful, Utah, produces plays and musicals using local talent, as he did.

K. Newell Dayley served as a member of the Brigham Young University Music Faculty and also the General Music Committee of the Church. Brother Dayley, an excellent trumpet player, became chairman of the Brigham Young University Music Department. He composed music for the pageants *III Nephi* and *Kirtland* and the soundtrack of the show at the Polynesian Cultural Center in Hawaii. He said, "I have a deep love for children's music and feel that some of our most important work ought to be focused in that direction."[50]

Laurie Huffman was raised in Utah where she attended Brigham Young University. Her talents in writing poetry and lyrics were used in the Young Women organization, and she continues to write and teach personal and family history writing. She was asked to collaborate with Brother Dayley on the words of this song.

The 1982 Children's Sacrament Meeting Presentation included an additional verse emphasizing service for the song. The verse was included in the *Children's Songbook* but because of the length of the song the following chorus, was not: "In this I will follow him: Give all I have for him; To feel my Savior's love, To know my Savior loves me."

The additional chorus works well in a solo performance but increases the teaching time of an already long song.

See also **Dayley**: Every Star Is Different, 142 (music); Home, 192 (music); Hum Your Favorite Hymn, 152 (music); The World Is So Big, 235 (music); *Hymns,* Lord, I Would Follow Thee, 220 (music).

THIS IS MY BELOVED SON, 76

Words: Marvin K. Gardner (1952–) LDS
Music: Vanja Y. Watkins (1938–) LDS

The scripture references to this song mark three places where Heavenly Father presented his son. **Marvin K. Gardner**, the author, said:

> As Church members, we often bear our testimonies of the Savior. In the scriptures, our Heavenly Father has also borne his testimony of

Jesus Christ: "This is my Beloved son, Hear Him!" One day, I was thinking how wonderful it would have been to be present at the River Jordan, in the Nephite city of Bountiful, or in the Sacred Grove, and to hear the Father speak these words of testimony. And then I realized that as we read of these events in the scriptures, we can be there in our minds and hear the Father's words. More importantly, any time we read the scriptures with a sincere heart, the Holy Ghost can bear witness to us of the Father's testimony of Jesus Christ.[51]

As a young boy, Brother Gardner served as a Primary pianist when he was just eleven years old. He studied music and taught English composition at Brigham Young University and Spanish at the Missionary Training Center in Provo. He worked as a freelance writer and editor for the Church Missionary Department and for Deseret Book and served as a member of the General Church Music Committee, helping edit much of the 1985 *Hymns*.

Vanja (VON-yuh) **Yorgason Watkins** said that when Marvin is inspired with something he feels strongly about, then it inspires her. And when he feels strongly, it comes out in lovely verses. He felt it was important for children to know of the episodes when Heavenly Father introduced his Son on earth.[52] Sister Watkins was a television and classroom music teacher, and Brigham Young University faculty member. She served as Primary general board music chairman and then as a member of the General Church Music Committee. The index of authors and composers shows her to be the greatest contributor to the songbook. She has credit lines for arrangements, words, music, and words and music—fourteen songs plus the thirteen Articles of Faith, making a total of twenty-seven credits. Many of her songs are favorites according to the survey, and all are of high quality musicianship.

See also **Watkins**: Easter Hosanna, 68 (words and music); Families Can Be Together Forever, 188 (music); For Thy Bounteous Blessings, 21 (arrangement); I Want to Be Reverent, 28 (music); I Will Be Valiant, 162 (words and music); I Will Follow God's Plan, 164 (words and music); It's Autumntime, 246 (arrangement); Latter-day Prophets, 134 (music); Thank Thee for Everything, 10 (words); The Articles of Faith, 122–132 (music); The Sacrament, 72 (words and music); The Things I Do, 170 (music); To Be a Pioneer, 218 (arrangement); Truth from Elijah, 90 (words and music); *Hymns*, Families Can Be Together Forever, 300 (music); Press Forward Saints, 81 (music).

PART THREE

See also **Gardner**, Marvin: *Hymns*, Press Forward, Saints, 81 (words); Thy Holy Word, 279 (words).

THE CHURCH OF JESUS CHRIST, 77

Words and music: Janice Kapp Perry (1938–) LDS

The *Children's Songbook* Committee felt it would be helpful to have a song containing the name of the Church so that children could practice the name correctly. **Janice Perry** filled our request in an interesting way. She said she was taking a nap one afternoon and awoke with the strong impression that there should be a song containing the full name of the Church. She knew the songs for the new Primary songbook had already been selected, but she began writing anyway. She completed a two-verse song and sent it to the committee. We were thrilled and suggested a few ideas that we had thought of, and asked if she could make some adjustments. We had hoped to include some of the ideas in the three-fold mission of the Church, which had recently been introduced. In the end, the song had one verse and began just the way Janice first wrote it, "I belong to The Church of Jesus Christ of Latter-day Saints."

Sister Perry played drums in her family orchestra. She studied music at Brigham Young University and was a member of the Utah Composer's Guild. She composed the LDS musical *It's a Miracle*, sixteen songbooks and albums, and musical presentations for Church auxiliaries. Her brother, Gary, is an artist and illustrates the covers for her songbooks. She sang in the Tabernacle Choir and then served a full-time mission with her husband in South America. In spite of nerve damage in her hand, she continues to compose, focusing now on music for the Spanish members of the Church. She was honored as an Outstanding Brigham Young University Alumnus for her tremendous contributions to the music of the Church.

Author's Note: I met Janice in the Composer's Guild where we both were hanging on every word Janene Brady said about self-publishing. Janice has remained humble and soft-spoken through her successful music career and continues to share her talents.

See also **Perry**: A Child's Prayer, 12 (words and music); I Love to See the Temple, 95 (words and music); I Pray in Faith, 14 (words and music); I'm Thankful to Be Me, 11 (music); I'm Trying to Be Like Jesus, 78 (words and music); Love Is Spoken Here, 190 (words and music); Mother, Tell Me the Story, 204 (words and music); The Word of Wisdom, 154 (words and music); We'll Bring the World His Truth, 172 (words and music); *Hymns*, As Sisters in Zion, 309 (music).

I'M TRYING TO BE LIKE JESUS, 78

Words and music: Janice Kapp Perry (1938–) LDS

Janice Perry was asked by local Church leaders to write a song on kindness for a regional Primary conference. She said, "As I pondered and prayed about that subject I felt sure the best way to approach it was to plant the idea in the children's hearts of trying to become like the kindest man who ever lived, our Savior Jesus Christ."[53] The result was a song that Michael F. Moody, chairman of the Church Music Committee at the time, said contained "the essence of the gospel." The song was first published in the *Ensign*.

Sister Perry was born in Ogden, Utah, and raised in Vale, Oregon. She received her musical training at Brigham Young University and has composed songs, musicals, and five sacred cantatas, two of which have been performed in the Salt Lake Tabernacle. Many of her songs have been published in the Church magazines.

See also **Perry**: A Child's Prayer, 12 (words and music); I Love to See the Temple, 95 (words and music); I Pray in Faith, 14 (words and music); I'm Thankful to Be Me, 11 (music); Love Is Spoken Here, 190 (words and music); Mother, Tell Me the Story, 204 (words and music); The Church of Jesus Christ, 77 (words and music); The Word of Wisdom, 154 (words and music); We'll Bring the World His Truth, 172 (words and music); *Hymns*, As Sisters in Zion, 309 (music).

HAD I BEEN A CHILD, 80

Words: Mabel Jones Gabbott (1910–2004) LDS
Music: Darwin Wolford (1936–) LDS

The message of this art song is similar to "I Think When I Read That Sweet Story of Old," but the setting is the Book of Mormon rather than the New Testament. It is from a children's cantata about the Book of Mormon called "Song of Cumorah," and can also be a lovely solo.

In the back of the *Children's Songbook*, there are several pages called *Using the Songbook*. Page 303 gives an explanation of every symbol and term used in the songs. *Ten.*, the abbreviation for *tenuto*, is marked in the third measure from the end of this song. Because this is the only use of the term in the book, I thought perhaps it could be removed. Brother

PART THREE

Wolford assured me it was necessary for the correct expression, and so it is explained in that section.

Mabel Jones Gabbott, the author, has worked on the staffs of the Church magazines and as a member of the YWMIA General Board and the General Church Music Committee. She chaired the Hymnbook Text Committee for the 1985 hymnbook. She was a very small lady with a very large talent for writing. She has written the words for sixteen Primary songs and four hymns. She lived in Bountiful, Utah, and grew roses and cherries. She said, "I love to hear children sing."[54]

Darwin Wolford was a music professor at BYU–Idaho and holds a PhD in organ and composition. He is widely published, and his works have been performed by the Mormon Tabernacle Choir and the Utah Symphony. He served on the General Church Music Committee and the 1985 Hymnbook Executive Committee. We are very much indebted to him for his expertise in simplifying and refining the songs for the 1989 *Children's Songbook*. It was a monumental time commitment with no recognition, yet he gave cheerful service on the project. Batches of songs would be mailed to him with suggestions, and he was always able to fill the need. The high musical standard of the book can be credited to his careful scrutiny and advice.

See also **Gabbott**: Baptism, 100 (words); Before I Take the Sacrament, 73 (words); Did Jesus Really Live Again?, 64 (words); Father Up Above, 23 (words); Had I Been a Child, 80 (words); Have a Very Happy Birthday!, 284 (words); Have a Very Merry Christmas!, 51 (words); He Sent His Son, 34 (words); My Country, 224 (words); Samuel Tells of the Baby Jesus, 36 (words); Sleep, Little Jesus, 47 (words); The Family, 194 (words); There Was Starlight on the Hillside, 40 (words); To Think about Jesus, 71 (words); We Are Reverent, 27 (words); Who Is the Child, 46 (words); *Hymns*, In Humility, Our Savior, 172 (words); Lord, Accept Into Thy Kingdom, 236 (words); Rejoice, Ye Saints of Latter Days, 290 (words); We Have Partaken of Thy Love, 155 (words).

See also **Wolford**: Beautiful Savior, 62 (arrangement); I Am a Child of God, 2 (arrangement); I Have a Family Tree, 199 (music); In Quietude, 191 (music); Keep the Commandments, 146 (arrangement); Mary's Lullaby, 44 (arrangement); Our Chapel Is a Sacred Place, 30 (music); Stars Were Gleaming, 37 (arrangement); Supplication, 297 (music); Teach Me to Walk in the Light, 177(obbligato); Thanks to Thee, 6 (music); The Lord Gave Me a Temple, 153 (music); *Hymns*, Sons of

STORIES OF THE CHILDREN'S SONGBOOK

Michael, He Approaches, 51 (music); We Listen to a Prophet's Voice, 22 (music).

WHEN HE COMES AGAIN, 82

Words and music: Mirla Greenwood Thayne (1907–1997) LDS

Mirla Thayne was elected to the Writer's hall of Fame of the League of Utah Writers. She tells children, "Do you know that in your wonderful brain is a tiny recorder that records and holds tight to the music you hear? Beautiful music comes from our Heavenly Father and is given to you to inspire you and lead you closer to Him." When Sister Thayne was preparing a presentation for her Provo ward's spring conference, she realized that she would need short speaking parts for the youngest children. She quickly wrote twelve two-line parts, which became one poem about the Second Coming. She said that later as she sat at her piano, "A tune formed in my mind to be transformed to my fingers." She found that the words the little children had spoken "were a perfect match" to the tune she was playing.[55] The song was printed in *The Children's Friend*, and became a favorite all over the world. For many years, her song "When He Comes Again," was available as an illustrated storybook.

Some copyrights prohibit copying or performing without permission because the song may be a source of income to its author. On this particular song, an agreement was made which now allows it to be copied from the *Children's Songbook*. Options were available for authors to either handle requests for use of their songs themselves or have the Church administer royalties and make decisions about requests to publish or record a song. There had not been a copyright office in the Church when the previous songbook was published, so there was extensive research needed to make everything currently "legal."

PART THREE

The Gospel

"[Memorize] some of the inspiring songs of Zion and then, when the mind is afflicted with temptations, [sing] aloud, to keep before your mind the inspiring words and crowd out the evil thoughts."[56]
—President Ezra Taft Benson (1899–1994)

This is the largest section of the book and contains 81 songs. They are grouped according to the following topics: the Restoration, temples and family history, first principles of the gospel, scriptures, Church leaders, the commandments, missionary work, and a few songs appropriate for leaders. As we categorized songs for the gospel section, we realized that the basic topics of the gospel are love and service, or being kind and choosing the right.

The idea for the double-page picture for the gospel section came from a beloved Norman Rockwell painting with two children reading and a collage of the characters they are reading about in the background. We suggested that Sister Luch portray something from the Old Testament, the New Testament, and the Latter-days. She did a masterful job showing the mother reading the scriptures to her children and the stories coming alive in their minds. The children needed to be dressed simply and the furnishings drawn plainly so that they would not portray an unreal, glamorous image of "the typical Mormon." For that reason, the fancy wallpaper under the wainscoting was eliminated from the original sketch.

AN ANGEL CAME TO JOSEPH SMITH, 86

Words: Anna Johnson (1892–1979) LDS
Music: A. Laurence Lyon (1934–2006) LDS

Anna Johnson was a special feature writer for the *Deseret News* and the author of "Hopscotch Valley," a children's column. Many books of her poetry were published, and **Alexander Schreiner**, tabernacle organist, wrote tunes for over a hundred of them. She also worked in the office of the YWMIA. One of her hobbies was collecting foreign dolls. The dolls represented children everywhere, in whom she was interested. The collection was given to the Primary Children's Hospital in Salt Lake City, Utah.

A melody by **Dr. Alexander Schreiner** was originally used for two poems by Sister Johnson: "An Angel Came to Joseph Smith" and "We Bow Our Heads." According to the survey, "We Bow Our Heads" is one of the most well-used prayer songs. It seemed that the other poem deserved separate music. Laurence Lyon was asked to write new music. When he sent his ideas, he explained that the natural feel of the words seemed to suggest a change of meter in the song, from three-quarter to two-quarter and back. He had not meant to make it "difficult" and tried the two-quarter measure with three beats (as in the first measure). He felt it worked best with the meter change. After we tried it both ways, we agreed—there is a definite charm to the change. The real difficulty is convincing music leaders that it is possible for them to lead it correctly! If you can sing the meter change in "Come, Come Ye Saints," you will be able to sing this song as well.

Laurence Lyon, the composer, was born in Holland while his father, T. Edgar Lyon, was mission president. He later served a mission to Holland as a young man. He received a doctorate in composition from Eastman School of Music and has more than one hundred published compositions, many performed by the Tabernacle Choir. He served on the Sunday School General Board and the General Church Music Committee.

See also **Johnson**: A Smile Is Like the Sunshine, 267 (words); I Think the World Is Glorious, 230 (words); Jesus Is Our Loving Friend, 58 (words); My Flag, My Flag, 225 (words); We Bow Our Heads, 25 (words).

See also **Lyon**: Christmas Bells, 54 (words and music); How Will They Know?, 182 (arrangement); I Have Two Ears, 269 (music); Little Pioneer Children, 216 (words and music); We Are Reverent, 27 (music); Whenever I Think about Pioneers, 222 (music); *Hymns*, Each Life That Touches Ours for Good, 293 (music); Saints, Behold How Great Jehovah, 28 (music).

THE GOLDEN PLATES, 86

Words: Rose Thomas Graham (1876–1967) LDS
Music: J. Spencer Cornwall (1888–1983) LDS

When *The Children Sing* was being compiled, there was a need for songs with specific Mormon messages. The compilers contacted **Rose Thomas Graham**, a poet, for possible texts. Apparently Sister Graham was a tiny lady who lived in a tiny house. She was a member of the

PART THREE

National League of American Pen Women, the Art Barn Poets, and other writer's groups. Her poems for children appeared in local and national publications.

"The Golden Plates" was selected from a collection of Rose Graham's poems, and **J. Spencer Cornwall** was asked to write music for her words. When Brother Cornwall was only four years old, he learned to play music on a pump organ. Because his legs were too short to reach the pedals, his brother pumped them for him. Spencer was so eager to learn that he would have a lesson in the morning, practice in the afternoon, and then go running back the next morning for another lesson. Besides becoming music supervisor of the Salt Lake Elementary School District, he also directed the Tabernacle Choir for twenty-three years. He thought making music was a wonderful reason for people to get together. He said, "My greatest pleasure was in teaching children to learn to sing and to discover the joy of making their own music." Music was his life, and when he was ninety-five years old, he was still composing.[57]

The best marriage of words and music occurs when the natural musical accent matches the word accent. The third measure of the second verse placed the unimportant word *a* on the first beat of the measure, which is the strongest accent in the measure. "A godly man" felt awkward when sung. Since the song was about the plates, rather than Nephi, it was a good solution to change that phrase to "Written in days of old." You can feel how nicely that sings.

We received a letter of concern about the word *found* in verse one. One meaning of *found* might imply that Heavenly Father was searching for someone to fulfill this important assignment. The double meaning of the word suggests, rather, that Joseph was found faithful by Heavenly Father, as a bishop might find a young man faithful and worthy to serve a mission.

See also **Cornwall**: *Hymns*, Softly Beams the Sacred Dawning, 56 (music).

THE SACRED GROVE, 87

Words: Joan D. Campbell (1929–) LDS
Music: Hal K. Campbell (1927–) LDS

Joan D. Campbell was born in England and worked in the woolen mills as a weaver before coming to America. She said, "Hal and I sang to our children when they were very tiny. We sing to our grandchildren and teach them all kinds of activity songs. Children learn very quickly and love to listen and participate."[58] She has been chairman of the Cedar City Music Arts Guild.

Her husband, **Hal K. Campbell**, said, "This song is intended to examine the setting of the lovely spring morning and the sacred encounter with deity by the young boy, Joseph Smith." Brother Campbell earned a doctorate in music and has taught music history, theory, and composition along with piano at Southern Utah State College at Cedar City, Utah. He says, "There is an important place for uplifting music on earth and in heaven. Primary music has the potential to reinforce gospel subjects and children's testimonies."[59]

See also **Campbell**: The Priesthood Is Restored, 89 (words and music).

ON A GOLDEN SPRINGTIME, 88

Words: Virginia Kammeyer (1925–1999) LDS
Music: Crawford Gates (1921–) LDS

Children can easily identify with the miracles of spring, and hopefully will transfer that same faith to the resurrection and the restoration. **Virginia Kammeyer** was asked to write a poem making a parallel between the awakening of springtime, the resurrection, and the restoration of the gospel. The song is listed under each of these topics in the index.

Sister Kammeyer had visited Israel and said, "We saw the tomb which Church leaders feel is the place where Christ was resurrected. There was the same holy feeling there as in the Sacred Grove where Joseph prayed." Her poem captured those feelings. She said, "The songs sung in Primary are among the most beautiful in the Church. They tell of our love for Jesus and his church. A song to Jesus is like a prayer set to music."[60]

After the words were approved, we approached **Crawford Gates** about a melody and accompaniment. He agreed, and we mailed the poem to him. The song was composed, he said, on the way to a rehearsal for the Beloit Symphony Orchestra, which he conducts. He said he hoped to give the children a touch of "richness of imagination with a unique flavor."[61] It was suggested that the high C in the middle of "springtime" was melodically difficult for children, but Brother Gates said his grandchildren had been able to sing it—and so we used it with confidence.

Author's Note: When Dr. Gates conducted "Sand in Their Shoes" at Brigham Young University, I was rehearsal accompanist. The orchestra, lead soloists, and everyone in the opera workshop were seated behind me. Dr.

PART THREE

Gates had his score laid out across the top of the piano and was conducting over me. He was very energetic, and I thought I might possibly be stabbed with his baton before it was over! The musical was performed outdoors in the stadium and the sound of the "Mormon Battalion" actors marching on the track to his inspiring music was electrifying.

Dr. Gates served as a missionary in the Eastern States and on the MIA General Board and the General Church Music Committee. He received his PhD from Eastman School of Music, and was a Brigham Young University music faculty member for sixteen years. He has been music director of the Beloit Janesville Symphony Orchestra and the Rockford Symphony. His music has been performed by major U.S. orchestras, and he received a Grammy award for his album entitled *The Lord's Prayer*. Dr. Gates composed "Promised Valley" for the Utah Centennial celebration as well as the musical score for the Hill Cumorah Pageant. He is a noted and revered director and composer, with more than 650 works.

See also **Kammeyer**: Pioneer Children Were Quick to Obey, 215 (words).

See also **Gates**: Baptism, 100 (music); *Hymns*, Our Savior's Love, 113 (music); Ring Out, Wild Bells, 215 (music).

THE PRIESTHOOD IS RESTORED, 89

Words: Joan D. Campbell, (1929–) LDS
Music: Hal K. Campbell, (1927–) LDS

The author, **Joan D. Campbell**, was born in England, and worked in the woolen mills as a weaver before coming to America. She said, "Hal and I sang to our children when they were very tiny. We sing to our grandchildren and teach them all kinds of activity songs. Children learn very quickly and love to listen and participate."[62] She has been chairman of the Cedar City Music Arts Guild.

Her husband, **Hal K. Campbell**, wrote the piano accompaniment as though it were a trumpet fanfare heralding the important restoration of the priesthood. He simplified the piano part for this collection. Brother Campbell earned a doctorate in music and has taught music history, theory, composition, and piano at Southern Utah State College at Cedar City, Utah. He says, "There is an important place for uplifting music on earth and in heaven. Primary music has the potential to reinforce gospel subjects and children's testimonies."[63]

See also **Campbell**: The Sacred Grove, 87 (words and music).

TRUTH FROM ELIJAH, 90

Words and music: Vanja Y. Watkins, (1938–) LDS

Vanja (VON-yuh) **Yorgason Watkins** was a music classroom and television teacher. She served as Primary general board music chairman and then as a member of the General Church Music Committee. For many years, Sister Watkins was a favorite teacher at the Brigham Young University Church Music Workshops. She also was a faculty member at the university. The index of authors and composers shows her to be the greatest contributor to the songbook. She has credit lines for arrangements, words, music, and words and music—fourteen songs plus the thirteen Articles of Faith, making a total of twenty-seven entries.

There were no songs on genealogy messages in the Primary music resources until 1983 when the sacrament meeting presentation addressed that topic. This song was composed to help fill that need. Vanja skillfully wrote a melody that "turns" along with the words. The key also turns from minor to major as a positive conclusion.

See also **Watkins**: Easter Hosanna, 68 (music); Families Can Be Together Forever, 188 (music); For Thy Bounteous Blessings, 21 (arrangement); I Want to Be Reverent, 28 (music); I Will Be Valiant, 162 (words and music); I Will Follow God's Plan, 164 (words and music); It's Autumntime, 246 (arrangement); Latter-day Prophets, 134 (music); Thank Thee for Everything, 10 (words); The Articles of Faith, 122–132 (music); The Sacrament, 72 (words and music); The Things I Do, 170 (music); This Is My Beloved Son, 76 (music); To Be a Pioneer, 218 (arrangement); *Hymns*, Families Can Be Together Forever, 300 (music); Press Forward Saints, 81 (music).

THE HEARTS OF THE CHILDREN, 92

Words and music: Patricia Kelsey Graham (1940–) LDS

Pat Graham served as the chairman of the 1983 Children's Sacrament Meeting Presentation. Because there were no Primary songs on genealogy topics, she suggested that a new song based on Malachi 4:5–6 could be written. She imagined the song to be of the caliber of "If With All Your Hearts" by Mendelssohn or "Baptism" by Crawford Gates. When the program was written, she inquired about the "new song." Somehow, it had not been requested.

Author's Note: I was very disappointed and then overwhelmed as I was asked to draft a song—and submit it the next week! I had been immersed in

PART THREE

the study and preparation of the program and was filled with ideas but felt terribly inadequate. I prayed earnestly for help in creating something worthy and then went to work. After spending most of the weekend at the piano, I emerged with a simple melody and an obbligato for flute or violin. I heard the song sung many times that year as I visited Primary Sacrament meeting programs, and I finally realized that my simple offering was adequate and had served the purpose. I learned that the Lord really does strengthen us as we do all we can. But I always wondered what might have been.

Sister Graham majored in commercial art and wanted to be an animated cartoonist—then she discovered teaching. She taught children in public school, in church, in her private piano studio, and at the preparatory division of the University of Utah Music Department. She was called to serve on the Primary general board when she was expecting her sixth child and completing a master's degree in education with emphasis on children's music.

Author's Note: During that time, I felt compelled to compose, and sometimes would stay up all night to finish a project. Looking back, I see that writing and publishing my own songs served as the tutoring I needed for my assignment to chair the Children's Songbook *Committee. Now I write when asked, but I am not driven. I am grateful for the opportunity I had to consecrate my time and talents for the children of the Church.*

See also **Graham**: I Am Like a Star, 163 (words and music); Picture a Christmas, 50 (words and music); The Nativity Song, 52 (words and music); We Are Different, 263 (words and music).

FAMILY HISTORY—I AM DOING IT, 94
(originally GENEALOGY—I AM DOING IT)

Words and music: Jeanne P. Lawler, (1924–) LDS

Jeanne Lawler practices what she preaches. She has served several missions for the Church, the latest being a temple mission in Sweden. She wrote this song after having worked for some time on her four-generation charts. Sister Lawler said, "I especially liked the idea of meeting every one of [my ancestors] someday, and I could just visualize myself saying, 'You belong to me . . . and I belong to you.'"[64]

Originally the words to verse two said, "People living now and the ones who've died *are on my pedigree.*" Now it says what should be done— "*can all be sealed to me.*" Sister Lawler loves to write musical theater and oratorios for children. She tells music leaders to "teach with enthusiasm and sing more and talk less. Children will remember thoughts set to music longer than conversation."⁶⁵

See also **Lawler**: Hinges, 277 (music); I Often Go Walking, 202 (music); The Holy Ghost, 105 (words and music); When Jesus Christ Was Baptized, 102 (words and music).

I LOVE TO SEE THE TEMPLE, 95

Words and music: Janice Kapp Perry (1938–) LDS

As a child, **Janice Kapp Perry** loved to travel to the Idaho Falls Temple to do baptisms for the dead. "I Love to See the Temple" reflects her feelings on those trips. Now she lives in Provo, Utah, and can see the temple from her home. After her tiny baby died, she was especially grateful that their family had been sealed. She is reminded of that blessing every time she sees the spire of the temple. She said, "The temple always gives me comfort because our sealing there ensures we will have that child again in eternity if we are worthy."⁶⁶

The song was first printed in *Supplement to More Songs*, 1982 edition, and included an introduction. It was also published in the children's sacrament meeting presentation.

Sister Perry was born in Ogden, Utah, and raised in Vale, Oregon. She received her musical training at Brigham Young University and has composed songs, musicals, and five sacred cantatas, two of which have been performed in the Salt Lake Tabernacle. Many of her songs have been published in the Church magazines.

See also **Perry**: A Child's Prayer, 12 (words and music); I Pray in Faith, 14 (words and music); I'm Thankful to Be Me, 11 (music); I'm Trying to Be Like Jesus, 78 (words and music); Love Is Spoken Here, 190 (words and music); Mother, Tell Me the Story, 204 (words and music); The Church of Jesus Christ, 77 (words and music); The Word of Wisdom, 154 (words and music); We'll Bring the World His Truth, 172 (words and music); *Hymns*, As Sisters in Zion, 309 (music).

FAITH, 96

Words: Beatrice Goff Jackson (1943–) LDS
Music: Michael Finlinson Moody (1941–) LDS

Bea Jackson said, "Faith is sometimes difficult to understand. I feel the Lord wants the Primary children . . . to learn about faith in everyday terms so they will know that they already have the beginnings of faith." Sister Jackson plays piano, violin, string bass, and alto recorder and has

PART THREE

played with many orchestras and symphonies. She is a schoolteacher and has said, "I know the Lord accomplishes his work by using ordinary people who are willing and obedient."[67]

The composer, **Michael Moody**, said, "Music is a tool for building families in good ways. It can bring a sweet spirit into the home. We sing before scripture reading, before meals, and on our way in the car. It keeps gospel messages in the minds of the children."[68] Brother Moody earned a doctorate in church music from the University of Southern California, and was employed as executive secretary of the General Church Music Committee for five years. He became the chairman of the music division of the Church in 1977 and directed the preparation of the 1985 hymnbook. He coached wisely during the preparation of the 1989 *Children's Songbook*. President Moody served a mission in France, spent three years as mission president in Haiti, and was called with his wife, Maria, to a music mission at the Brigham Young University Jerusalem Center.

See also **Moody**: Have a Very Happy Birthday!, 284 (music); Have a Very Merry Christmas!, 51 (music); He Sent His Son, 34 (music); Sleep, Little Jesus, 47 (music); Teacher, Do You Love Me?, 178 (words and music); There Was Starlight on the Hillside, 40 (music); Who Is the Child?, 46 (music); *Hymns*, Testimony, 137 (music).

GOD'S LOVE, 97

Words: Elizabeth Cushing Taylor
Music: Grace Wilbur Conant (1858–1948)

In 1939, children's poet **Elizabeth Cushing Taylor** published a number of her works in a collection entitled *Happiness to Share*. "God's Love" was included in that collection and also printed in *Picture Story Paper*, copyrighted by Stone and Pierce.

Composer and musical editor **Grace Wilbur Conant** studied piano, harmony, and composition in Boston and Paris. Her kindergarten and school part-songs were published in magazines and periodicals. She compiled and edited *Songs for Little People* in 1905. Several songs in the children's music resources of the Church are from this source. She also edited the musical department of *Kindergarten Review*.

The song is used by permission of the Presbyterian Board of Christian Education who hold the 1930 copyright for *Primary Music and Worship*, published by Westminster Press, Philadelphia, Pennsylvania. We suggested a title change to the first line to more easily identify the song, but the copyright contract required that it remain the same.

REPENTANCE, 98

Words: Sylvia Knight Lloyd (1933–) LDS
Music: Robert P. Manookin (1918–1997) LDS

Sylvia Lloyd received her elementary education and early childhood degree from the University of Utah. She taught in Salt Lake City schools and later managed the office of an architectural firm. She is the daughter-in-law of Leah Ashton Lloyd, composer of "I Think When I Read That Sweet Story of Old," 56, and "Reverence," 27.

Robert Manookin composed the music for Sister Lloyd's poem. He removed some of the original dissonance when he simplified his music but did not remove the charm. Brother Manookin served a mission in Germany and served with his wife in the Manila Philippines, Sydney Australia, and New Zealand Temples. He composed the New Zealand Temple Pageant music and the dedicatory music for the Orson Hyde Memorial Gardens in Jerusalem. He earned a BA, MA, and PhD in music theory, composition, and conducting, and has published numerous compositions, some having been performed by the Tabernacle Choir. After serving in teaching and administrative positions, he was named Professor Emeritus of Music at Brigham Young University. Dr. Manookin served on the General Church Music Committee and contributed six hymns to the 1985 hymnbook.

See also **Manookin**: A Prayer Song, 22 (words and music); Our Bishop, 135 (words and music); *Hymns*, Like Ten Thousand Legions Marching, 253 (music); Rise, Ye Saints, and Temples Enter, 287 (music); Saints of Zion, 39 (music); See the Mighty Priesthood Gathered, 325 (music); Thy Will, O Lord, Be Done, 188 (music); We Have Partaken of Thy Love, 155 (music).

HELP ME, DEAR FATHER, 99

Words and music: Frances K. Taylor (1870–1952) LDS

Frances Kingsbury Thomassen Taylor studied piano, organ, harmony, and counterpoint at the University of Utah and Columbia University. She was prominent as an early childhood educator and songwriter in the Salt Lake Valley. Sister Taylor served as a member and secretary of the General Primary Association for eight years. The Deseret Sunday School Union published her songbook, *Kindergarten and Primary Songs*, for use in the Junior Sunday Schools of the Church.

Because there was only one other song about repentance, two lines

PART THREE

were added to make a "repentance" verse in this one. Because we teach forgiveness as part of repentance, this felt very appropriate. I hope Sister Taylor would approve. In addition, the accompaniment was simplified and the title was changed to the first line. In the last line, "nearer" is sung twice rather than holding "to" for three beats as in the original.

See also **Taylor**: Daddy's Homecoming, 210 (music); The Dearest Names, 208 (words and music).

BAPTISM, 100

Words: Mabel Jones Gabbott (1910–2004) LDS
Music: Crawford Gates (1921–) LDS

The original, beautiful accompaniment to "Baptism" was referred to as "the hardest song" for pianists to play in *Sing With Me*. A simplification had been given in the 1981 CTR A manual (page 198) and it was further simplified and fingering added for this collection.

Mabel Jones Gabbott was one of nine children. She received her education at the University of Idaho and the University of Utah. She served a mission to the Northwestern States, and then became secretary to Elder LeGrand Richards. She worked on the staffs of the Church magazines and as a member of the YWMIA General Board and the General Church Music Committee, and chaired the 1985 Hymnbook Text Committee. She was a very small lady with a very large talent for writing, and her poems have been used as words for sixteen Primary songs and four hymns. Sister Gabbott lived in Bountiful, Utah, where she grew roses and cherries. She said, "I love to hear children sing."[69]

Crawford Gates served as a missionary in the Eastern States, and was a member of the MIA General Board and the General Church Music Committee. He received his PhD from Eastman School of Music, and was a Brigham Young University music faculty member for sixteen years. He has been music director of the Beloit Janesville Symphony Orchestra and the Rockford Symphony. His music has been performed by major U.S. orchestras, and he has received a Grammy award for his album *The Lord's Prayer*. Brother Gates composed "Promised Valley" for the Utah Centennial celebration, and included this beautiful "Baptism" song in his musical score for *The Hill Cumorah Pageant*. He is a noted and revered musical director and composer with more than 650 works.

See also **Gabbott**: Before I Take the Sacrament, 73 (words); Did Jesus Really Live Again?, 64 (words); Father Up Above, 23 (words); Had I Been a Child, 80 (words); Have a Very Happy Birthday!, 284 (words);

Have a Very Merry Christmas!, 51 (words); He Sent His Son, 34 (words); My Country, 224 (words); Samuel Tells of the Baby Jesus, 36 (words); Sleep, Little Jesus, 47 (words); The Family, 194 (words); There Was Starlight on the Hillside, 40 (words); To Think about Jesus, 71 (words); We Are Reverent, 27 (words); Who Is the Child, 46 (words); *Hymns,* In Humility, Our Savior, 172 (words); Lord, Accept Into Thy Kingdom, 236 (words); Rejoice, Ye Saints of Latter Days, 290 (words); We Have Partaken of Thy Love, 155 (words).

See also **Gates**: On a Golden Springtime, 88 (music); *Hymns,* Our Savior's Love, 113 (music); Ring Out, Wild Bells, 215 (music).

WHEN JESUS CHRIST WAS BAPTIZED, 102

Words and music: Jeanne P. Lawler (1924–) LDS

Jeanne Lawler served in the U.S. Coast Guard and then received an associate degree in music from Glendale California College. She and her daughter joined the Church, and moved to Provo, Utah, where Sister Lawler graduated from Brigham Young University at age fifty-seven. She has served proselyting and temple missions. Sister Lawler loves to write musical theater and oratorios for children. She tells music leaders to "teach with enthusiasm and sing more and talk less. Children will remember thoughts set to music longer than conversation." [70] She also said:

> Often I would wonder what it was like when Jesus Christ was baptized . . . and I wish I had been there and heard the voice from heaven and saw what others saw, and felt what they felt at that great event. That is why I wrote this song, and I wanted to put those feelings in the hearts of children who are going to be baptized or are reflecting on the time they were baptized.[71]

A second verse was added to make this message personal. Brother Moody emphasized the importance of singing what we should *do* and suggested verses be added to several songs so that they were more of a commitment.

See also **Lawler**: Family History—I Am Doing It, 94 (words and music); Hinges, 277 (music); I Often Go Walking, 202 (music); The Holy Ghost, 105 (words and music).

WHEN I AM BAPTIZED, 103

Words and music: Nita Dale Milner (1952–2004) LDS

PART THREE

In 1986, this song was a Church music contest winner entitled "Rainbows: A Baptism Song." There were many songs about baptism, and without a different focus the song could not be considered. We approached **Nita Milner** about revising the words with a virtue inference. After several suggestions she consented to the changes. That was fortunate, as the song has definitely become a favorite. The title now emphasizes the message, and the song is listed in the topic index under "baptism" and "morality."

Sister Milner taught piano and said, "The music you store inside of you is something no one can take away and can help you go through times in your life that may be difficult. I believe that music is a gift from our Heavenly Father to comfort us, teach us, and make our lives happier."[72] She had improved health after a kidney transplant and expressed her gratitude through her music.

At the songbook celebration, the authors and composers had an opportunity to meet and sign each other's books.

Author's Note: Sister Milner wrote in my book, "Thanks for your help." Without the adaptation this lovely song would not have been included in the book.

I LIKE MY BIRTHDAYS, 104

Words: Wallace F. Bennett (1898–1993) LDS
Music: Tracy Y. Cannon (1879–1961) LDS

In the 1940s, **Wallace F. Bennett** served on the General Church Music Committee and the Sunday School General Board. He was a fine bass soloist and his wife, Frances Grant (youngest daughter of President Heber J. Grant), accompanied him on the piano. When Frances served on the Primary general board, he was asked to write words for several children's songs. For many years he served as ward choir director, and near his birthday his ward would honor him by singing his hymn. He left his business, Bennett Glass and Paint Company, to serve as the U.S. Senator from Utah for twenty-four years.

Tracy Y. Cannon was invited to join the Tabernacle Choir when he was fifteen and later served as assistant organist for twenty-one years, playing for many choir radio broadcasts. He was chairman of the General Music Committee of the Church and established a training program for Church conductors and organists. He also was director of the McCune School of Music and Art in Salt Lake City.

See also **Bennett**: When We're Helping, 198 (words); *Hymns,* God of Power, God of Right, 20 (words).

See also **Cannon**: *Hymns,* Come, Let Us Sing an Evening Hymn, 167 (music); Come, Rejoice, 9 (words and music); God of Power, God of Right, 20 (music); How Beautiful Thy Temples, Lord, 288 (music); Jesus, Mighty King in Zion, 234 (music); Praise the Lord with Heart and Voice, 73 (words and music); The Lord Be with Us, 161 (music).

THE HOLY GHOST, 105

Words and music: Jeanne P. Lawler, (1924–) LDS

Jeanne P. Lawler served in the U.S. Coast Guard and then received an associate degree in music from Glendale California College. She and her daughter joined the Church and moved to Provo, Utah, where Sister Lawler graduated from Brigham Young University at age fifty-seven. She has served proselyting and temple missions.

Extensive word revision combined the ideas of the original second and third verses and included a personal commitment in this song. Music leaders appreciate fewer verses to teach, and a survey had shown that third and fourth verses are seldom used. Sister Lawler tells music leaders to "teach with enthusiasm and sing more and talk less. Children will remember thoughts set to music longer than conversation." [73] Sister Lawler loves to write musical theater and oratorios for children.

See also **Lawler**: Family History—I Am Doing It, 94 (words and music); Hinges, 277 (music); I Often Go Walking, 202 (music); When Jesus Christ Was Baptized, 102 (words and music).

THE STILL, SMALL VOICE, 106

Words and music: Merrill Bradshaw (1929–2000) LDS

Merrill Bradshaw composed over two hundred musical works including simple songs, symphonies, concertos, oratorios, and pageants. His works have been performed by symphonic groups in Utah, Mexico, Australia, and New Zealand. He served on the General Church Music Committee and chaired the initial work done on the 1985 hymnal. Dr. Bradshaw was composer-in-residence at Brigham Young University and taught for nearly forty years.

With the exception of this song and the following round, all other songs in the book have chord symbols (C, F, G7, etc.) above the melody line. Simplified chording, however, could not capture the unique sound of the modal accompaniment. Dr. Bradshaw preferred no chord symbols

PART THREE

rather than simplified chording. "Using the Songbook" section, pages 302–303 in the *Children's Songbook*, has an explanation of how to use chords when playing chord cassios and organs, guitar or autoharp.

See also **Bradshaw**: Listen, Listen, 107 (words and music); *Hymns*, We Will Sing of Zion, 47 (words and music).

LISTEN, LISTEN, 107

Words and music: Merrill Bradshaw (1929–2000) LDS

Merrill Bradshaw said, "Music gives us a way to communicate our testimony to God, especially those things that we feel too deeply to say in words. We worship not only when we are quiet and reverent, but also when we are joyful and happy and recognize the hand of the Lord in all things."[74] Dr. Bradshaw composed over two hundred musical works including simple songs, symphonies, concertos, oratorios, and pageants. His works have been performed by symphonic groups in Utah, Mexico, Australia, and New Zealand. He served on the General Church Music Committee and chaired the initial work done on the 1985 hymnal. Dr. Bradshaw was composer-in-residence at Brigham Young University and taught for nearly forty years.

With the exception of this song and the previous one, all other songs in the book have chord symbols (C, F, G7, etc.) above the melody line.

See also **Bradshaw**: The Still, Small Voice, 106 (words and music); *Hymns*, We Will Sing of Zion, 47 (words and music).

SEEK THE LORD EARLY, 108

Words and music: Joanne Bushman Doxey (1932–) LDS

Joanne Bushman Doxey and her husband served as mission presidents in Barcelona, Spain. While there, she said, "I was impressed as I read the scriptures ... that if children learned early to seek the Lord, they would be guided and protected throughout their lives."[75] Just before the Doxeys completed their mission, President Dwan Young contacted Joanne. She wanted someone who could understand the needs of children in the mission field. One of the first assignments given to Sister Doxey was to help write the 1984 Children's Sacrament Meeting Presentation. The scripture she had been impressed with prompted this song.

Author's Note: I always liked to sit by Joanne at board meetings. I had a new baby as well as teenagers, and I eagerly soaked up her comments about parenting and teaching. She always made me feel that it was possible to be a successful mother and serve in the Church.

STORIES OF THE CHILDREN'S SONGBOOK

Joanne said, "The most important of all activities and honors, the most time-consuming and most rewarding, has been the rearing of a righteous family."[76] She is the mother of eight children who enjoy singing together and collecting and playing musical instruments. Sister Doxey served as counselor to General Relief Society President Barbara Winder; chairman of Church Hostessing; and with her husband as counselor in the Salt Lake Temple presidency, and president of the Spain Madrid Temple.

See also **Doxey**: Where Love Is, 138 (words and music).

SEARCH, PONDER AND PRAY, 109

Words: Jaclyn Thomas Milne (1949–) LDS
Music: Carol Baker Black (1951–) LDS

Jaclyn Milne enjoys writing as a hobby and has collaborated with her friend, **Carol Black**. One of their compositions, "The Miracle of America," was performed at the Kennedy Center in Washington, DC at the nation's bicentennial celebration. Their song, "Search, Ponder and Pray," won the children's song category of the 1986 Church Music Contest, and was printed in the Children's Sacrament Meeting Presentation that year. The words teach what to do to gain a testimony, and the music causes a warm feeling when singing it. That is an example of the songbook preface statement, "As you sing, you may feel good inside. The Holy Ghost gives you warm feelings to help you understand that the words and messages of the songs are true."[77]

Sister Milne believes that Heavenly Father is always near. As a young child, she remembers being made well almost immediately after priesthood blessings. She attended Dixie Jr. and Weber State Colleges and has been successful in turning her writing hobby into published songs.

Sister Black began serving in the Church as the Primary pianist when she was twelve. When Primary was held after school, she would run from school to the Church to begin playing prelude music for the children as they entered the chapel. She said, "My parents provided me with the opportunity of taking piano lessons, but I have had no formal training in music theory or composition. I do, however, possess a great love for good music and a testimony of its influence in our lives."[78] She has been composing at the request of Sister Milne since 1985.

See also **Milne**: How Dear to God Are Little Children, 180 (words).
See also **Black**: How Dear to God Are Little Children, 180 (music).

PART THREE

FOLLOW THE PROPHET, 110

Words and music: Duane Hiatt (1937–) LDS

Primary boys and girls enjoyed the additional verses to "Book of Mormon Stories" which were added to the song for the 1988 Children's Sacrament Meeting Presentation. The Church Songbook Committee thought it might be worthwhile to have a song about Old Testament stories, with a Jewish flavor—like "Fiddler on the Roof." A memorable chorus could contain the main message of the song.

After deciding on the prophets to be included, **Duane Hiatt** was asked to create the song. Brother Hiatt had performed musical comedy professionally with the "Three D's" for sixteen years, and their songs were recorded for Capitol Records. Brother Hiatt has won awards for his work as a freelance radio and television scriptwriter, and was producer-director of television learning programs for Media Productions at Brigham Young University. He sang and played his guitar for nine verses with a catchy chorus that had a memorable "hook."

Author's Note: The song was notated from the recording he submitted and we chuckled over the clever verses he had sung. However, each verse needed to have the same number of syllables, and Correlation made some suggestions for word changes. During the editing process, Brother Hiatt's wife, Diane, passed away. I didn't feel that I could contact him about some of the suggestions and tried to find the solutions myself. I asked Lynn Elliott, a friend of my daughter, for input. Together we solved the problems, and now the friend is my son-in-law!

Brother Hiatt said, "Trying to entertain, educate, and inspire fifteen children in home evenings over the years has helped me develop an appreciation for what music and rhythm can do in teaching . . . . We've had good times pantomiming the situations in the verses, and then doing a little shuffle in the choruses."[79] He also recommends accompanying with guitar, banjo, mandolin, handclaps and finger snapping, or tambourine and other rhythm instruments.

Author's Note: While serving a mission in Detroit, Michigan, I wrote about two more prophets who were especially important to new converts: Joseph Smith and Gordon B. Hinckley. The children loved singing "Bitner" and after learning the verse could easily say President Hinckley's name. Over half the members of the Detroit River Branch were Spanish-speaking, and they were eager to learn new words. I submitted my ideas to the Friend, *and the President Hinckley verse was printed in the October 2006 magazine, pages 40–41.*

> Joseph Smith, a young boy asked which church was right.
> God, the Father, and His Son appeared in heav'nly light.
> He received the gold plates restoring gospel truth.
> Joseph organized the Church again upon the earth.
>
> Gordon Bitner Hinckley travels o'er the earth
> Making friends with kings and leaders of the world.
> Dedicating temples, waving with his cane
> Standing up for righteousness honors God's name.[80]

THE COMMANDMENTS, 112

Words: anonymous

Music: Charlene Anderson Newell (1937–) LDS

Charlene Newell graduated from BYU with honors, and then studied at the University of Utah, BYU–Hawaii, and the New England Conservatory of Music. Her compositions have been published in the *Friend*, *Sing With Me*, and the hymnbook. "A Woman's Prayer" won the 1977 Relief Society song contest, and was performed in the Tabernacle and at the dedication of the Nauvoo Monument to Women. Sister Newell is an outstanding pianist and taught music in Utah's Granite School District and private voice and organ lessons. She is married to Robert R. Newell, and they are the parents of twelve children.

See also **Newell**: He Died That We Might Live Again, 65 (music); Little Jesus, 39 (music); Your Happy Birthday, 283 (words and music); *Hymns*, A Key Was Turned in Latter Days, 310 (music).

THE BOOKS IN THE OLD TESTAMENT, 114

Words: anonymous

Music: George Kaillmark (1781–1835); hymn tune "Do What Is Right" adapted

George Kaillmark, an Englishman, originally wrote this tune for an excerpt written by Thomas Moore. President George Q. Cannon heard the text for "Do What Is Right" sung to Mr. Kaillmark's melody during a Scottish conference where he presided. President Cannon was so impressed with the message of hope and the urge to be "faithful and fearless" that he included the song in the twelfth edition of the Latter-day Saints' hymnbook, which was published in 1863. The tune became

PART THREE

popular in the United States with other words as well, such as "The Old Oaken Bucket" by Samuel Woodworth.

An anonymous person, perhaps a teacher, adapted this popular tune to the table of contents of the Old Testament to help children remember the order of the books. Additional melody notes were necessary to accommodate the extra syllables. Memorizing words and music together has proven to be a very successful teaching method.

THE BOOKS IN THE NEW TESTAMENT, 116

Words: anonymous
Music: Scottish folk song; adapted, W. W. Phelps (1792–1872) LDS tune of "Praise to the Man," arrangement

William Wines Phelps contributed twenty-six texts to the first hymnbook and assisted Emma Smith in revising and editing all the selections (see D&C 55). He was a scribe for the prophet Joseph in translating the book of Abraham and was a member of the First Presidency of the Church in Missouri. He crossed the plains to the Salt Lake Valley and served as a regent of the University of Deseret and a member of the Utah legislature. Fifteen of his original hymn texts are included in the 1985 hymnal, including the favorites "The Spirit of God," "Now Let Us Rejoice," "Redeemer of Israel," "Gently Raise the Sacred Strain," and "O God, the Eternal Father."

For more than fifty years, children in Primary and students in seminary have learned the order of the books in the New Testament by singing them to the Scottish folk song that Brother Phelps adapted for his text, "Praise to the Man." The phonetic pronunciation for "Philemon" was added below the text in the song.

See also **Phelps:** *Hymns* (words), Adam-ondi-Ahman, 49; Come, All Ye Saints of Zion, 38; Come, All Ye Saints Who Dwell on Earth, 65; Come, Let Us Sing an Evening Hymn, 167; Gently Raise the Sacred Strain, 146; Glorious Things Are Sung of Zion, 48; If You Could Hie to Kolob, 284; Joy to the World, 201 (alteration); Now Let Us Rejoice, 3; Now We'll Sing with One Accord, 25; O God, the Eternal Father, 175; Praise to the Man, 27; Redeemer of Israel, 6 (alteration); The Spirit of God, 2; We're Not Ashamed to Own Our Lord, 57.

BOOK OF MORMON STORIES, 118

Words and music: Elizabeth Fetzer Bates (1909–1999) LDS
Optional words: Nancy Daines Carter (1935–) LDS

STORIES OF THE CHILDREN'S SONGBOOK

Elizabeth Fetzer Bates, a piano teacher and the mother of six children, became totally blind in 1951. She accepted her blindness as a challenge and decided that she would learn to do everything that she could. In 1969, she wrote "Book of Mormon Stories" because she loved the Book of Mormon and was grateful for America. She thinks that children like this song because it is simple and true. It ranked either number one or two in three of the survey categories.

Author's Note: I interviewed Sister Bates in her home on Ninth South just above East High School in Salt Lake City. She played some of her other compositions for me and showed me artwork drawn by her grandchildren. She was extremely independent and very cheerful.[81]

The 1988 Children's Sacrament Meeting Presentation was about the Book of Mormon. Additional verses to this favorite song had been submitted by **Nancy K. Daines Carter** and were used in the program. They were a wonderful teaching tool and were included in the *Children's Songbook*. Sister Carter has a PhD in education and said, "If you want to learn something, sing it! Children will better understand the Book of Mormon if they can sing its stories."[82]

See also **Bates**: Pioneer Children Sang as They Walked, 214 (words and music).

THE BOOKS IN THE BOOK OF MORMON, 119

Words: adapted, Daphne Matthews (1917–2014) LDS

You might know other words to the tune used for singing this song. How appropriate that the tune "Ten Little Indians" is used for a song about Nephites and Lamanites. **Daphne Matthews** chose this familiar tune and adapted the list of fifteen books in the Book of Mormon's table of contents. The second verse, last phrase was originally "singing this is so fun." It was decided to have it match the first verse ("In the Book of Mormon") which emphasizes the message of the song, and also avoids the unimportant word *so* on an important musical accent.

Author's Note: My scripture quad is small and has no indented tabs down the side of the pages. As I look for scriptures, I always sing through this song to get to the right place. It works very well, and I notice I can keep up with others around me who are using tabs.

NEPHI'S COURAGE, 120

Words and music: Bill N. Hansen, Jr. (1952–) LDS and Lisa T. Hansen (1958–) LDS.

PART THREE

This favorite song was first published in the *Friend* magazine in 1986 when the focus of Primary was the Book of Mormon. It was written by a husband and wife team, **Bill N. Hansen, Jr.** and **Lisa Tensmeyer Hansen**, who like children to have fun when they sing. Brother Hansen, an attorney, said, "I believe that living the gospel can be fun as we develop our many talents in the service of others." Sister Hansen, a Kimball Scholar at BYU and mother of five, said, "I know the gospel of Jesus Christ is true. I felt the Spirit reveal this to me when I was eleven years old."[83]

It was suggested that this song have a third verse to apply the message to the child. The Hansen's responded with verse three, which is a good match for Nephi's commitment in the chorus.

THE ARTICLES OF FAITH, 122–132

Words: Joseph Smith (1805–1844) LDS
Music: Vanja Y. Watkins, (1938–) LDS

Joseph Smith, Jr. prayed to his Heavenly Father to know which church was right. He was visited by the Father and the Son, and became the first prophet of the restored Church of Jesus Christ. He was directed to the gold plates, which he translated and published as the Book of Mormon. The Prophet organized The Church of Jesus Christ of Latter-day Saints in 1830 and restored priesthood keys for baptism and temple work. His wife, Emma, compiled the first hymnal for the Church.

The Articles of Faith were written to tell the beliefs of the Church, and are included with Joseph Smith's history in the *Pearl of Great Price*. Members often memorize these statements so that they can express what they believe in a concise way.

After observing the success Primary leaders had as they taught handicapped children through music, President Naomi Shumway requested a musical setting for the Articles of Faith. Composers tried different approaches, changing the words to make rhymes or adding additional ideas. **Vanja** (VON-yuh) **Yorgason Watkins** tried and said it initially felt like trying to set the phone book to music! The words in the Articles of Faith do not rhyme, as most children's songs do, so she set the words to the melodies in the approximate rhythm you would speak them. She began with a single melody line for each, and found the appropriate personality of each article—some serious, some joyful. She was careful to match music and word accents, which helps with pronunciation of words like "paradisiacal" (tenth Article of Faith). Some were written during a family outing while her husband entertained their small children, and some were written on her parents' front porch while she was watering the yard.

The success of Sister Watkins' musical settings was proven when a group of mentally handicapped children successfully sang several of the songs at a Primary conference in the Tabernacle. Singing the Articles of Faith is an effective way to memorize them because the melody helps recall the words. Memorizing these songs is memorizing scripture, and once you sing them from memory you can't forget them.

Sister Watkins was a television music teacher before serving on the Primary general board and the General Music Committee of the Church. She has written music and words, or arranged a total of twenty-seven songs in this collection.[84]

See also **Watkins**: Easter Hosanna, 68 (words and music); Families Can Be Together Forever, 188 (music); For Thy Bounteous Blessings, 21 (arrangement); I Want to Be Reverent, 28 (music); I Will Be Valiant, 162 (words and music); I Will Follow God's Plan, 164 (words and music); It's Autumntime, 246 (arrangement); Latter-day Prophets, 134 (music); Thank Thee for Everything, 10 (words); The Sacrament, 72 (words and music); The Things I Do, 170 (music); This Is My Beloved Son, 76 (music); To Be a Pioneer, 218 (arrangement); Truth from Elijah, 90 (words and music); *Hymns*, Families Can Be Together Forever, 300 (music); Press Forward Saints, 81 (music).

LATTER-DAY PROPHETS, 134

Words: Cynthia Lord Pace (1955–) LDS
Music: Vanja Y. Watkins (1938–) LDS

Cynthia Lord Pace was one of ten children and became the accompanist for her father, a singer. After attending Brigham Young University and marrying, she suffered cancer of the lymph system. Following difficult years and spiritual blessings, she recovered. She said, "I think music is a deeper form of communication than talking, and it makes me feel wonderful things." Concerning the origin of her poem, "Latter-day Prophets," she related, "One very dedicated and concerned mother came to me . . . and asked me to write a song so her daughter could remember the names of the prophets. . . . I knelt down and poured out my heart to my Father in Heaven [in thanks] for my many blessings. I also asked him to help me write a little song to help this girl. At the close of my prayer the words to the first line of the song came: 'Latter-day prophets are:

PART THREE

number one, Joseph Smith, then Brigham Young,' with the impression, 'I have given you the first line, you write the rest!'"[85]

Sister Pace used the nursery tune "Here We Go 'Round the Mulberry Bush," for her melody. When the song was submitted to the *Friend* magazine, Vanja Watkins was asked to write original music for the poem. Originally, the current prophet was named in the last phrase of the song. Sister Watkins said, "After revising the words and music several times, it seemed appropriate to write the last line so that future names could be added with only minor revision. Perhaps the song will make it to the millennium!"[86]

Original:

(1980) A mighty man was Harold B. Lee,
And now we have named past prophets you see.
Our prophet today is loved by all; he's Spencer W. Kimball.
(1986) A mighty man was Harold B. Lee,
Ezra Taft Benson—we honor him.
All Latter-day prophets show the way.
We hear and follow their words today.
(1994) Ezra Taft Benson—we honor him.
Howard W. Hunter shows the way.
We hear and honor his words today.
(1995) Ezra Taft Benson, Howard W. Hunter,
Gordon B. Hinckley shows the way.
We hear and follow his words today.

Vanja (VON-yuh) **Yorgason Watkins** wrote the music for the 1980 publication of the song in the April *Friend*. She served as Primary general board music chairman and as a member of the General Church Music Committee. The index of authors and composers shows her to be the greatest contributor to the songbook with twenty-seven credit lines. Many are favorites and all are of quality musicianship.

See also **Watkins**: Easter Hosanna, 68 (words and music); Families Can Be Together Forever, 188 (music); For Thy Bounteous Blessings, 21 (arrangement); I Want to Be Reverent, 28 (music); I Will Be Valiant, 162 (words and music); I Will Follow God's Plan, 164 (words and music); It's Autumntime, 246 (arrangement); Thank Thee for Everything, 10 (words); The Articles of Faith, 122–132 (music); The Sacrament, 72 (words and music); The Things I Do, 170 (music); This Is My Beloved Son, 76 (music); To Be a Pioneer, 218 (arrangement); Truth from Elijah,

90 (words and music); *Hymns*, Families Can Be Together Forever, 300 (music); Press Forward Saints, 81 (music).

OUR BISHOP, 135

Words and music: Robert P. Manookin (1918–1997) LDS

Robert Manookin was serving as a bishop when he composed this song to explain the role of a bishop. He revised the accompaniment and added a second verse for the *Children's Songbook* collection. The time signature was changed from 4/4 to 2/2. He served a mission in Germany as a young man and temple missions with his wife to Manila, Phillipines; Sydney, Australia; and New Zealand. He composed the New Zealand Temple Pageant music and the dedicatory music for the Orson Hyde Memorial Gardens in Jerusalem. Dr. Manookin served on the General Church Music Committee and contributed six hymns to the 1985 hymnbook. After teaching and administrative positions, he was named Professor Emeritus of Music at Brigham Young University.

See also **Manookin**: A Prayer Song, 22 (words and music); Repentance, 98 (music); *Hymns*, Like Ten Thousand Legions Marching, 253 (music); Rise, Ye Saints, and Temples Enter, 287 (music); Saints of Zion, 39 (music); See the Mighty Priesthood Gathered, 325 (music); Thy Will, O Lord, Be Done, 188 (music); We Have Partaken of Thy Love, 155 (music).

LOVE ONE ANOTHER, 136

Words and music: Luacine Clark Fox (1914–2002) LDS

Luacine Clark Fox's beloved song is part of a cantata. The background music and dialogue surrounding "Love One Another" tells the Easter Story. Sister Fox explained how the song came to be:

It is always my habit to pray before doing any writing or composing. This I did while in the process of working on *Psalm of Easter*, from which "Love One Another" is taken. In searching the scriptures, I came to the words of the Savior at the Last Supper wherein he gave his new commandment to love one another. I knew that I had found the theme I wanted. As I jotted down the words in my notebook, taken from John 13:34–35, the melody to accompany them came into my mind, and I wrote it down as well. The final result of words and music was exactly the same as had come to me initially, with no variation whatsoever. It is my witness that whatever is of worth in the song came from the Lord.[87]

Sister Fox is the daughter of J. Reuben Clark, who was an Apostle and counselor to President David O. McKay. She feels that music is the most heavenly of all the arts, and says, "When we sing to Heavenly Father, it is like praying." She believes that "there can be no greater fulfillment in the exercise of a God-given talent than to use it in connection with the work of the Lord."[88] She wrote and appeared on a children's radio program, "Storytelling Time," and was active for many years as a writer for City Rep Children's Theater in Salt Lake. She also served on the YWMIA General Board, and she and her husband were missionaries in Nauvoo, Illinois.

Author's Note: Sister Fox brought a choir to Whittier Ward to perform her Easter cantata. I was sixteen and serving as the ward organist and had the blessing of accompanying her group. I treasure the copy of the original handwritten score she gave me.

Over the years, many people sent ideas for a second verse to Sister Fox. She did write another verse, although it has never been published. The syllables are not matched exactly to the original melody notes, but it is an appropriate follow-up message. Her idea was to sing verse one, verse two, and then verse one again.

> Thus spake the Savior unto His disciples.
> Thus speaks the Savior unto us all.
> May we endeavor, now and forever, This sacred counsel—to recall.

Jo Marie Borgeson Bray (1925–1988), a multi-instrumentalist and Utah native, prepared the arrangement to include an obbligato. It is effective to have children sing page 136 (in the Key of F) and then have the violin play the melody with children signing; then use *Hymns* page 301 (in the Key of G) with singing, signing, and violin obbligato (move up one step).

The deaf sign language was printed for this song as a model for the use of signing on other Primary songs. This beautiful hand language can be enjoyed by every child and teaches understanding beyond the words. The Special Needs Department of the Church has prepared videos and DVDs demonstrating American Sign for Primary Songs.

See also **Fox**: *Hymns*, Love One Another, 308 (words and music).

WHERE LOVE IS, 138

Words: Joanne Bushman Doxey (1932–) LDS and Norma B. Smith (1923–2010) LDS

Music: Joanne Bushman Doxey (1932–) LDS and Marjorie Castleton Kjar (1927) LDS

STORIES OF THE CHILDREN'S SONGBOOK

Joanne Doxey believes, "Music is a language of the Spirit and through it, we can all draw closer to each other and our Maker."[89] In 1969, she was asked to write a song for a Primary conference. "After praying for help," she said, "a pure flow of inspiration came with both words and music."[90] Since the song was written, Sister Doxey has served with her husband as mission president in Barcelona, Spain, as a member of the Primary general board, as a counselor in the general Relief Society presidency, and as head of Church hostessing.

Marjorie Kjar arranged the melody and piano accompaniment. Sister Kjar loves to have her family, including her grandchildren, sing together and believes that music can bring happiness to the soul. Sister Kjar teaches piano "to help children prepare to serve in the Church as musicians." She received a music degree from the University of Utah, and served for five years on the Primary general board, and then on the General Church Music Committee. She said, "The Lord has blessed me so abundantly that I desire only to serve Him by serving others in sharing my time, effort and talents." She and her husband also presided over a mission in New Zealand. Her advice to Church music directors and pianists is "to prepare ahead by learning the gospel messages of the songs. I strongly feel that the music director is her [own] best visual aid."[91]

The song "Where Love Is" became a favorite of both adults and children and has been sung on every occasion imaginable! There have been many versions of the song published, but Sister Doxey and Sister Kjar prepared this as the official "short" version. They have written many songs together, suggesting changes to each other and reworking the words and music until they are just right.

Norma B. Smith, a member of the Primary general board who was on the Conference Committee, had developed ideas for the song. She wrote her thoughts on a napkin while accompanying her husband on business. Sister Smith is talented in writing, public speaking, and singing. She also served as a counselor in the Young Women General Presidency.

See also **Doxey**, Joanne: Seek the Lord Early, 108 (words and music).

See also **Kjar**: Birds in the Tree, 241 (music); Come with Me to Primary, 255 (words and music); We Welcome You, 256 (music); Stand Up, 278 (music).

I'LL WALK WITH YOU, 140

Words: Carol Lynn Pearson (1939–) LDS

PART THREE

Music: Reid Nibley (1923–2008) LDS
Author's Note: As we were evaluating the songs from the survey, we began to make a topical index. We realized that we had no songs on special needs. A Primary board member, Carmen Pingree, said she wished we had a song that taught how to treat people with handicaps or differences that make people feel uncomfortable. We brainstormed about the content of such a song and wrote a sample message in free verse. We felt it should show the Savior's example and cause a feeling of commitment. When asked who might write the poem, Carmen suggested **Carol Lynn Pearson** *because of her concise and thought-provoking writing.*

Sister Pearson has a master's degree in theater from BYU, has taught drama and English at the college level, and has traveled as an actress and speaker. She is the author of books of poetry and plays such as the musical "My Turn on Earth." The international award-winning "Cipher in the Snow" is also her work. She was contacted in Walnut Creek, California, and agreed to help us. The sample was mailed to her, and while flying to Salt Lake for a rehearsal, she worked on the poem. When she dropped it off at the Church offices she said, "Feel free to revise or fix this in any way to fit your purpose."[92] We were delighted with her poem, and after one slight revision and approval from Correlation, it was ready to have music added.

Reid Nibley is sensitive to this topic because he has cared for a handicapped daughter. He returned his musical setting of the poem in less than three weeks and said he had wanted it to sound like "walking" in the left-hand accompaniment. The original accompaniment, however, was simplified—he is, after all, a concert pianist! Dr. Nibley began studying piano at age six and eventually gave concerts throughout the United States, Canada, Europe, Japan, and New Zealand for fifty years. He holds a doctor of musical arts degree from the University of Michigan, and was artist-in-residence at BYU for sixteen years. He also served on the General Church Music Committee.

Author's Note: It is difficult to "make" a favorite song. You never know if what you have requested will be successful. A neighbor of mine told me that her daughter had a new favorite song in Primary—"I'll Walk With You." Her daughter has an arm that hasn't grown right, and this song helped her to feel okay about it. That is a true measure of the success of the song.

See also **Nibley**: I Know My Father Lives, 5; *Hymns*, I Know My Father Lives, 302.

EVERY STAR IS DIFFERENT, 142

Words: John C. Cameron (1951–)
Music: K. Newell Dayley (1939–) LDS

Originally, this song was composed in the style of musical theater. The ideas of several verses were compressed into a second verse for the *Children's Songbook* emphasizing the importance of being who you alone can be. In June of 1990, a newspaper article told about the graduation exercises of the Hartvigsen School for the handicapped. The young man who was president of the graduating class had chosen to use the words of the second verse as part of his talk. The message had come full circle and was useful to those it was intended to strengthen.

K. Newell Dayley served as a member of the Brigham Young University Music Faculty and also the General Music Committee of the Church. Brother Dayley is an excellent trumpet player and became chairman of the Brigham Young University Music Department. He composed music for the musicals *III Nephi* and *Kirtland* and the soundtrack of the show at the Polynesian Cultural Center in Hawaii. He said, "I have a deep love for children's music and feel that some of our most important work ought to be focused in that direction."[93]

There is no information on the author, **John Cameron**.

See also **Dayley**: Home, 192 (music); Hum Your Favorite Hymn, 152 (music); I Feel My Savior's Love, 74 (words and music); The World Is So Big, 235 (music); *Hymns,* Lord, I Would Follow Thee, 220 (music).

SHINE ON, 144

Words and music: Joseph Ballantyne (1868–1944) LDS

Joseph Ballantyne was born in Ogden Valley, Utah, the son of Richard Ballantyne, the founder of the Sunday School of the Church. He studied music in New York, and with musicians from Chicago, New York, London, and Paris. Brother Ballantyne directed the Ogden Tabernacle Choir, and then chaired the music committee for the Deseret Sunday School Board. During this time, he wrote many children's songs. His song "Shine On" was first printed in 1905 in both the *Deseret Sunday School Songbook* and *The Primary Song Book*. When Brother Ballantyne moved to Long Beach, California, he directed the Los Angeles Stake choir and the choir at St. Anthony's Church. He also taught private voice lessons.

See also **Ballantyne, Joseph**: Jesus Once Was a Little Child, 55

PART THREE

(music); Little Purple Pansies, 244 (music); Oh, Hush Thee, My Baby, 48 (words and music); Stand for the Right, 159 (words and music).

A SPECIAL GIFT IS KINDNESS, 145

Words and music: Sharon Steed (1935–) LDS

Sharon Mann Steed grew up on a farm and learned from her mother how to sing and perform. She studied voice and piano and later taught both in her home. Sister Steed attended Weber State College, graduated from Excelsis Beauty School, and was employed as secretary of the Ogden City Schools. Sister Steed sang with the Weber State College Symphonic Choir. Her sweet song about kindness was number 31 on the 1983 survey of Primary songs.

KINDNESS BEGINS WITH ME, 145

Words and music: Clara Watkins McMaster (1904–1997) LDS

Clara McMaster was the eleventh child in her family, and learned to love music at an early age. She sang and accompanied others on the piano as she grew up in Brigham City, Utah. For twenty-two years, she was a member of the Tabernacle Choir. Sister McMaster feels that "Music is a rich gift of God, and it is in the world to make the lives of His children happier and better."[94]

Sister McMaster served on the Primary general board for fourteen years, and was music chairman much of that time. She and her husband, J. Stuart McMaster, received the 1978 Franklin S. Harris Fine Arts Award from Brigham Young University for their musical contributions to the Church and community. They also presided over the Independence, Missouri Mission.

See also **McMaster**: Choose the Right Way, 160 (words and music); My Heavenly Father Loves Me, 228 (words and music); Remember the Sabbath Day, 155 (words and music); Reverently, Quietly, 26 (words and music); Teach Me to Walk in the Light, 177 (words and music); *Hymns*, Teach Me to Walk in the Light, 304 (words and music).

KEEP THE COMMANDMENTS, 146

Words and music: Barbara A. McConochie (1940–) LDS
Arrangement: Darwin Wolford (1936–) LDS

When Harold B. Lee became the President of the Church, he was asked if he had a message for the world. "Keep the commandments" was the reply he gave at the press conference announcing him as the new prophet. **Barbara McConochie** used those words for the message of this song. Because it was included in the 1985 hymnbook, another version was needed for this book. Sister McConochie thought of many possible ideas. Since first writing the song, she has coped with many difficulties. She has learned that keeping the commandments doesn't mean you won't have problems but rather that you can be strong enough to meet the tests. As she tossed and turned in her bed suffering with tendonitis, she thought of Abraham 3:24–25: "And we shall prove them herewith." Her new second verse expresses that idea, and she also added an obbligato for voice or instrument. Darwin Wolford made the arrangement of her work for the *Children's Songbook*.

Sister McConochie taught piano and was ward organist at the age of thirteen. She has been a high-school English teacher and has raised a combined family of nine children. She said, "If we strive to keep the commandments, life will be sweet to us even in our most dire trials. True peace will come to each individual, family, and nation only as we learn obedience to the laws of our Heavenly Father. . . . Keeping the commandments is the anchor for our safety amidst the storm."[95]

Darwin Wolford was a music professor at BYU–Idaho and holds a PhD in organ and composition. He is widely published, and his works have been performed by the Mormon Tabernacle Choir and the Utah Symphony. He served on the General Church Music Committee and the 1985 Hymnbook Executive Committee. We are very much indebted to him for his expertise in simplifying and refining the songs for the 1989 *Children's Songbook*. It was a monumental time commitment with no recognition, yet he gave cheerful service on the project. Batches of songs would be mailed to him with suggestions, and he was always able to fill the need. The high musical standard of the book can be credited to his careful scrutiny and advice.

See also **McConochie**: You've Had a Birthday, 285 (words and music).

See also **Wolford**: Beautiful Savior, 62 (arrangement); Had I Been a Child, 80 (music); I Am a Child of God, 2 (arrangement); I Have a Family Tree, 199 (music); In Quietude, 191 (music); Mary's Lullaby, 44 (arrangement); Our Chapel Is a Sacred Place, 30 (music); Stars Were Gleaming, 37 (arrangement); Supplication, 297 (music); Teach Me to Walk in the Light, 177(obbligato); Thanks to Thee, 6 (music); The Lord Gave Me a Temple, 153 (music); *Hymns*, Sons of Michael, He Approaches, 51 (music); We Listen to a Prophet's Voice, 22 (music).

PART THREE

I WANT TO LIVE THE GOSPEL, 148

Words: Naomi Ward Randall (1908–2001) LDS
Music: Roy M. Darley (1918–2003) LDS

Naomi Randall served for twenty-eight years on the Primary general board, four of those as First Counselor to General Primary President LaVern Parmley. She said the whole purpose of the song "I Want to Live the Gospel" was to help us try to live each day a little better. Singing "I will try" and then remembering to do it is a good way to practice living the gospel. "My deep conviction that all children have an innate desire to learn of our Heavenly Father and to live by his teachings prompted the lyrics," she said. "Even though we sometimes make mistakes, we try again and again to do as our Savior taught."[96]

Sister Randall believes that "we can learn the gospel through songs," and that "the truths that are sung into our hearts will help us at critical times in our lives."[97] As a child, she made up rhymes, jingles, and stories and grew up to use her imagination writing for the *Children's Friend* and serving on the editorial board, which she did for more than thirteen years. She created the "Barnabee Bumbleberry" series and a children's Bible story series. After the death of her husband, she served a mission to Washington, DC.

A choir of children once performed at a luncheon of former Primary general board members. When Naomi Randall was introduced as the composer of the song they had sung, the children swarmed around her asking for her autograph. She obliged by writing on anything that they handed her, including paper napkins!

Roy Darley, a former tabernacle organist, wrote the music. In that assignment, he gave a series of ten organ lessons in the Assembly Hall to people who were called to be ward organists.

Author's Note: When I was 14 years old, I had the opportunity to learn from him. The classes were held once a week, and it was both wonderful and terrifying when it was my turn to play the assigned hymns. The pipe organ seemed huge in comparison to the small electric Hammond organ I played in Whittier Ward. But with his encouragement and suggestions, we all grew in our calling.

He served for thirty-seven years as Tabernacle organist, giving over 6,000 organ recitals—many of them during the lunch hour. He served an Eastern States Mission and a mission to New Zealand with his wife.

Brother Darley was on the YMMIA General Board for twenty-five years, and also served as a temple worker.

See also **Randall**: I Am a Child of God, 2 (words).

I BELIEVE IN BEING HONEST, 149

Words: Ruth Muir Gardner (1927–1999) LDS
Music: Lyall J. Gardner (1926–2012) LDS

Ruth Muir Gardner liked to read and write poetry and stories, play and teach piano, and work crossword puzzles. She taught English and business subjects at the high school level and taught piano lessons in her home. Sister Gardner served for fourteen years on the Primary general board, called first by LaVern Parmley and then Dwan Young. As music chairman, she taught annually at the BYU Church Music Workshops.[98]

When a new song was needed for the 1987 Children's Sacrament Meeting Program, Ruth wrote a text and her husband, **Lyall Gardner,** composed the music. Brother Gardner received an MA degree in musicology and organ, and studied at the Eastman School of Music, Brigham Young University, the University of Utah, and the University of Michigan. He managed the Church Consultation Center and served as a member of the General Music Committee. Brother and Sister Gardner served a full-time mission to Florida even though Lyall had suffered a stroke.

See also **Gardner**, Ruth: Families Can Be Together Forever, 188 (words); Go The Second Mile, 167 (words and music); To Be a Pioneer, 218 (words and music); We Welcome You, 256 (words); *Hymns*, Families Can Be Together Forever, 300 (words); Go Forth With Faith, 263 (words).

See also **Gardner**, Lyall: *Hymns*, Go Forth With Faith, 263 (music).

I'M GLAD TO PAY A TITHING, 150

Words and music: Ruth Benson Lehenbauer (1933–) LDS

Ruth Lehenbauer studied piano and loved composing. She earned money accompanying dance classes and served a mission in Germany. She graduated with a master's degree in French from Brigham Young University and taught French and German at Utah State University in Logan. She and her husband lived in Dearborn, Michigan, where they raised their six children. They returned to Logan where she continues to write.

Sister Lehenbauer said the inspiration for the words was "the thought

PART THREE

that children need to understand the reasons behind paying tithing, one being gratitude and the other being to acknowledge God in all things."[99] The title originally was "I Pay My Tithing," and was changed to "I'm Glad to Pay a Tithing."

I WANT TO GIVE THE LORD MY TENTH, 150

Words and music: Lonnie Dobson Adams (1942–) LDS

Lonnie Adams earned a master's degree in music from the University of Utah and has accompanied dance classes and taught private piano. She also performs as a soloist. Her grandmother gave her a mosaic container for her tithing and taught her that if she was faithful in paying her tithing, she would always have enough money. Sister Adams wrote her testimony of the principle of tithing in this song.

I AM GLAD FOR MANY THINGS, 151

Words and music: Moiselle Renstrom (1889–1956) LDS

K. Moiselle Renstrom wrote both words and music to thirteen songs included in this collection. She was born in Huntsville, Utah, and taught school in Salt Lake, Weber, and Davis Counties. She was a gifted teacher, and her songs for little children encourage them to pretend and move with the music (like "Once There Was a Snowman").

As we were evaluating songs, we noticed that her work required no changes. Sister Renstrom knew the range for children's voices, wrote so that it was easy to play, taught well with her rhymes, and was doctrinally accurate. This song is from her collection *Merrily We Sing*, which along with *Musical Adventures* and *Rhythm Fun*, have been used by early childhood teachers everywhere.[100]

See also **Renstrom**: A Happy Family, 198 (words and music); A Happy Helper, 197 (words and music); A Prayer, 22 (words and music); I Love to Pray, 25 (words and music); Jesus Loved the Little Children, 59 (words and music); Jesus Said Love Everyone, 61 (words and music); Little Seeds Lie Fast Asleep, 243 (words and music); Once There Was a Snowman, 249 (words and music); Rain Is Falling All Around, 241 (words and music); The World Is So Lovely, 233 (words and music); To Get Quiet, 275 (words and music); Two Little Eyes, 268 (words and music).

HUM YOUR FAVORITE HYMN, 152

Words: Marilyn Price Adams (1926–) LDS

STORIES OF THE CHILDREN'S SONGBOOK

Music: K. Newell Dayley (1939–) LDS

The text was difficult for children and so was simplified to be age-appropriate. **Marilyn Price Adams** grew up in California and Arizona before moving to a farm in Layton, Utah. She became a member of the Young Women General Board and a Lambda Delta Sigma national officer. Her poem, "Hum Your Favorite Hymn," was originally published in *Songs of the Heart* (page 89), a collection of music for young men and young women. The song was shortened and simplified for Primary. The original chorus included such eloquent phrases as "Resound a note, expound a quote," which was changed to "And you will find it clears your mind." Sister Adams said she hopes that the children who sing her song will enjoy it as much as she enjoyed the music in Primary when she was a little girl.

K. Newell Dayley served as a member of the Brigham Young University Music Faculty and also the General Music Committee of the Church. Brother Dayley is an excellent trumpet player and became chairman of the Brigham Young University Music Department. He composed music for the musicals *III Nephi* and *Kirtland*, and the soundtrack of the show at the Polynesian Cultural Center in Hawaii. He said, "I have a deep love for children's music and feel that some of our most important work ought to be focused in that direction."[101]

See also **Dayley**: Every Star Is Different, 142 (music); Home, 192 (music); I Feel My Savior's Love, 74 (words and music); The World Is So Big, 235 (music); *Hymns*, Lord, I Would Follow Thee, 220 (music).

THE LORD GAVE ME A TEMPLE, 153

Words: Donnell Hunter LDS (1930–)
Music: Darwin Wolford LDS (1936–)

Donnell Hunter has been a temple worker in both Idaho Falls and Hawaii for over twenty years. He has a master's in fine arts from the University of Montana and taught at Ricks College (BYU–Idaho), BYU, and BYU–Hawaii. More than two hundred fifty of his poems are published in over one hundred different magazines throughout the United States.

The song was originally written for *Sing With Me*. The composer, **Darwin Wolford,** revised the beginning pitch, changed the key, and simplified the accompaniment. He also suggested that the original second verse of Brother Hunter's poem be considered, which had not been used previously. The verse seemed vital for this generation and was included to strengthen children against substance abuse.

Darwin Wolford was a music professor at BYU–Idaho and holds a PhD in organ and composition. He is widely published, and his works have been performed by the Mormon Tabernacle Choir and the Utah Symphony. He served on the General Church Music Committee and the 1985 Hymnbook Executive Committee, and the 1989 *Children's Songbook* Committee.

See also **Wolford**: Beautiful Savior, 62 (arrangement); Had I Been a Child, 80 (music); I Am a Child of God, 2 (arrangement); I Have a Family Tree, 199 (music); In Quietude, 191 (music); Keep the Commandments, 146 (arrangement); Mary's Lullaby, 44 (arrangement); Our Chapel Is a Sacred Place, 30 (music); Stars Were Gleaming, 37 (arrangement); Supplication, 297 (music); Teach Me to Walk in the Light, 177(obbligato); Thanks to Thee, 6 (music); *Hymns*, Sons of Michael, He Approaches, 51 (music); We Listen to a Prophet's Voice, 22 (music).

THE WORD OF WISDOM, 154

Words and Music: Janice Kapp Perry (1938–) LDS

"In Our Lovely Deseret" had been sung by the children in the very first Primary and was included in the 1985 hymnbook. Part of the song's message taught children to despise "tea and coffee and tobacco." That was as close to a song on the word of wisdom as there was. **Janice Kapp Perry** responded to a request for a two-part song on the subject. She said, "Though it seems very simple in its final form, I researched the subject extensively before attempting to reduce it to the simplest terms for the children."[102] Inspired by the words of Elder John A. Widtsoe in his book *A Principle with a Promise*, Sister Perry created a message focused on the blessings that come from keeping this commandment. Singing the two verses together gives children an experience with vocal harmony.

Sister Perry was born in Ogden, Utah, and raised in Vale, Oregon. She played sports and percussion in high school. After attending Brigham Young University and having her family, a sports injury helped bring her musical talents to fruition. Beginning with original songs for a roadshow, she has created musicals, sacred cantatas (two of which have been performed in the Salt Lake Tabernacle), songbooks, and recordings. Many of her songs have been published in Church magazines.

See also **Perry**: A Child's Prayer, 12 (words and music); I Love to

See the Temple, 95 (words and music); I Pray in Faith, 14 (words and music); I'm Thankful to Be Me, 11 (music); I'm Trying to Be Like Jesus, 78 (words and music); Love Is Spoken Here, 190 (words and music); Mother, Tell Me the Story, 204 (words and music); The Church of Jesus Christ, 77 (words and music); We'll Bring the World His Truth, 172 (words and music); *Hymns*, As Sisters in Zion, 309 (music).

REMEMBER THE SABBATH DAY, 155

Words and music: Clara Watkins McMaster (1904–1997) LDS

Clara McMaster was the eleventh child in her family, and she learned to love music at an early age. She sang and accompanied others on the piano as she grew up in Brigham City, Utah. For twenty-two years she was a member of the Tabernacle Choir. Sister McMaster feels that "Music is a rich gift of God, and it is in the world to make the lives of His children happier and better."[103]

Sister McMaster served on the Primary general board for fourteen years and was music chairman much of that time. She and her husband, J. Stuart McMaster, received the 1978 Franklin S. Harris Fine Arts Award from Brigham Young University for their musical contributions to the Church and community. They also presided over the Independence, Missouri Mission.

See also **McMaster**: Choose the Right Way, 160 (words and music); Kindness Begins with Me, 145 (words and music); My Heavenly Father Loves Me, 228 (words and music); Reverently, Quietly, 26 (words and music); Teach Me to Walk in the Light, 177 (words and music); *Hymns*, Teach Me to Walk in the Light, 304 (words and music).

THE CHAPEL DOORS, 156

Words and music: Dorothy Little Read (1920–) LDS

Dorothy Read said, "It was in Primary that I learned about . . . children's characteristics at a given age, gospel principles at a child's level of understanding, the importance of music as a teaching tool in church . . . I loved serving in the Primary."[104] She has written songs, poems, and programs; taught piano and organ; and published a series of music study books. She and her husband served a mission to the Oakland California Temple Visitor's Center.

Often only one verse of a prayer song is sung, and "The Chapel Doors" originally had two verses with good concepts. The solution was to combine the first half of the first verse with the second half of the

PART THREE

second verse to emphasize the positive things we do—"We gather here on the Sabbath day, to learn of Jesus, to sing and pray."

WHEN I GO TO CHURCH, 157

Words and music: Faye Glover Petersen (1914–2009)

Faye Glover Petersen studied piano and voice even though she claimed to be a tomboy. She worked at the State School Board Office in youth corrections and also at Zions Bank.

Author's Note: Locating a maiden name and birth date of a "Petersen" seemed like trying to find a needle in a haystack. At a committee meeting where we had been reviewing names we were still trying to find, it was suggested that I contact Robert Cundick for possible clues. After the meeting I got on the elevator and there was Brother Cundick! I asked him if he might possibly know Faye Petersen, a composer I needed to locate. He said, "Why yes I do. For years, my wife and I have met regularly in a dinner group with her. Would you like her address or phone number?" and he reached into his pocket for his directory. This sort of thing was happening so often that I began to depend on it. I know for certain that Heavenly Father answers our prayers through others.

To simplify the look of the song, the phrase repeated in all verses was printed only once ("When I go to church"). This was done throughout the book.

See also **Petersen**: Because It's Spring, 239 (words and music).

DARE TO DO RIGHT, 158

Words: anonymous

Music: Arranged by A. C. Smyth (1840–1909) LDS

The 1905 edition of the *Primary Songbook* contained "Dare to Do Right" and so has every songbook since. **Adam Craik Smyth**, the arranger, was born in Manchester and immigrated to Utah as a young man. He was a teacher, composer, choir leader, and choral instructor in Salt Lake City and Cache County, Utah. His Juvenile Opera Company performed in the Salt Lake Theatre, and he produced the popular Gilbert and Sullivan operettas of the day. When he moved to Manti, he became a recorder in the temple and a local choir director.

See also **Smyth**: *Hymns*, Come Along, Come Along, 244 (music); Come, Thou Glorious Day of Promise, 50 (music); Joseph Smith's First Prayer, 26 (adapted music); Zion Stands with Hills Surrounded, 43 (music).

STAND FOR THE RIGHT, 159

Words and music: Joseph Ballantyne (1868–1944) LDS

Joseph Ballantyne was born in Ogden Valley, Utah, the son of Richard Ballantyne, who founded the Sunday School of The Church of Jesus Christ of Latter-day Saints. He studied music in New York and with musicians from Chicago, New York, London, and Paris. Brother Ballantyne directed the Ogden Tabernacle Choir, and then chaired the music committee for the Deseret Sunday School Board. During this time, he wrote many children's songs, including "Stand for the Right." The song was first printed in *The Primary Song Book* in 1939 and also appeared in the *Deseret Sunday School Songbook*. For the 1989 songbook, the music was simplified and the direction *slower* added in the penultimate (next to last) measure for emphasis.

When he moved to Long Beach, California, Brother Ballantyne directed the Los Angeles Stake choir, the choir at St. Anthony's Church, and the choir that performed at the San Diego World's Fair in 1935. He also taught private voice lessons.

See also **Ballantyne**: Jesus Once Was a Little Child, 55 (music); Little Purple Pansies, 244 (music); Oh, Hush Thee, My Baby, 48 (words and music); Shine On, 144 (words and music).

CHOOSE THE RIGHT WAY, 160

Words and music: Clara Watkins McMaster (1904–1997) LDS

While serving on the Primary general board, **Clara Watkins McMaster** was asked to compose a class song for the CTR Primary age children. Her ability as a singer helped her create a song everyone loves to sing. The message is appropriate to all ages, and the initials CTR have taken on a life of their own.

Sister McMaster was the eleventh child in her family. She learned to love music at an early age; she sang and accompanied others on the piano as she grew up in Brigham City, Utah. For twenty-two years she was a member of the Tabernacle Choir. Sister McMaster feels that "Music is a rich gift of God, and it is in the world to make the lives of His children happier and better."[105]

For fourteen years, Sister McMaster served on the Primary general board and was music chairman. Often, she and her husband, J. Stuart McMaster, performed duets together. In 1978, they received the Franklin S. Harris Fine Arts Award from Brigham Young University for

PART THREE

their musical contributions to the Church and community. They also presided over the Independence, Missouri Mission.

See also **McMaster**: Kindness Begins with Me, 145 (words and music); My Heavenly Father Loves Me, 228 (words and music); Remember the Sabbath Day, 155 (words and music); Reverently, Quietly, 26 (words and music); Teach Me to Walk in the Light, 177 (words and music); *Hymns*, Teach Me to Walk in the Light, 304 (words and music).

I PLEDGE MYSELF TO LOVE THE RIGHT, 161

Words: Margaret Mann (1890–1950)

Music: Wolfgang Amadeus Mozart (1756–1791)

There is no information about the author. Perhaps someone matched the poem she wrote to this melody written by Mozart. Before copyright laws existed, songs were printed using the work of a writer or composer without asking permission.

Mozart was a boy-genius. He picked up his father Leopold's violin and was able to play without any instruction. Leopold Mozart was a fine musician in Salzburg, Austria, and when Wolfgang was four years old, he gave him piano lessons. Little Mozart composed his own pieces when he was five, and many are in books that piano students study today. His older sister, Nannerl, called him "Wolfie" and they gave concerts together, often for kings and queens. He was a concert pianist, an organist, a conductor, and a composer. Unfortunately, he never received a well-paid position and struggled constantly against poverty. Mozart believed his talent was a gift from God. He said, "God is ever before my eyes. I realize His omnipotence and I fear His anger; but I also recognize His love, His compassion, and His tenderness towards His creatures." Mozart's motivation to compose was internal and not dependent on the praise or recompense of others. He wrote in a letter, "Let us put our trust in God and console ourselves with the thought that all is well, if it is in accordance with the will of the Almighty, as He knows best what is profitable and beneficial to our temporal happiness and our eternal salvation."[106] Mozart had enormous energy for composing. He worked out the ideas in his mind, and then wrote as though by dictation—never changing any of the notes he had written. His barber complained about the difficulty of dressing Mozart's hair, as he would dash to write down ideas as they came, leaving the barber to run after him. Once, when he had no money to give a beggar, he took the man to a coffeehouse and quickly wrote a Minuet and Trio, which he gave to the man with a letter to a publisher. The beggar received five guineas as a result.

Mozart's health had always been fragile, and he died at the early age of thirty-five. He had written more than six hundred works, including church requiems, operas, symphonies, concertos, sonatas, and chamber and choral pieces. During the suffering of his last year, he was working on a requiem and sang dictation for it the night before he died.

See also **Mozart**: Prelude in F, 298 (music).

I WILL BE VALIANT, 162

Words and music: Vanja Y. Watkins (1938–) LDS

In 1981, new class manuals were prepared for the Sunday consolidated schedule. **Vanja** (VON-yuh) **Yorgason Watkins** was asked to write the Valiant class song, and said she would begin as soon as the committee sent her the words. They said they needed her to write the words, and the message should include keeping baptismal covenants. There was not a lot of time, and Sister Watkins prayed and fasted and agonized over the words. A few couplets came, but she needed a good beginning. She walked into her bedroom and noticed a paper on her dresser with a quotation from Joseph Fielding Smith. She read, "Our young people are among the most blessed and favored of our Father's children. Their spirits have been reserved to come forth in this day when the gospel is on earth, and when the Lord needs valiant servants to carry on his great Latter-day work."[107] She wept as she recognized the answer to her prayer. These words were the first line she needed, and they had been given to her in this quotation. She felt it was a little miracle, because no one in the family knew how the precious paper got on her dresser.[108]

Sister Watkins served as Primary general board music chairman and then as a member of the General Church Music Committee. She has credit lines on twenty-seven entries in the *Children's Songbook*. Many are favorites and all are of quality musicianship.

See also **Watkins**: Easter Hosanna, 68 (words and music); Families Can Be Together Forever, 188 (music); For Thy Bounteous Blessings, 21 (arrangement); I Want to Be Reverent, 28 (music); I Will Follow God's Plan, 164 (words and music); It's Autumntime, 246 (arrangement); Latter-day Prophets, 134 (music); Thank Thee for Everything, 10 (words); The Articles of Faith, 122–132 (music); The Sacrament, 72 (words and music); The Things I Do, 170 (music); This Is My Beloved Son, 76 (music); To Be a Pioneer, 218 (arrangement); Truth from Elijah,

PART THREE

90 (words and music); *Hymns*, Families Can Be Together Forever, 300 (music); Press Forward Saints, 81 (music).

I AM LIKE A STAR, 163

Words and music: Patricia Kelsey Graham (1940–) LDS

Pat Graham's first assignment as a member of the Primary general board was to write a short, simple song for four- and five-year-old Star children. The song was to contain concepts taught in the new class manuals.

Author's Note: As I thought of music appealing to this age group, the nursery tune "Twinkle, Twinkle Little Star" came to mind. I played it high on the piano to sound like a music box with an Alberti bass, and had my five-year-old son, Matt, sing my ideas, and I wrote down what evolved. Over the years, I have been delighted to hear little children sing this song. I have been richly repaid for my effort."

In October of 1987, I was assigned to visit and speak in Primaries in Minneapolis, Minnesota. When I attended the Bloomington Ward, the music leader had the children sing my little star song for me. After they finished, the leader stood still for a minute, and then with tears in his eyes he said to the children, "Did you feel that, boys and girls? You sang so sweetly you brought the spirit of our Heavenly Father into our Primary." I will never forget the reverence of those little children as they followed the direction of their sensitive music leader. We were all moved by the singing but moved even more by a Priesthood leader who explained the presence of our Heavenly Father's Spirit to the children.

I received a thank you note from Rachel Woolley, a former piano student of mine. She was attending college away from home and was having a discouraging day. Words of the "Star Song" came to her and as she sang "for I know Heavenly Father loves me," she was comforted. She wrote to thank me for composing the song.

Debbie Stewart told me she grew up thinking she was an important person, a "star," because of the message of this little song. I'm glad that children can gain confidence by singing these positive messages into their hearts. I was delighted to learn that Heather Back, a piano student of mine, had been the model for the picture Beth Whittaker (her neighbor and one of the songbook artists) drew for this page in the book. I have had many "pay-days" through this happy song.

Luana Lish, an emergency medical technician (EMT), was called to a serious accident involving a family and their van. She was attempting to stabilize the head of a small boy who was critically injured and thrashing about. Fearful that he might hurt himself further, she asked Heavenly Father to bless her to know how to calm Ryan and ease his pain. She received the impression to sing to him. She worried how professional it would look to have an EMT singing in an ambulance over a critically injured patient. As he cried out again she held his head, leaned close to his ear, and began, "I am like a star shining brightly, Smiling for the whole world to see." As she sang, Ryan became quiet. She and his distraught mother continued to sing other songs until the emergency trauma team at the hospital took over. "I will always remember an answered prayer when my little patient quieted instantly in response to songs he loved, songs that reminded him of how much his Heavenly Father loves him. . . . the beauty and simplicity of a few Primary songs will forever remain in my memory as a gentle and profound miracle."[109]

Sister Graham has a master's degree in education with emphasis on children's music. She was an elementary school teacher and has taught piano and organ for over forty years. She loves to accompany musicians and play for receptions. During her eight years on the Primary general board, she originated and wrote the monthly Sharing Time page for the *Friend* and chaired the 1989 *Children's Songbook*.

See also **Graham**: Picture a Christmas, 50 (words and music); The Hearts of the Children, 92 (words and music); The Nativity Song, 52 (words and music); We Are Different, 263 (words and music).

I WILL FOLLOW GOD'S PLAN FOR ME, 165

Words and music: Vanja Yorgason Watkins (1938–) LDS

Mabel Gabbott wrote a text with this title in answer to a request for a new song for the Merrie Miss classes in Primary. Her words were given to **Vanja** (VON-yuh) **Yorgason Watkins**. While she was working on the project, some additional ideas were given to her, and the text was adjusted and added to. When she spoke to Mabel about the changes, she agreed with the additions but requested that only Vanja's name appear as author. Sister Watkins said, "With just one name on the song, it appears that I did the whole thing, and I didn't. Mabel deserves the credit for being the originator of the text and I would like that to be known."[110] Both of these women have given so freely of their talents and truly are not concerned with who gets the credit.

A visitor in her home once asked Sister Watkins, "Is this the piano where you compose all of your songs?" "Hardly," she answered. "Ideas

PART THREE

come in the car, while walking, even sitting under a tree. I start with the words, which suggest the rhythm and the melody. Then I harmonize it. If it doesn't flow I may change the melody. It requires re-working and revising."[111]

The index of authors and composers shows Vanja to have credit lines for fourteen songs plus the thirteen Articles of Faith, making a total of twenty-seven entries. She said she never anticipated having such a wonderful opportunity to write for the children of the Church and expressed her gratitude for the blessing of serving in this way.

The words originally were "I will" but Correlation suggested "I can" instead, which was how the song was first published. This applied to "I Can Be Valiant" as well. In March of 1986, our committee discussed the possibility of changing the words "I can" to "I will" as requested by the composer. There was concern about the impact on other materials and curriculum. In the 1988 October Conference, President Michaelene (MY-kul-een) Grassli announced the change and discussed the importance of making commitments.

Rebecca Amyot, a young mother in the Rochester Michigan Ward, received comfort through the song when she was having chemotherapy treatments after surgery. Her husband had taken her to the clinic for an IV and to regulate her blood pressure. She was weak and allergic to the anti-nausea drugs and even though she knew she was not going to die, she secretly thought that it wasn't a bad idea. She wrote, "It was at this point that I thought of the song, 'I Will Follow God's Plan For Me.' The song was like bearing my testimony privately to Heavenly Father that I was thankful for my life and that I trusted him in everything. I sang the song over and over to help me hang on for five more minutes at a time until the hours passed and I was able to go home. I knew the Lord was with me. Even now when I sing the song, I remember that day and feel again my testimony of the Lord's love for me."[112]

See also **Watkins**: Easter Hosanna, 68 (words and music); Families Can Be Together Forever, 188 (music); For Thy Bounteous Blessings, 21 (arrangement); I Want to Be Reverent, 28 (music); I Will Be Valiant, 162 (words and music); It's Autumntime, 246 (arrangement); Latter-day Prophets, 134 (music); Thank Thee for Everything, 10 (words); The Articles of Faith, 122–132 (music); The Sacrament, 72 (words and music); The Things I Do, 170 (music); This Is My Beloved Son, 76 (music); To Be a Pioneer, 218 (arrangement); Truth from Elijah, 90 (words and music);

STORIES OF THE CHILDREN'S SONGBOOK

Hymns, Families Can Be Together Forever, 300 (music); Press Forward Saints, 81 (music).

A YOUNG MAN PREPARED, 166

Words and music: Daniel L. Carter (1955–) LDS

As a young boy in Idaho, **Daniel L. Carter** often cried when he listened to the beautiful music of the Tabernacle Choir at conference time. He said, "I always yearned to be able to share my testimony and feelings of the gospel through music."

When Brother Carter was asked to write a song to help prepare boys to receive the priesthood, he worried about his ability to write something that boys would enjoy singing. "After several weeks of working and rewriting, an idea for the music came, and I felt sure that this song could help boys."[113]

It is exciting to have music with the majesty of a "Star Wars March" applied to a message for the young men of the Church. In an effort to extend the use of the song to Deacons, the words "I'm a Blazer" are optional.

Brother Carter has a degree in musical composition, has served as a member of the General Church Music Committee, and works in the Church Music Editing and Publishing Division. He has been very involved in translations of the Primary songs and music typesetting. Compositions by Brother Carter include numerous published choral pieces as well as a beautiful sacrament hymn.

See also **Carter**: The Shepherd's Carol, 40; *Hymns*, As Now We Take the Sacrament, 169 (music).

GO THE SECOND MILE, 167

Words and music: Ruth Muir Gardner (1927–1999) LDS

Ruth Gardner was an asset on Primary committees because of her writing and music skills. For the 1981 Sacrament meeting presentation, she wrote, "Go the Second Mile." Sister Gardner liked to read and write poetry and stories, play and teach piano, and work crossword puzzles. She taught English and business subjects on a high-school level, and piano lessons in her home. Sister Gardner was called to serve on the Primary general board by LaVern Parmley and then Dwan Young and served for fourteen years. As music chairman, she taught annually at the BYU Church Music Workshops.

See also **Gardner**, Ruth: Families Can Be Together Forever, 188

PART THREE

(words); I Believe in Being Honest, 149 (words); To Be a Pioneer, 218 (words and music); We Welcome You, 256 (words); *Hymns*, Families Can Be Together Forever, 300 (words); Go Forth with Faith, 263 (words).

I WANT TO BE A MISSIONARY NOW, 168

Words and music: Grietje Terburg Rowley (1927–) LDS

Because **Grietje** (GREE-chuh) **Rowley** is a convert to the Church, missionary work is very important to her. She said, "I love the children and know that Heavenly Father expects them to do great things. I wrote 'I Want to Be a Missionary Now' to show children how they can bring happiness to others."[114] She thinks that the songs we learn in Primary can bring us joy and comfort forever. For over twenty-five years Sister Rowley played the piano for children at church. When she writes songs, she tries to make them easy to sing, easy to play, and easy to remember. She has written over one hundred scripture melodies, making musical arrangements for scriptures that are important to her. She writes every day and says it is more fun than washing dishes.

Sister Rowley served on the General Music Committee and the *Children's Songbook* Committee. She simplified, transposed, offered helpful suggestions, and proofed the notation of the words, markings, and notation of every song *three* times! Often when I was discouraged, she would remind me that this book was important to our Father in Heaven and that he would help us to do it in the best way.

See also **Rowley**: A Smile is Like the Sunshine, 267 (music); Distant Bells, 299 (music); Each Sunday Morning, 290 (music); Roll Your Hands, 274 (arrangement); Samuel Tells of the Baby Jesus, 36 (music); *Hymns*, Be Thou Humble, 130 (words and music).

I HOPE THEY CALL ME ON A MISSION, 169

Words and music: Newel Kay Brown (1932–) LDS

Newel Kay Brown likes to oil paint and teach piano. He also teaches theory and composition at North Texas State University. When he was a young boy, his mother accompanied him at the piano while he sang his favorite song, "A Mormon Boy" (also President Benson's favorite childhood song). When he was asked to write a song about missionary work, he wanted it to be fun to sing and to help shape testimonies. The cowboy bass reminds us that he lives in Texas. He said, "My dream of a song which would lay a part in the motivation of young men and women to share the gospel has been realized."[115] He called it "The little 'cowboy' tune" which was written in Arkadelphia, Arkansas. The melody was written into the accompaniment when the song was simplified for the *Children's Songbook*.

DeAnn Hickman Giles suggested alternate words so the song would be appropriate for older missionaries:

> I hope they call me on a mission when I've *retired* a *year* or two.
> I hope by then I will be ready to teach and preach and work as missionaries do.
> I hope that I can share the gospel with those *with whom I'll spend my time*.
> I want to be a missionary and serve and help the Lord while I am in my *prime*.

See also **Brown**: My Country, 224; *Hymns*, With Songs of Praise, 71 (music).

THE THINGS I DO, 170

Words: L. Clair Likes (1908–1998) LDS
Music: Vanja Y. Watkins (1938–) LDS

Clair Likes grew up on an isolated dry farm in Idaho, and eventually earned a teaching certificate and a master's degree in theater. He has written and directed many pageants and plays, and served for twenty-one years on the YMMIA drama committee. He said the words for this song were inspired by the scriptures. "James and Paul seemed to point out the best, perhaps the only way that children could be missionaries: James with his 'Shew me thy faith without thy works, and I will shew thee my faith by my works' (James 2:18), and Paul with his admonition to Timothy, 'Be thou an example of the believers, in work, in conversation, in charity, in spirit, in faith, in purity' (1 Timothy 4:12)."[116]

Vanja (VON-yuh) **Yorgason Watkins** was always singing when she was a little girl. Her parents would hear her in bed at night singing and singing until she fell asleep. She composed piano pieces and also loved to play for others to sing. Vanja did not know Clair Likes but was asked to compose music for his poem for the 1975 Children's Sacrament Meeting Presentation. She decided to write the melody using only the notes in the pentatonic scale. This scale has five tones and corresponds to the notes played on the black keys of a piano. For example, the notes you use to play "Peter, Peter, Pumpkin Eater" and other childhood songs are the intervals of the pentatonic scale. From his work collecting folksongs,

PART THREE

Zoltan Kodaly, a Hungarian composer and educator, observed that children all over the world naturally sing the intervals so-mi, so-la-so, and mi-re-do without instruction. So she wrote the melody using the "children's intervals."

Sister Watkins has BA and MA degrees in music education, and was a television teacher and primary grade music coordinator for the Ogden City schools. She became Primary general board Music Chairman and then a member of the General Church Music Committee. The index of authors and composers shows her to be the greatest contributor to the songbook with credit lines for arrangements, words, music, and words and music—fourteen songs plus the thirteen Articles of Faith, making a total of twenty-seven entries. Many are favorites according to the survey and all are of high quality musicianship.

See also **Watkins**: Easter Hosanna, 68 (words and music); Families Can Be Together Forever, 188 (music); For Thy Bounteous Blessings, 21 (arrangement); I Want to Be Reverent, 28 (music); I Will Be Valiant, 162 (words and music); I Will Follow God's Plan, 164 (words and music); It's Autumntime, 246 (arrangement); Latter-day Prophets, 134 (music); Thank Thee for Everything, 10 (words); The Articles of Faith, 122–132 (music); The Sacrament, 72 (words and music); This Is My Beloved Son, 76 (music); To Be a Pioneer, 218 (arrangement); Truth from Elijah, 90 (words and music); *Hymns*, Families Can Be Together Forever, 300 (music); Press Forward Saints, 81 (music).

WE'LL BRING THE WORLD HIS TRUTH, 172

Words and music: Janice Kapp Perry (1938–) LDS

A Provo stake requested a stirring missionary song for a 200-voice children's choir to sing at a stake conference. These children were from strong families and would carry the responsibility of sharing the gospel. **Janice Kapp Perry** responded with what has become the theme song of many missions around the world. The following additional verse was written for a Primary sacrament presentation: "We are God's children, we have received the blessings promised to Abraham's seed./We'll share the gospel, this is our quest 'til ev'ry nation on earth is blessed."

The Perry family is a missionary family. Their children served missions to Belgium; Korea; Washington, DC; and Argentina, and Brother and Sister Perry served in Chile. Composing music to strengthen testimonies is another way that Sister Perry has served a unique mission.

This song has three entries in the *Children's Songbook* index: the first line (We have been born); the title (We'll Bring the World His Truth), and the subtitle, in this case the way the children identify the song, (Army of Helaman). Some song titles for the *Children's Songbook* were adjusted to state the message or subject of the song or to help them be identified more easily.

See also **Perry**: A Child's Prayer, 12 (words and music); I Love to See the Temple, 95 (words and music); I Pray in Faith, 14 (words and music); I'm Thankful to Be Me, 11 (music); I'm Trying to Be Like Jesus, 78 (words and music); Love Is Spoken Here, 190 (words and music); Mother, Tell Me the Story, 204 (words and music); The Church of Jesus Christ, 77 (words and music); The Word of Wisdom, 154 (words and music); *Hymns*, As Sisters in Zion, 309 (music).

CALLED TO SERVE, 174

Words: Grace Gordon, altered (1873–1956)
Music: Walter G. Tyler (1855–1933)

The motivating power of this stirring song was felt when missionaries from the Missionary Training Center marched down the aisles in the Assembly Hall on Temple Square. They carried the flags of many different countries and sang "Called to Serve" for area presidents, regional representatives, and mission presidents. The message was so convincing that the song was added to the 1985 hymnbook. The *LDS Church News*, August 11, 1985, page 16, stated, "The impact of this experience was so moving that tears were flowing and deep emotions were stirred. It was an unforgettable spiritual moment."

"Called to Serve" has been in Primary songbooks since 1920. Initially it was used as a song for leaders rather than for children. The original text had three verses and was shortened to verse one and three only for *Sing With Me*. Several word alterations were made for the 1985 hymnbook and the *Children's Songbook*: "Sons of *God, and* children of a King" made more inclusive with "Sons and *daughters*, children of a King"; "homage" to "*praises*"; and "Joy our strength will be" to "*God* our strength will be." The alto and the accompaniment were simplified for this edition.

Grace Gordon is a pseudonym for the author, Elsie Duncan Yale, who was born in Brooklyn, New York, and died in San Bernadino, California. She had poetry published in children's magazines. Several of her poems were set to music and included in the 1927 and 1939 Primary songbook editions. The composer, **Walter G. Tyler**, also used the pen name **Adam Geibel**. An incorrect eyewash prescription caused him to lose his sight as an infant, yet he developed the ability to play tunes he heard traveling musicians play. His family emigrated from Germany to Philadelphia when he was seven, and he became musical director at Temple University. He founded a music publishing house and eventually composed approximately 3,000 works, including "Stand Up, Stand Up for Jesus," the ballad "Kentucky Babe," and the hymn "Behold! A Royal Army," which is included in the 1985 hymnbook.

Author's Note: When my husband and I served a mission to Detroit, I wrote an alternate verse for couples. We planned actions and performed it for the young missionaries, who thought we were good sports to sing about being senior couples:

CALLED TO SERVE
Adapted: Patricia Kelsey Graham (1940–) LDS

1. Couples who have recently retired,
   Heard the prophet's missionary call.
   With the love and faith that are required,
   We responded one and all.

   CHORUS
   Couples serving missions, called to serve both far and near,
   Couples serving missions leave our home and fam'ly dear.
   Couples lengthen shuffles wave our comfort zone goodbye
   God our strength will be,
   Together we can serve at least one year!

2. Couples who are getting slightly older,
   Left our canes and rocking chairs behind.
   New responsibilities to shoulder, challenges of every kind.

   CHORUS

See also **Tyler**: *Hymns*, Behold! A Royal Army, 251 (music); Called to Serve, 249 (music).

TELL ME, DEAR LORD, 176
Words: M.E.P.
Music: Carl Harold Lowden (1883–1963)

The author apparently wanted to be unknown and gave only initials. The song first appeared in Primary materials in 1920. "Anoint my eyes to understand Thy word" was changed to "help me to understand Thy loving word." Correlation suggested that it would be more correct to address this prayer to "Heavenly Father," rather than "Dear Lord." Various attempts were made, but all felt awkward. Because it was a suggestion rather than an absolute request, the words remained unchanged and the song could still be used.

Harold Lowden was organist at Linden Baptist and the First Methodist/Episcopal Churches in Camden, New Jersey, from 1920–1954. He wrote songs that appeared in their church songbooks, including "Living for Jesus." Heidelberg Press published a Christmas program written by him in 1919, and Lowden directed and accompanied a choir of his own.

TEACH ME TO WALK IN THE LIGHT, 177

Words and music: Clara Watkins McMaster (1904–1997) LDS
Obbligato: Darwin Wolford (1936–) LDS

Clara Watkins McMaster was assigned to compose a song for the Primary choir to sing at the April 1958 General Conference. She said, "The scriptures are filled with this great important message—'walk in the light'—and I have often gone to the scriptures for guidance and direction in my assignments." For twenty-two years, Sister McMaster was a member of the Tabernacle Choir. She feels that "Music is a rich gift of God, and it is in the world to make the lives of His children happier and better."[117] Sister McMaster served on the Primary general board for fourteen years and was music chairman for many of them. She and her husband, J. Stuart McMaster, received the 1978 Franklin S. Harris Fine Arts Award from Brigham Young University for their musical contributions to the Church and community. They also presided over the Missouri Independence Mission.

Darwin Wolford was a music professor at BYU–Idaho and holds a PhD in organ and composition. He is widely published, and his works have been performed by the Mormon Tabernacle Choir and the Utah Symphony. He served on the General Church Music Committee and the 1985 Hymnbook Executive Committee. We are very much indebted to him for his expertise in simplifying and refining the songs for the 1989 *Children's Songbook*. It was a monumental time commitment with no recognition, yet he gave cheerful service on the project. Batches of songs would be mailed to him with suggestions, and he was always able to fill the need. The high musical standard of the book can be credited to his careful scrutiny and advice.

See also **McMaster**: Choose the Right Way, 160 (words and music); Kindness Begins with Me, 145 (words and music); My Heavenly Father

PART THREE

Loves Me, 228 (words and music); Remember the Sabbath Day, 155 (words and music); Reverently, Quietly, 26 (words and music); *Hymns*, Teach Me to Walk in the Light, 304 (words and music).

See also **Wolford**: Beautiful Savior, 62 (arrangement); Had I Been a Child, 80 (music); I Am a Child of God, 2 (arrangement); I Have a Family Tree, 199 (music); In Quietude, 291 (music); Mary's Lullaby, 44 (arrangement); Our Chapel Is a Sacred Place, 30 (music); Stars Were Gleaming, 37 (arrangement); Supplication, 297 (music); Thanks to Thee, 6 (music); The Lord Gave Me a Temple, 153 (music); *Hymns*, Sons of Michael, He Approaches, 51 (music); We Listen to a Prophet's Voice, 22 (music).

TEACHER, DO YOU LOVE ME? 178

Words and music: Michael Finlinson Moody (1941–) LDS

In 1986, the Primary had an opportunity to prepare a satellite fireside. It was felt that a song could be used under the storyline and would be helpful in restating the theme of the broadcast. To explain what was needed and ask who might be given this assignment, the Primary Music Committee met with **Michael Moody**, the general music chairman. He said he would like to think about it overnight. The next day, he returned with the first draft of this tender song. He was the right one to create the piece.

Brother Moody said, "Music is a tool for building families in good ways. It can bring a sweet spirit into the home. We sing before scripture reading, before meals, and on our way in the car. It keeps gospel messages in the minds of the children."[118] He earned a doctorate in church music from the University of Southern California and was employed as executive secretary of the General Church Music Committee for five years. As chairman of the Church's music division since 1977, he directed the preparation of the 1985 hymnbook and coached the preparation of the 1989 *Children's Songbook*. He served a mission in France, spent three years as mission president in Haiti, and is now serving with his wife, Maria, on a music mission at the Brigham Young University Jerusalem Center.

See also **Moody**: Faith, 96 (music); Have a Very Happy Birthday, 284 (music); Have a Very Merry Christmas!, 51 (music); He Sent His Son, 34 (music); Sleep, Little Jesus, 47 (music); There Was Starlight on the Hillside, 40 (music); Who Is the Child?, 46 (music); *Hymns*, Testimony, 137 (music).

STORIES OF THE CHILDREN'S SONGBOOK

HOW DEAR TO GOD ARE LITTLE CHILDREN, 180

Words: Jaclyn Thomas Milne (1949–) LDS
Music: Carol Baker Black (1951–) LDS

Jaclyn Milne enjoys writing as a hobby and has collaborated with her friend, **Carol Black**. One of their compositions, "The Miracle of America," was performed at the Kennedy Center in Washington, DC, at the nation's bicentennial celebration. They have been recognized in the *Ensign* music contests. Sister Milne believes that Heavenly Father is always near. As a young child, she remembers being made well almost immediately after priesthood blessings. She attended Dixie Jr. and Weber State Colleges and has been successful in turning her writing hobby into published songs.

Sister Black began serving in the Church as the Primary pianist when she was twelve. When Primary was held after school, she would run from school to the Church to begin playing prelude music for the children as they entered the chapel. She said, "My parents provided me with the opportunity of taking piano lessons, but I have had no formal training in music theory or composition. I do, however, possess a great love for good music and a testimony of its influence in our lives."[119] She has been composing at the request of Sister Milne since 1985.

See also **Milne**: Search, Ponder, and Pray, 109 (words).
See also **Black**: Search, Ponder, and Pray, 109 (music).

HOW WILL THEY KNOW? 182

Words and music: Natalie W. Sleeth (1930–1992)
Arrangement: A. Laurence Lyon (1934–2006) LDS and Natalie W. Sleeth (1930–1992)

To complete the songbook, we had hoped to include a few songs for leaders about the importance of teaching children. As I sat with my music committee in April Conference 1987, we heard the Tabernacle Choir sing an SATB arrangement of "How Will They Know?" We all looked at each other as we felt the same prompting—that song should be in the book! When a song is already in print, it is sometimes difficult to obtain permission to change it, and we needed a much simpler arrangement. We contacted Sonos Publishing and learned that **Natalie Sleeth** was in poor health. It was suggested that we submit an arrangement to her and ask if she would approve its use. **Lawrence Lyon** agreed to prepare an SSA simplification which was sent to Mrs. Sleeth in Denver,

PART THREE

Colorado. She revised it and gave permission to include it in the songbook as long as making copies would be prohibited. That notice is at the bottom of the song, and we feel blessed to have use of it.

Natalie Sleeth is well-known for "Joy in the Morning," "Baby, What You Goin' to Be?" and many other choral pieces. She said, "When my son had young children of his own, I became aware of how the way he was raised (by my husband and me) was reflected in the way he and his wife were raising their children. . . . I generalized this idea into an expression of the need for teaching those within our care what we feel is important in life."[120] She wrote "How Will They Know?" after she and her husband had gathered their family to tell them of their health problems. Her husband died soon after, and she passed away several years following the work on the arrangement.

Laurence Lyon, the arranger, was born in Holland while his father, T. Edgar Lyon, was mission president. He returned later as a missionary himself. Brother Lyon earned a doctorate in composition from Eastman School of Music and taught college courses in composition, theory, piano, violin, and music history. He has more than one hundred published compositions, many performed by the Tabernacle Choir. One of his most-loved arrangements is "Consider the Lilies," by Roger Hoffman. He served on the Sunday School General Board and the General Church Music Committee.

See also **Lyon**: Christmas Bells, 54 (words and music); I Have Two Ears, 269 (music); Little Pioneer Children, 216 (words and music); We Are Reverent, 27 (music); Whenever I Think about Pioneers, 222 (music); *Hymns,* Each Life That Touches Ours for Good, 293 (music); Saints, Behold How Great Jehovah, 28 (music).

STORIES OF THE CHILDREN'S SONGBOOK

Home and Family

"Music has boundless powers for moving families toward greater spirituality and devotion to the gospel. Hymns can also help us withstand the temptations of the adversary." [121]
—1985 *Hymns*

Rounds, descants, and two-part songs have been included in this section to challenge and appeal to the older children in Primary. Following songs about the family in general, there are songs about grandparents, mothers, and fathers. Alternate words encourage the exchange of names (mother, father, grandma) to bring relevance for a child with a single parent.

The divider pages portray a Korean family holding home evening about genealogy. It is important that cultures are accurately represented. The artwork was submitted to the International Department of the Church and they approved the authenticity of the clothing, furnishings, and food in the picture.

FAMILIES CAN BE TOGETHER FOREVER, 188

Words: Ruth Muir Gardner (1927–1999) LDS
Music: Vanja Yorgason Watkins (1938–) LDS

In 1981, while **Ruth Muir Gardner** was serving as music chairman of the Primary general board, she was asked to help write a sacrament meeting presentation about temples. She liked to read and write poetry and stories, work crossword puzzles, and had been a high school English and business teacher. She began thinking of all the things children should know about temple work and her words became a poem. Ruth made a melody for her words but was not satisfied with it. She felt this was a very important subject and needed dignified music. She asked her friend, **Vanja** (VON-yuh) **Yorgason Watkins**, a former Primary general board Member, to set the words to music. Vanja was serving on the General Music Committee and called this "a sweet opportunity." She prepared many versions, and always felt the song ended too soon. Finally, the idea came to emphasize the last statement, as it bears repeating. She said, "The Lord blessed me as I worked, and I completed the song for the children's sacrament meeting presentation."[122] The song became a

PART THREE

favorite and was number 11 on the 1983 Primary survey. Because it is also in the 1985 hymnbook, the song received a new treatment for the *Children's Songbook*. It was simplified by the composer and the introduction was deleted.

Author's Note: One of the gifts of music is that it can provide comfort and assurance. I always think of Michael Sorenson whenever this song is sung. He was just four years old when he drowned. Michael had been sealed to his parents, and I was grateful to play this beautiful new song about eternal families at his funeral. The message seemed even more personal because the author of the song lived in our ward. Over the years, grandchildren have also sung the song at funerals to honor their grandparents.

See also **Gardner**, Ruth: Families Can Be Together Forever, 188 (words); Go the Second Mile, 167 (words and music); I Believe in Being Honest, 149 (words); To Be a Pioneer, 218 (words and music); We Welcome You, 256 (words); *Hymns*, Families Can Be Together Forever, 300 (words); Go Forth with Faith, 263 (words).

See also **Watkins**: Easter Hosanna, 68 (music); Families Can Be Together Forever, 188 (music); For Thy Bounteous Blessings, 21 (arrangement); I Want to Be Reverent, 28 (music); I Will Be Valiant, 162 (words and music); I Will Follow God's Plan, 164 (words and music); It's Autumntime, 246 (arrangement); Latter-day Prophets, 134 (music); Thank Thee for Everything, 10 (words); The Articles of Faith, 122–132 (words); The Sacrament, 72 (words and music); The Things I Do, 170 (music); This Is My Beloved Son, 76 (music); To Be a Pioneer, 218 (arrangement); Truth from Elijah, 90 (words and music); *Hymns*, Families Can Be Together Forever, 300 (music); Press Forward Saints, 81 (music).

FAMILY PRAYER, 189

Words and music: DeVota Mifflin Peterson (1910–1996) LDS

DeVota Peterson said, "Our family knelt before meals to pray. We'd turn our plates upside down, turn our chairs away from the table, and then kneel at the chairs for the blessing on the food. At night before bedtime, we knelt with our parents for evening prayer. This time we joined hands in a circle and thanked our Heavenly Father for his many blessings to us. It was easy for me to express my sentiments in words and music because of the example set for me by my family."[123]

Sister Peterson became the Primary pianist at the age of fourteen, and played the piano in a dance band in high school. She studied at the

McCune School of Music, and after receiving a teacher's diploma she taught in Malad, Idaho, and Salt Lake City, Utah. She believes "Good music is a noble and inspiring gift from God. A child will long remember the hours spent singing in Primary, and with parents, brothers, and sisters in the warmth of the family circle."[124]

LOVE IS SPOKEN HERE, 190

Words and music: Janice Kapp Perry (1938–) LDS

Janice Perry's two-part song was the first place winner of the *Ensign* song-writing contest in 1980. She said, "I decided to write about two things that gave me a feeling of peace and security in that (my) home —hearing my mother's prayer and seeing my father's priesthood. I wrote one verse about each of them which could be sung at the same time over a common harmonic structure. This was my first experiment with counter melodies."[125] Sister Perry played sports and percussion in high school and studied music at Brigham Young University. A sports injury and a call from her bishop to write a roadshow with original music launched her composition career. After joining the Utah Composer's Guild, she composed the LDS musical *It's a Miracle,* sixteen songbooks and albums, and musical presentations for Church auxiliaries. She sang in the Tabernacle Choir and then served a full-time mission with her husband in South America. In spite of nerve damage in her hand, she continues to compose, focusing now on music for the Spanish members of the Church. She was honored as an Outstanding Brigham Young University Alumnus for her tremendous contributions to the music of the Church.

See also **Perry**: A Child's Prayer, 12 (words and music); I Love to See the Temple, 95 (words and music); I Pray in Faith, 14 (words and music); I'm Thankful to Be Me, 11 (music); I'm Trying to Be Like Jesus, 78 (words and music); Mother, Tell Me the Story, 204 (words and music); The Church of Jesus Christ, 77 (words and music); The Word of Wisdom, 154 (words and music); We'll Bring the World His Truth, 172 (words and music); *Hymns,* As Sisters in Zion, 309 (music).

HOME, 192

Words: Caroline Eyring Miner (1907–1999) LDS
Music: K. Newell Dayley (1939–) LDS

Caroline Eyring Miner was born in Colonial Juarez, Mexico, a sister of Camilla Eyring Kimball. She earned a master's degree from her

PART THREE

studies at Brigham Young University and Utah State University. Sister Miner taught high school English and authored many books of poetry and prose. One of her books is about her sister, Camilla. For nearly twenty years she was a member of the YWMIA General Board. About this song she said, "I want to emphasize the loving influence gentle music and words can impart in the home and for our Heavenly Father."[126]

K. Newell Dayley served as a member of the Brigham Young University Music Faculty and also the General Music Committee of the Church. Brother Dayley is an excellent trumpet player, and became chairman of the Brigham Young University Music Department. He composed the music for two musicals, *III Nephi*, and *Kirtland*, and the soundtrack for the Hawaiian Polynesian Cultural Center. He said, "I have a deep love for children's music and feel that some of our most important work ought to be focused in that direction."[127]

See also **Dayley**: Every Star Is Different, 142 (music); Hum Your Favorite Hymn, 152 (music); I Feel My Savior's Love, 74 (words and music); The World Is So Big, 235 (music); *Hymns*, Lord, I Would Follow Thee, 220 (music).

SING YOUR WAY HOME, 193

Words and music: traditional song; arranged

"Sing Your Way Home" was in *Sing With Me*, the previous Primary songbook. It was arranged by Gladys Pitcher with a piano accompaniment and an additional voice line for the melody. The arrangement required a royalty from the copyright holder, but the words and melody were in Public Domain. Since the decision had been made to put melody lines into the accompaniments of songs in the *Children's Songbook*, it saved both space and money to have a new arrangement, which the Church could copyright. The new arrangement added additional scale passages in the accompaniment, and an optional descant in the last two measures which provides a challenge for older girls (or leaders) to add harmony.

THE FAMILY, 194

Words: Mabel Jones Gabbott (1910–2004) LDS
Music: Richard Wallace Clinger (1946–) LDS

Mabel Jones Gabbott, the author, said, "This is one of my favorite songs because it is so personal. Though my five are grown now and enjoying families of their own, they still come together on Monday nights to my home in Bountiful. We still believe that when the family gets together, it seems that nothing can go wrong."[128]

Sister Gabbott was one of nine children. She received her education from the University of Idaho and the University of Utah. She served a mission to the Northwestern States and then became a secretary to Elder LeGrand Richards. She worked on the staffs of the Church magazines, was a member of the YWMIA General Board and the General Church Music Committee, and chaired the 1985 Hymnbook Text Committee. Sister Gabbott was a very small lady with a very large talent for writing, and her poems were used for sixteen Primary songs and four hymns. She said, "I love to hear children sing."[129]

Richard Wallace Clinger is the head of the music department at a private school, directs a musical performing group, and arranges and accompanies the Sacramento Music Circus. He teaches piano at Sacramento City College, and he and his wife organized an International Children's Chorus.

See also **Gabbott**: Baptism, 100 (words); Before I Take the Sacrament, 73 (words); Did Jesus Really Live Again?, 64 (words); Father Up Above, 23 (words); Had I Been a Child, 80 (words); Have a Very Happy Birthday!, 284 (words); Have a Very Merry Christmas!, 51 (words); He Sent His Son, 34 (words); My Country, 224 (words); Samuel Tells of the Baby Jesus, 36 (words); Sleep, Little Jesus, 47 (words); There Was Starlight on the Hillside, 40 (words); To Think about Jesus, 71 (words); We Are Reverent, 27 (words); Who Is the Child, 46 (words); *Hymns*, In Humility, Our Savior, 172 (words); Lord, Accept Into Thy Kingdom, 236 (words); Rejoice, Ye Saints of Latter Days, 290 (words); We Have Partaken of Thy Love, 155 (words).

FAMILY NIGHT, 195

Words and music: Carol Graff Gunn (1929–) LDS

Carol Gunn wrote about some of the things that her family did for family night. She wanted to tell about the love that grows as families enjoy being together. Her gift for playing the piano "by ear" helped her to serve as Primary organist at the age of twelve and then ward organist by age sixteen. She was able to play although she had only three formal lessons. Sister Gunn taught piano in her home and also studied composition with Dr. LeRoy Robertson at the University of Utah.

Besides writing songs for her family to sing, Sister Gunn has written original music and words for roadshows and musicals to honor her

PART THREE

ancestors. Some of her work has been published in the *Friend*. Sister Gunn helped to organize the Utah Composer's Guild and served as an officer for many years, helping many other composers. We were officers together in the guild, and I am one of those who benefited from her encouragement. During the preparation of *Sing With Me*, she and Sharon Nielson, the president of the guild, were called to serve on the Ad Hoc Committee and gave valuable service to the project. Sister Gunn and her husband also served a mission in Australia.

See also **Gunn**: My Dad, 211 (words and music).

SATURDAY, 196

Words and music: Rita S. Robinson (1920–2011) LDS
Arrangement: Chester W. Hill (1912–1997) LDS

Rita S. Robinson's father died when she was three years old. Although her mother was not a member of The Church of Jesus Christ of Latter-day Saints, she sent Rita to meetings because the Church had been important to her father. After graduating with honors from the University of Utah, Rita taught school and later worked as a master welder for the Navy during World War II. She published twenty-seven songs for children in a collection called *I Like to Sing*. After her husband's death, she served a mission in California.

Chester W. Hill played piano for priesthood meeting when he was ten years old. Brother Hill composed in his early teens, and after studying music at Brigham Young University, Juilliard School of Music, and Columbia Teacher's College, he taught at Ricks College (BYU–Idaho) and Brigham Young University. He served as director of concerts at the Washington, DC chapel. He prepared the original arrangement of Sister Robinson's words and melody.

See also **Robinson**: Hosanna, 66 (words and music).

A HAPPY HELPER, 197

Words and music: Moiselle Renstrom (1889–1956) LDS

K. Moiselle Renstrom was born in Huntsville, Utah, and taught school in Salt Lake, Weber, and Davis Counties. Sister Renstrom was asked to compose songs for little children for the 1940 publication, *Merrily We Sing*. A picture shows her at an upright piano, her hair in beautiful finger waves, with little children seated on the floor around her. She was a gifted teacher and many of her songs for little children encourage them to pretend and move with the music. She wrote both words and music to thirteen songs that have survived to this collection. As we were evaluating songs, we noticed that her work required no changes from the original. She knew the range for children's voices, wrote so that it was easy to play, taught well with her rhymes, and was doctrinally accurate. *Merrily We Sing* and two other collections of her work, *Musical Adventures* and *Rhythm Fun*, have been used by early childhood teachers all over the world.[130]

See also **Renstrom**: A Happy Family, 198 (words and music); A Prayer, 22 (words and music); I Am Glad for Many Things, 151 (words and music); I Love to Pray, 25 (words and music); Jesus Loved the Little Children, 59 (words and music); Jesus Said Love Everyone, 61 (words and music); Little Seeds Lie Fast Asleep, 243 (words and music); Once There Was a Snowman, 249 (words and music); Rain Is Falling All Around, 241 (words and music); The World Is So Lovely, 233 (words and music); To Get Quiet, 275 (words and music); Two Little Eyes, 268 (words and music).

QUICKLY I'LL OBEY, 197

Words: Thelma J. Harrison (1906–) LDS
Music: Russian folk tune
Optional ostinato: Patricia Haglund Nielsen (1936–2009) LDS

Thelma Harrison said, "Music is one of the lovely gifts with which our Heavenly Father has blessed us. . . . The healing words of hymns slip into our minds to bless us in times of sorrow or to guide us in our actions."[131] Her service on the Primary general board for sixteen years included writing curriculum for younger age groups and writing for the *Children's Friend*. She was an elementary school teacher, and gifted in both writing and telling stories. Her poem was matched to a Russian folk tune.

The words of the second phrase were revised to be the same in all verses, which makes the song easier to teach and allows parents to be human (originally, "*For mother knows* just what is best," was changed to "*I want to do* just what is best"). Interestingly, we received a letter suggesting that, because of child abuse concerns, it was not good to teach a child to always obey their parents. After counseling with priesthood advisors, it was determined that the positive example of parents should be held as the norm.

For many years, **Pat Nielsen** taught at the Brigham Young University Church Music Workshops, sharing her expertise as a music educator.

PART THREE

She received her MA in music education at Teachers College, Columbia University. To keep the interest of older children during songs directed to younger children, Sister Nielsen composed ostinatos (a repeated pattern) as a challenge. We were grateful to make use of two of her patterns. Brother and Sister Nielsen are serving as Family History specialists, and she says the skills of being a music leader have helped her to keep the attention of her computer students.

See also **Nielsen**: Oh, Hush Thee, My Baby, 48 (ostinato, words and music).

A HAPPY FAMILY, 198

Words and music: Moiselle Renstrom (1889–1956) LDS

K. Moiselle Renstrom wrote both words and music to thirteen songs included in this collection. She was born in Huntsville, Utah, and taught school in Salt Lake, Weber, and Davis Counties. Sister Renstrom was a gifted teacher, and her songs for little children encourage them to pretend and move with the music. She had the gift of "becoming as a little child" and was thrilled by the accomplishments of her students. She knew the range for children's voices, wrote so that it was easy to play, taught well with her rhymes, and was doctrinally accurate. A year before she died, she wrote a number of little songs and sermons for Junior Sunday School children at the request of the General Church Music Committee. Her songbooks, *Merrily We Sing*, *Musical Adventures*, and *Rhythm Fun* have been used by early childhood teachers everywhere.[132]

See also **Renstrom**: A Happy Helper, 197 (words and music); A Prayer, 22 (words and music); I Am Glad for Many Things, 151 (words and music); I Love to Pray, 25 (words and music); Jesus Loved the Little Children, 59 (words and music); Jesus Said Love Everyone, 61 (words and music); Little Seeds Lie Fast Asleep, 243 (words and music); Once There Was a Snowman, 249 (words and music); Rain Is Falling All Around, 241 (words and music); The World Is So Lovely, 233 (words and music); To Get Quiet, 275 (words and music); Two Little Eyes, 268 (words and music).

WHEN WE'RE HELPING, 198

Words: Wallace F. Bennett (1898–1993) LDS
Music: German folk song

While Frances Bennett was serving on the Primary general board (with President May Anderson and President May Hinckley) she asked her husband to write words for several children's songs. "When We're Helping" was printed in Primary materials in 1939. Wallace F. Bennett was a fine bass soloist and his wife, Frances (the youngest daughter of President Heber J. Grant), accompanied him on the piano. Their son, Senator Robert Bennett, said the family always joked about how hard their father worked to write the second verse (la la la la la la la . . .). In the 1940s, Brother Bennett served on the General Church Music Committee and the Sunday School General Board. For many years he served as ward choir director, and every year near his birthday his ward would honor him by singing his hymn. He said that "music is essential to the building of an emotional element in service in the Church."[133] He left his business, Bennett Glass and Paint, to serve as United States senator from Utah for twenty-four years.

See also **Bennett**: I Like My Birthdays, 104 (words); *Hymns*, God of Power, God of Right, 20 (words).

I HAVE A FAMILY TREE, 199

Words: Mary Ellen Jex Jolley (1926–) LDS
Music: Darwin Wolford (1936–) LDS

Mary Ellen Jex Jolley was inspired to write this poem by her love for her relatives. She has 125 first cousins and they have many reunions. Her words make it sound like they are having a good time being together! Sister Jolley served on the editorial board of the *Children's Friend* and was a member of the Sunday School General Board. She also was a writer on a missionary tract committee.

Darwin Wolford was a music professor at BYU–Idaho and holds a PhD in organ and composition. He is widely published, and his works have been performed by the Mormon Tabernacle Choir and the Utah Symphony. He served on the General Church Music Committee and the 1985 Hymnbook Executive Committee. We are very much indebted to him for his expertise in simplifying and refining the songs for the 1989 *Children's Songbook*. It was a monumental time commitment with no recognition, yet he gave cheerful service on the project. Batches of songs would be mailed to him with suggestions, and he was always able to fill the need. The high musical standard of the book can be credited to his careful scrutiny and advice.

See also **Wolford**: Beautiful Savior, 62 (arrangement); Had I Been a Child, 80 (music); I Am a Child of God, 2 (arrangement); In Quietude, 291 (music); Keep the Commandments, 146 (arrangement); Mary's

PART THREE

Lullaby, 44 (arrangement); Our Chapel Is a Sacred Place, 30 (music); Stars Were Gleaming, 37 (arrangement); Supplication, 297 (music); Teach Me to Walk in the Light, 177(obbligato); Thanks to Thee, 6 (music); The Lord Gave Me a Temple, 153 (music); *Hymns*, Sons of Michael, He Approaches, 51 (music); We Listen to a Prophet's Voice, 22 (music).

GRANDMOTHER, 200

Words and music: Nonie Nelson Sorensen (1925–) LDS

While reviewing the topics needed, it seemed there should be a companion to the activity song, "When Grandpa Comes." **Lenora (Nonie) Sorensen**, who has eleven children of her own and many musical grandchildren, was asked to write a grandmother song. We suggested a rocking chair rhythm and perhaps several verses with a repeated phrase. Alternating the word *grandfather* extends the use of the song. Sister Sorensen said, "I love to sing fun songs, too; and I love to hear my grandchildren sing to me."[134]

Nonie served on the YWMIA General Board and composed selections for *Songs of the Heart*. She taught modern dance at the University of Utah and likes to write musical theater based on true stories of her ancestors. For fourteen years, she and her husband spent their summers serving music missions in Nauvoo. While she was fulfilling her duties, her husband, Maynard, began carving award-winning ducks. Sister Sorensen's assignment was to write and prepare short musicals that were given daily in the visitor's center and the social hall.

WHEN GRANDPA COMES, 201

Words and music: Marian Major (1899–1985)

The author/composer, **Lorrain E. Watters**, published under the pseudonym "**Marian Major**." He studied at Julliard School of Music and taught and directed music education in Iowa public schools for many years. He also edited the Ginn and Co. music series, *Our Singing World* and *The Magic Of Music*.

The Mormon Youth Chorus recorded this song for an album with the word change "hooray!" rather than "we're gay," which has taken on negative connotations since the song was written in 1949. The *Children's Songbook* is consistent with the recording and used the same word change.

I OFTEN GO WALKING, 202

Words: Phyllis Luch (1937–1995) LDS
Music: Jeanne P. Lawler (1924–) LDS

Phyllis Luch, the major artist for the songbook, wrote about her mother in the words for this song. She explains, "My mother was mentally ill. . . . Nearly the only time she was at peace was in the fields and meadows. . . . She knew the names of wildflowers, which as a child I thought was amazing."[135] The song is used to express love for mothers on Mother's Day and is often used at funerals. The introduction was revised to give the pitch. Ironically, there was no room on the page to include a picture! Sister Luch said, "Music has great power to lift the spirit. I'm sure great composers were inspired by God and numbers of people have been drawn closer to heaven through music.[136]

Jeanne P. Lawler thinks music leaders should "teach with enthusiasm and sing more and talk less. Children will remember thoughts set to music longer than conversation."[137] Sister Lawler served in the U.S. Coast Guard and then received an associate degree in music from Glendale California College. She and her daughter joined the Church and moved to Provo, Utah, for schooling. She wrote "Sing Unto the Lord," a musical based on Isaiah. This fulfilled part of the requirements for her Brigham Young University degree, which she completed at age fifty-seven. She has served proselyting and temple missions.

See also **Lawler**: Family History—I Am Doing It, 94 (words and music); Hinges, 277 (music); The Holy Ghost, 105 (words and music); When Jesus Christ Was Baptized, 102 (words and music).

MY MOTHER DEAR, 203

Words and music: Becky-Lee Hill Reynolds (1944–) LDS

Becky-Lee Hill Reynolds, the author and composer, was able to compose at a young age, which was a family "gift." Her grandmother, Maryhale Woolsey, was also an author and wrote the words for the Utah favorite, "Springtime in the Rockies," as well as several Primary songs in previous collections. Sister Reynolds attended the University of Utah and also served a mission to France. She is the mother of five children.

This sweet song was often overlooked as a Mother's Day message—probably because the first line title "Like Sunshine in the Morning," had placed it with nature songs. The last two measures became the new title, and "colorful and gay" and its rhyme were changed to avoid adverse reactions from children.

See also **Reynolds**: Heavenly Father, While I Pray, 23 (words and music).

MOTHER, TELL ME THE STORY, 204

Words and music: Janice Kapp Perry (1938–) LDS

Janice Kapp Perry has written many two-part songs that give children the opportunity to experience singing harmony. This one is a mother and child bedtime duet. "I remembered the many times my mother told me of where I came from, why I'm here, where I'm going, and how she loved me," she said. "I always felt peace at these times."[138] The Primary music committee suggested an idea for an optional verse, and Sister Perry wrote additional words telling of Jesus nearness and His watching over us as we sleep. The song is a comforting lullaby containing gospel truths.

Janice played drums and sports in high school. She studied music at Brigham Young University and was a member of the Utah Composer's Guild. She composed the LDS musical *It's a Miracle*, sixteen songbooks and albums, and musical presentations for Church auxiliaries. She sang in the Tabernacle Choir and then served a full-time mission with her husband in South America. In spite of nerve damage in her hand, she continues to compose, focusing now on music for the Spanish members of the Church. She was honored as an Outstanding Brigham Young University Alumnus for her tremendous contributions to the music of the Church.

See also **Perry**: A Child's Prayer, 12 (words and music); I Love to See the Temple, 95 (words and music); I Pray in Faith, 14 (words and music); I'm Thankful to Be Me, 11 (music); I'm Trying to Be Like Jesus, 78 (words and music); Love Is Spoken Here, 190 (words and music); The Church of Jesus Christ, 77 (words and music); The Word of Wisdom, 154 (words and music); We'll Bring the World His Truth, 172 (words and music); *Hymns*, As Sisters in Zion, 309 (music).

MOTHER DEAR, 206

Words: Maud Belnap Kimball (1889–1971) LDS
Music: Mildred Tanner Pettit (1895–1977) LDS. Arranged.

Maud Belnap Kimball taught school in Ogden, Utah. She had singing leads in operas and concerts, and was an active civic and political leader. Sister Kimball was the social service director of the Salt Lake General Hospital, and a clerk in the county recorder's office. **Mildred Pettit** had ancestors who were Mayflower pilgrims, and some of whom were original Utah pioneers. She studied piano, pipe organ, and composition at the McCune School of Music and also attended the Latter-day Saints College in Salt Lake City. Sister Pettit taught school and then married a medical school graduate. She served for thirty-five years in the Primary, with four of those years on the Primary general board. During that time, she wrote many programs and songs for children. She has composed 145 musical selections.

See also **Pettit**: Beauty Everywhere, 232 (music); Father, I Will Reverent Be, 29 (music); I Am a Child of God, 2 (music); *Hymns*, I Am a Child of God, 301 (music); The Light Divine, 305 (music).

DEAREST MOTHER, I LOVE YOU, 206

Words and music: Vernon J. LeeMaster (1904–2001) LDS

Vernon J. LeeMaster grew up on a dry farm in Moab, Utah. At age eleven, he was called as ward organist. Later, he studied at the McCune School of Music in Salt Lake, Brigham Young University, and the University of Southern California, which culminated in a master's degree in music. After teaching, he became supervisor of music in the Salt Lake City Schools for twenty-one years. He also served on the Sunday School general board and sang with the Tabernacle Choir.

Brother LeeMaster encourages those who teach children to sing to cultivate their natural, pure, sweet voices, rather than harsh, loud singing. He said, "Directing the all-city festivals in the Tabernacle with hundreds of angelic voices . . . is not soon forgotten. The sweet voices of children singing [create] a beauty unsurpassed."[139]

MOTHER, I LOVE YOU, 207

Words and music: Lorin F. Wheelwright (1909–1987) LDS

Lorin F. Wheelwright said he loved his mother dearly and wrote this song as a tribute to her. He became Junior Sunday School pianist at age ten when he lived in Ogden, Utah. He financed his education with his piano and organ abilities and received a doctorate degree from Columbia University. He became music supervisor for the Salt Lake City schools in 1937. Brother Wheelwright served as a member of the Sunday School General Board and associate editor of the *Instructor* magazine. His arrangement of "Beautiful Savior" (the Crusader's Hymn) was included in *The Children Sing,* published in 1951. He was president of Pioneer Music Press, which printed the work of many Latter-day Saint composers. Dr. Wheelwright was dean of the College of Fine Arts and Communication at Brigham Young University, and also an assistant to President Dallin H. Oaks.

See also **Wheelwright**: *Hymns*, Help Me Teach with Inspiration, 281 (words and music); O Love That Glorifies the Son, 295 (words and music); Oh, May My Soul Commune with Thee, 123 (words and music).

THE DEAREST NAMES, 208

Words and music: Frances K. Taylor (1870–1952) LDS

Frances Kingsbury Thomassen Taylor studied piano, organ, harmony, and counterpoint at the University of Utah and Columbia University. She was prominent as an early childhood educator and songwriter in the Salt Lake Valley. Sister Taylor served as a member and secretary of the General Primary Association for eight years. The Deseret Sunday School Union published her songbook, *Kindergarten and Primary Songs*, for use in the Junior Sunday Schools of the Church.

Originally, this song was written in three quarter time. However, it was tiring to conduct even at a moderate tempo—a feeling of "beating the song to death." The meter was changed to six beats per measure to allow a relaxed two-beat conducting pattern, which gives the desired "tender" mood. The second verse can be sung alone for a Father's Day program.

See also **Taylor**: Daddy's Homecoming, 210 (music); Help Me, Dear Father, 99 (words and music).

FATHERS, 209

Words: Dawn Hughes Ballantyne (1932–1995) LDS
Words and music: Joyce Mills Jensen (1936–2002) LDS

Dawn Hughes Ballantyne said, "I have loved to sing since I was very young. My mother was a songwriter and used to write songs for me to sing. My father was a singer and one of my fondest memories is of sitting on his knee and singing songs with him. I especially loved Primary songs."[140] She grew up in Bountiful, Utah, attended Brigham Young University, and served a mission to the Gulf States. She performs with several musical and drama groups.

Joyce Mills Jensen liked to draw, write poetry, and compose music. She decided to choose one of those creative things and do it as well as she could. She read many books on composing and then studied music composition and harmony at Brigham Young University. She taught music to troubled teens and used music therapy in nursing homes. Sister Jensen received first place awards in the National Mu Phi Epsilon Music Composition Contest; the Utah Academy of Arts, Sciences, and Letters Contest; the Relief Society Song Contest; and the Utah Composer's Guild Competition.

DADDY'S HOMECOMING, 210

Words: anonymous
Music: Frances K. Taylor, (1870–1952) LDS

Frances Kingsbury Thomassen Taylor studied piano, organ, harmony, and counterpoint at the University of Utah and Columbia University. She was prominent as an early childhood educator and songwriter in the Salt Lake Valley. Sister Taylor served as a member and secretary of the General Primary Association for eight years. The Deseret Sunday School Union published her songbook, *Kindergarten and Primary Songs*, for use in the Junior Sunday Schools of the Church.

Author's Note: The holding power of a simple song was manifest to me when a mother in Westland, Michigan, told of an experience she had with her estranged son. Over the years, the son had ignored the mother's attempts to stay close to him. On Father's Day, the mother emailed the words of "Daddy's Homecoming" to her son and told how she remembered him singing the song and doing the actions with his father. The son responded and expressed how he had loved those close times with his family and that he could still sing the song.

See also **Taylor**: Help Me, Dear Father, 99 (words and music); The Dearest Names, 208 (words and music).

MY DAD, 211

Words and music: Carol Graff Gunn (1929–) LDS

Carol Gunn wrote a song for her three little boys to sing to their father. She said they "loved their dad and wanted to be with him every chance they got."[141] Her gift for playing the piano "by ear" helped her to serve as Primary pianist at the age of twelve and then ward organist at age sixteen. She was able to play although she had only three formal lessons. Carol taught piano and studied composition with Dr. LeRoy Robertson at the University of Utah. Besides writing songs for her family to sing, she has written original music and words for roadshows and musicals to

PART THREE

honor her ancestors. Her work has been published in the *Friend* magazine. Sister Gunn helped to organize the Utah Composer's Guild and served as an officer for many years, encouraging other composers. During the preparation of *Sing With Me*, she and Sharon Nielson, the president of the guild, gave valuable assistance on the Ad Hoc Committee. Brother and Sister Gunn served a mission in Australia.

See also **Gunn**: Family Night, 195 (words and music).

STORIES OF THE CHILDREN'S SONGBOOK

Heritage

"It's the song ye sing, and the smiles ye wear,
That's a-makin' the sun shine everywhere." [142]
—James Whitcomb Riley
(1849–1916), U.S. poet

There are eleven pioneer and patriotic songs in section V, the smallest section in the book. The nine pioneer songs might only be used once a year but they tell an important part of Church history and are the heritage of all members no matter where they live. The patriotic songs are generic and are appropriate to be sung in any country. The wonderful pictures were drawn by Beth Whittaker.

PIONEER CHILDREN SANG AS THEY WALKED, 214

Words and music: Elizabeth Fetzer Bates (1909–1999) LDS

Elizabeth Fetzer Bates earned two bachelor's degrees and two master's degrees in social work and music from the University of Utah after she became blind. Elizabeth also served two missions—one to the Northern States and another to Washington State with her husband. She was the mother of six children and a piano teacher. When she became totally blind at age forty-two, she accepted it as a challenge and decided that she would learn to do everything she could. She learned Braille, and since she could no longer read music, she learned to compose music. For her master's thesis, she invented a typewriter code so that blind musicians could write down their music to be transcribed by a sighted person. Sister Bates came to believe that everyone should write a song.[143] "Heavenly Father has created so many lovely things that we should sing as we walk along!" she said. "We can always be happy if we remember to be grateful."[144]

Sister Bates visited Ruth May Fox and "asked her to tell about when she was a pioneer in 1864. She (Ruth May) said they enjoyed walking across the plains, sang as they walked, sang and danced in their group in the evenings, and held meetings on Sunday. When I returned home, I wrote the song . . . we are all pioneers–we've never been in today before."[145]

See also **Bates**: Book of Mormon Stories, 118 (words and music).

PART THREE

PIONEER CHILDREN WERE QUICK TO OBEY, 215

Words: Virginia Maughan Kammeyer (1925–1999) LDS
Music: Lynn Shurtleff (1939–) LDS

Virginia Maughan Kammeyer grew up in Logan, Utah, and later received a BA degree in English and Speech. She lived with her husband and six children in the Seattle area. She said, "The songs sung in Primary are among the most beautiful in the Church. They tell of our love for Jesus and his church. A song to Jesus is like a prayer set to music."[146]

Lynn Richard Shurtleff said, "The stories of the pioneer children had an influence on my childhood. I always used to wonder if I could ever be like those children. This song gave me a chance to express some of that admiration."[147] Brother Shurtleff received his MA in music theory from Brigham Young University and his PhD after studying at Indiana University and Vienna, Austria. His missionary service took him to Uruguay, Paraguay, Argentina, and Brazil, and he served as a member of the General Music Committee for four years. His compositions include choral works, chamber orchestra, symphony, and pageants. Dr. Shurtleff founded the Prune Hollow Choral Society and is chairman of the music department of Santa Clara University where he received the Distinguished Faculty Award.

See also **Kammeyer**: On a Golden Springtime, 88 (words).

See also **Shurtleff**: *Hymns*, Father, This Hour Has Been One of Joy, 154 (music).

LITTLE PIONEER CHILDREN, 216

Words and music: A. Laurence Lyon (1934–2006) LDS

Before **Laurence Lyon** was three years old he said, "Mommy, someday I want to 'piano' in the Sunday School."[148] By the time he was ten, he played piano, violin, and viola. Brother Lyon was born in Holland while his father, T. Edgar Lyon, was mission president. He later served a mission himself to the Netherlands. He received a doctorate in composition from Eastman School of Music and taught college courses in composition, theory, piano, violin, and music history. Dr. Lyon has more than one hundred published compositions, many performed by the Tabernacle Choir. He served on the Sunday School General Board and the General Church Music Committee.

The melody was written into the accompaniment to simplify the song. The words "and gay" were changed to "were they" and "gaily singing" to "often singing." Singing the song in a round creates a pleasant harmony of thirds.

See also **Lyon**: Christmas Bells, 54 (words and music); How Will They Know?, 182 (arrangement); I Have Two Ears, 269 (music); We Are Reverent, 27 (music); Whenever I Think about Pioneers, 222 (music); *Hymns,* Each Life That Touches Ours for Good, 293 (music); Saints, Behold How Great Jehovah, 28 (music).

WESTWARD HO! 217

Words: Miriam H. Kirkell
Music: Marcia Davidson

The publishers of *Childcraft* commissioned **Miriam Kirkell** to write words for a song in a 1937 publication. Mrs. Kirkell was an American poet, and the song was printed in *Art and Music,* Volume 13 of *Childcraft.* Receiving a commission for writing intimates that the person is a reliable and established author. Many people write for a hobby, but being asked to write and being paid for it sets one apart as a professional. The use of the song for the *Children's Songbook* was negotiated by the copyright department of the Church. No information is available on the composer.

TO BE A PIONEER, 218

Words and music: Ruth Muir Gardner (1927–1999) LDS
Arranged: Vanja Yorgason Watkins (1938–) LDS

Ruth Muir Gardner wrote this song for a Primary 1977 summer program. The descant creates a challenge for older children. Sister Gardner liked to read and write poetry and stories, play and teach piano, and work crossword puzzles. She taught English and business subjects on a high-school level, and piano lessons in her home. Sister Gardner served on the Primary general board for fourteen years with President LaVern Parmley, and then President Dwan Young. As music chairman, she taught annually at the Brigham Young University Church Music Workshops. Even after her husband Lyall suffered a stroke, they served a mission to Florida.

Sister Gardner asked **Vanja** (VON-yuh) **Yorgason Watkins** to arrange her words, melody, and descant. The left-hand accompaniment has a "western" sound, which is appropriate for a pioneer song. Vanja did a lot of singing and accompanying as she was growing up. Her parents sacrificed so she could attend BYU, where she majored in music education. She loved learning the rules of music theory, which became the

PART THREE

springboard to her writing. Sister Watkins said, "I discovered that by being obedient to the rules, I could write successfully. As I was doing my student teaching with a high school choir, I had the strong feeling that what I could best contribute should be with younger children. This was a turning point that has made all the difference."[149] Sister Watkins became coordinator of primary grade music in the Ogden City Schools, served as Primary general board music chairman, and was a member of the General Church Music Committee. Twenty-seven entries are listed by her name in the author/composer index of the *Children's Songbook*. She says her motive for writing is her love of children, her love of music, and her love of the gospel.

See also **Gardner**, Ruth: Go the Second Mile, 167 (words and music); Families Can Be Together Forever, 188 (words); I Believe in Being Honest, 149 (words); We Welcome You, 256 (words); *Hymns*, Families Can Be Together Forever, 300 (words); Go Forth With Faith, 263 (words).

See also **Watkins**: Easter Hosanna, 68 (words and music); Families Can Be Together Forever, 188 (music); For Thy Bounteous Blessings, 21 (arrangement); I Want to Be Reverent, 28 (music); I Will Be Valiant, 162 (words and music); I Will Follow God's Plan, 164 (words and music); It's Autumntime, 246 (arrangement); Latter-day Prophets, 134 (music); Thank Thee for Everything, 10 (words); The Articles of Faith, 122–132 (music); The Sacrament, 72 (words and music); The Things I Do, 170 (music); This Is My Beloved Son, 76 (music); Truth from Elijah, 90 (words and music); *Hymns*, Families Can Be Together Forever, 300 (music); Press Forward Saints, 81 (music).

THE OXCART, 219

Words and music: anonymous

The first printing of "The Oxcart" in Church resources was in the *Children's Friend*, July 1949. Perhaps it was an early pioneer song, which, like many other folk songs, was passed on without knowing the origin. It is the only pioneer song in this collection that uses the word *ox* which creates a teaching opportunity.

THE HANDCART SONG, 220

Words: John Daniel Thompson McAllister (1827–1910) LDS
Words: Lucile Cardon Reading (1909–1982) LDS
Music: John Daniel Thompson McAllister (1827–1910) LDS, arranged

One of the difficult tasks in compiling the songbook was to correctly credit the authors and composers. Sometimes the research brought rewarding experiences.

Author's Note: Several months before the printing deadline, I attended the funeral of composer **Mary Jane Davis** *who wrote "The Prophet Said to Plant a Garden." I almost didn't go because a water pipe had broken in our basement and we were in quite a mess. However, I had been inspired by Mary Jane's valiant life and I felt impressed to be there. Wylene Fotheringham, a neighbor and one of the speakers, told of the things that Mary Jane loved. She mentioned her family, music, and her heritage, and what an inspiration her forebears had been, particularly* **John Daniel Thompson McAllister** *who had written "The Handcart Song." I wept as I realized it was more than a coincidence that this composer's name had come to my attention in this way. I came very close to missing it!*

Mary Jane's husband later explained that Daniel McAllister had been serving a mission in Ireland when he composed "The Handcart Song." He recorded the words in his journal and said the song was written to motivate the saints to immigrate to Utah. Brother Davis loaned the journal to submit as proof of authorship, and once again the importance of the songbook was confirmed by a small miracle.

Daniel McAllister had to leave his home in Delaware when he joined the Church because his father was so bitter. The young convert married and traveled to Salt Lake City with a wagon and five yoke of cattle. Later, he served a mission in Scotland and Wales and was responsible for 376 immigrants aboard the *Manchester*. As he helped a handcart company in Iowa, he taught his song to those pioneers who sang it as they pushed and pulled their handcarts to the Salt Lake Valley. Other groups that followed sang the song to lift their spirits. In the valley, Brother McAllister worked on the Salt Lake Tabernacle as a carpenter, acted as chief of the fire department, and played with a brass band. He moved his family to St. George where he served as president of the St. George Temple and participated in the ordinance work for the founding fathers. In 1877, President Wilford Woodruff recorded in his journal, "I baptized brother McAllister for 21, including General Washington & his forefathers and all the Presidents of the United States that were on my list except Buchanan, Van Buren and Grant."[150] He later moved to Manti, Utah.

Lucile Cardon Reading was a capable writer, educator, secretary, and editor. She was called to the Primary general board in 1962 and then served for seven years as a counselor to President LaVern Parmley. She was managing editor of the *Friend* until her death.

Sister Reading wrote a verse for children of today, and it was combined with the original chorus by Brother McAllister. The original song had been published without a credit line in many resources. In a school songbook, a descant had been added. That idea grew into the optional new descant for this version. Now Brother McAllister's merry melody has revised words, accompaniment, and a new descant, and so the credit line says "arranged."

Covered Wagons, 221

Words: Anne Kaelin (1917–1995)
Music: Richard Randolph (1911–1969), arranged

Doris F. Fisher used the pen name **Anne Kaelin** for the lyrics she wrote. Mrs. Fisher grew up in Queens, New York, and studied in Massachusetts. She obtained a master's degree in math from Columbia University and taught high school mathematics. Her husband, **William R. Fisher**, used the pseudonym **Richard Randolph**. He was a professor of music at Lowell University and became head of the music department and then assistant dean of the graduate school. The William Fisher Hall at the University is named for this respected educator.

William Fisher compiled the third-grade book for the series *This Is Music for Today*, published by Allyn and Bacon, which included this song and many others that he and his wife had written. The melody was written into the accompaniment for this arrangement. Notice who holds the copyright for the lyrics.

WHENEVER I THINK ABOUT PIONEERS, 222

Words: Della Dalby Provost (1910–1973) LDS
Music: A. Laurence Lyon (1934–2006) LDS

Della Dalby Provost taught kindergarten and high school art, and then completed a master's degree in elementary education from Brigham Young University. She taught in the Brigham Young University Education Department and supervised student teachers. Sister Provost served on the Primary general board and wrote many stories for the *Children's Friend*. She also wrote lessons for Family Home Evening manuals, and then served on the Church Correlation Committee. Her poem, with music by Brother Lyon, was printed in the *Sing With Me* songbook.

Laurence Lyon, the composer, was born in Holland while his father, T. Edgar Lyon, was mission president. He later served his own mission there. He received a doctorate in composition from Eastman School of Music. He has more than one hundred published compositions, many performed by the Tabernacle Choir. "Consider the Lilies" by Roger Hoffman is an example of the beauty of Dr. Lyon's arrangements. He served on the Sunday School General Board and the General Church Music Committee.

There was extensive word editing to align the words of both verses with the music. One verse was deleted to make the song easier, and Brother Lyon simplified his original music.

See also **Lyon**: Christmas Bells, 54 (words and music); How Will They Know? 182 (arrangement); I Have Two Ears, 269 (music); Little Pioneer Children, 216 (words and music); We Are Reverent, 27 (music); *Hymns*, Each Life That Touches Ours for Good, 293 (music); Saints, Behold How Great Jehovah, 28 (music).

MY COUNTRY, 224

Words: Mabel Jones Gabbott (1910–2004) LDS
Music: Newel Kay Brown (1932–) LDS

The love of liberty and homeland exists everywhere and can be shared through the universal language of music. With worldwide Church membership, there was a need for patriotic songs that could be sung in any country—a generic message that would be appropriate regardless of the degree of political freedom of a country. A generic flag was used in the picture.

Mabel Jones Gabbott said, "The words of the song refer to geographical differences in the lands we live in, not political boundaries; children everywhere can find kinship with the descriptions of these lands."[151] Sister Gabbott served a mission to the Northwestern States and then used her writing skills on the staffs of the Church magazines. She was a member of the YWMIA General Board and the General Church Music Committee, and chaired the Hymnbook Text Committee for the 1985 hymnbook. Sixteen of her poems have been used for Primary songs in this collection, and four others are lyrics for hymns in the hymnbook.

Newell Kay Brown composed an energetic march as a new musical setting for Sister Gabbott's poem. He explains, "The mildly syncopated rhythm of the song results from an attempt to match the natural spoken rhythm of the text." He suggests speaking the words first so that "such phrases as 'I sing it with pride' will fall very naturally into place when

PART THREE

the children are asked to sing the words."[152] Dr. Brown is a professor of music at the University of North Texas and remembers singing many solos as a young boy.

See also **Gabbott**: Baptism, 100 (words); Before I Take the Sacrament, 73 (words); Did Jesus Really Live Again?, 64 (words); Father Up Above, 23 (words); Had I Been a Child, 80 (words); Have a Very Happy Birthday!, 284 (words); Have a Very Merry Christmas!, 51 (words); He Sent His Son, 34 (words); Samuel Tells of the Baby Jesus, 36 (words); Sleep, Little Jesus, 47 (words); The Family, 194 (words); There Was Starlight on the Hillside, 40 (words); To Think about Jesus, 71 (words); We Are Reverent, 27 (words); Who Is the Child, 46 (words); *Hymns*, In Humility, Our Savior, 172 (words); Lord, Accept Into Thy Kingdom, 236 (words); Rejoice, Ye Saints of Latter Days, 290 (words); We Have Partaken of Thy Love, 155 (words).

See also **Brown**: I Hope They Call Me on a Mission, 169 (words and music); *Hymns*, With Songs of Praise, 71 (music).

MY FLAG, MY FLAG, 225

Words: Anna Johnson (1892–1979) LDS
Music: Alexander Schreiner (1901–1987) LDS

Anna Johnson was a special feature writer for the *Deseret News* and the author of "Hopscotch Valley," a children's column. Many books of her poetry were published, and Brother Schreiner, tabernacle organist, wrote tunes for over one hundred of them. She also worked in the office of the YWMIA. One of Sister Johnson's hobbies was collecting foreign dolls. To her, the dolls represented children everywhere in whom she was interested. The collection was given to the Primary Children's Hospital in Salt Lake City, Utah.

Alexander Schreiner was born in Nürnberg, Germany, and played the piano at the age of five. At age eight, he became a Church organist. He also studied the violin. He came to Salt Lake City at the age of eleven and played his first recital in the Tabernacle while in his teens. Soon after, he was appointed Tabernacle organist and held the position for 53 years. He excelled as organist, composer, arranger, writer, and concert artist and millions of people heard his organ broadcasts from the Tabernacle. Dr. Schreiner earned the first PhD given in music at the University of Utah. He composed the music for nine hymns in the 1985 *Hymns*.[153]

See also **Johnson**: A Smile Is Like the Sunshine, 267 (words); An

Angel Came to Joseph Smith, 86 (words); I Think the World Is Glorious, 230 (words); Jesus Is Our Loving Friend, 58 (words); We Bow Our Heads, 25 (words).

See also **Schreiner**: I Think the World Is Glorious, 230 (music); Jesus Is Our Loving Friend, 58 (music); We Bow Our Heads, 25 (music); *Hymns,* Behold Thy Sons and Daughters, Lord, 238 (music); God Loved Us, So He Sent His Son, 187 (music); Holy Temples on Mount Zion, 289 (music); In Memory of the Crucified, 190 (music); Lead Me into Life Eternal, 45 (music); Lord, Accept into Thy Kingdom, 236 (music); Thy Spirit, Lord, Has Stirred Our Souls, 157 (music); Truth Eternal, 4 (music); While of These Emblems We Partake, 174 (music).

PART THREE

Nature and Seasons

"When we rejoice in beautiful scenery, great art, and great music, it is but the flexing of instincts acquired in another place and another time." [154]
—Elder Neal A. Maxwell (1926–2004)

The songs in Nature and Seasons help us appreciate the beauty and wonder of our Heavenly Father's creations, and to recognize His hand in the world around us. Some of the timeless favorites, such as "Give, Said the Little Stream" and "Little Purple Pansies" help to bind us to our parents and grandparents. Someday our children will sing those songs to their children.

Virginia Sargent prepared the delightful small artwork. Scripture references were not given to specific seasonal songs, or to the songs in the "Fun and Activity" section. But "Man is that he might have joy" might have served for the entire group!

MY HEAVENLY FATHER LOVES ME, 228

Words and music: Clara Watkins McMaster (1904–1995) LDS

Clara McMaster was the eleventh child in her family and sang and accompanied others on the piano as she grew up in Brigham City, Utah. She said, "I'm grateful that as a child we had an orchestra, and a chorus in our family. It was easy because we had no radios, TV, or movies. I was born on a farm, and I knew the sounds in the barnyard. When I was called to the Primary general board, I was told that the children needed a song to teach them that their Heavenly Father loves them. I didn't really know how to do that. The Lord answered my prayers through the song of a bird. All I would have to do to write this song was to bear my testimony. This was my way of saying to the children that my Heavenly Father loves me. It wasn't my song. It was something brought into my heart many years ago. I'm grateful that the children still want to sing my song."[155] The beginning pitch of the song was raised an octave to help children sing in their head voices. Because Sister McMaster and her husband performed duets often, she naturally wrote memorable melodies that were easy to harmonize. The melody for the words "I'm glad that I live in this beautiful world" was incorrectly notated as an ascending scale in *Sing With Me*. It was originally written as it now appears, with optional cue notes that may be sung by high voices or played by the piano.

Sister McMaster said, "Music is a rich gift of God, and it is in the world to make the lives of His children happier and better."[156] She was a member of the Tabernacle Choir for twenty-two years and served fourteen years on the Primary general board. Clara and her husband, J. Stuart McMaster, presided over the Independence, Missouri Mission. They received the 1978 Franklin S. Harris Fine Arts Award from Brigham Young University for their musical contributions to the Church and community.

See also **McMaster**: Choose the Right Way, 160 (words and music); Kindness Begins with Me, 145 (words and music); Remember the Sabbath Day, 155 (words and music); Reverently, Quietly, 26 (words and music); Teach Me to Walk in the Light, 177 (words and music); *Hymns*, Teach Me to Walk in the Light, 304 (words and music).

GOD IS WATCHING OVER ALL, 229

Words: Nellie Poorman
Music: Franz Schubert (1797–1828) arranged

The original title of the poem by **Nellie Poorman** was "Loving Care," and it was matched to a melody written by Franz Schubert. The song was published in *Tuning Up*, by Silver, Burdett & Ginn Inc. in 1936.

Franz Schubert was a child prodigy born in Vienna, Austria. He played the viola in his family string quartet and studied organ and theory. Franz won a scholarship to the Imperial Court Chapel Choir when he was eleven, and after his voice changed he spent several years teaching with his schoolmaster father. He devoted most of his time to composing symphonies, string quartets, and his unique *Lieder*, which were romantic songs based on poems.

In a café one evening, Schubert read aloud the words of a poem by Shakespeare which begins, "Hark, hark, the lark." A melody came to his mind and he wanted to write it down, but had no paper. A friend gave him a menu and scratched some music staves on the back of it. In the candlelight, the young composer wrote rapidly. Franz and his friends gathered around a piano later that night, and his new composition was sung for the first time—one of the most beautiful songs of the nineteenth century.

PART THREE

Schubert gave up teaching for composing and lived in poverty because he lacked the ability to promote himself and his works. He said, "It sometimes seems to me as if I did not belong to this world at all."[157] He acknowledged that his talent was God-given and shared it with a group of friends who called themselves the Schubertians. They enjoyed many evenings together playing games, dancing to his music, and singing his beautiful melodies. He wrote over 600 songs, as many as four in a day. Some favorites are "Serenade," "Ave Maria," and "Who Is Sylvia?" It is said that he slept with his glasses on so that he wouldn't have to look for them to begin composing in the morning. One close friend wrote, "Schubert had a devout nature and believed firmly in God and the immortality of the soul. His religious sense is also clearly expressed in many of his songs. At the time when he was in want he in no way lost courage, and if, at times, he had more than he needed he willingly shared it with others who appealed to him for alms."[158] He died of a fever diagnosed as typhus, the disease common in the city slums. He was only 31, and sadly, his music did not become popular until after his death. As he had wished, he was buried close to his hero, Ludwig van Beethoven.

See also **Schubert**: Andante, 294 (music); Impromptu, 288 (music).

I THINK THE WORLD IS GLORIOUS, 230

Words: Anna Johnson (1892–1979) LDS
Music: Alexander Schreiner (1901–1987) LDS

This song is one of the few in the *Children's Songbook* with open measures. That means the type is set according to the poem rather than the music. Usually, the eighth note "pickups" would be included with the last measure of each line to make the counting easier for the pianist. The layout following the poem helps the singer, rather than the accompanist. The 1985 hymnbook always favors the singer, as more people will read the songs than will play them. Flip through the pages of the hymnbook and you will see this to be the case (for example, "How Firm a Foundation," 85). It usually takes more space for this layout, but aids memory as the rhymes are more obvious. In the *Children's Songbook*, "The Handcart Song," 220, has open measures—can you find any others?

The author, **Anna Johnson**, was a special feature writer for the *Deseret News* and the author of "Hopscotch Valley," a children's column. Many books of her poetry were published, and Dr. Schreiner, tabernacle organist, wrote tunes for over a hundred of them. She also worked in the office of the YWMIA. One of Sister Johnson's hobbies was collecting foreign dolls. To her, the dolls represented children everywhere in whom she was interested. The collection was given to the Primary Children's Hospital in Salt Lake City, Utah.[159]

Alexander Schreiner was born in Nürnberg, Germany, and played the piano at age five. He studied the violin when he was eight, and also became a Church organist. Alexander immigrated to Salt Lake City at age eleven, and played his first recital in the Tabernacle while in his teens. Soon after, he was appointed Tabernacle organist, a position he held for 53 years. He excelled as organist, composer, arranger, writer, and concert artist, and millions of people heard his organ broadcasts from the Tabernacle. Dr. Schreiner earned the first PhD given in music at the University of Utah, and was awarded four additional honorary doctorates.

See also **Johnson**: A Smile Is Like the Sunshine, 267 (words); An Angel Came to Joseph Smith, 86 (words); Jesus Is Our Loving Friend, 58 (words); My Flag, My Flag, 225 (words); We Bow Our Heads, 25 (words).

See also **Schreiner**: My Flag, My Flag, 225 (music); Jesus Is Our Loving Friend, 58 (music); We Bow Our Heads, 25 (music); *Hymns,* Behold Thy Sons and Daughters, Lord, 238 (music); God Loved Us, So He Sent His Son, 187 (music); Holy Temples on Mount Zion, 289 (music); In Memory of the Crucified, 190 (music); Lead Me into Life Eternal, 45 (music); Lord, Accept into Thy Kingdom, 236 (music); Thy Spirit, Lord, Has Stirred Our Souls, 157 (music); Truth Eternal, 4 (music); While of These Emblems We Partake, 174 (music).

ALL THINGS BRIGHT AND BEAUTIFUL, 231

Words: Cecil Frances Alexander (1818–1885)
Music: Old English tune, arranged.

Cecil Frances Alexander was born in County Wicklow, Ireland. She helped establish a school for the deaf and was very involved in religious education. Her *Hymns for Little Children* was published in seventy or more editions, and the earnings were donated to an Irish school for the handicapped. She married the Reverend William Alexander, who became archbishop of Ireland for the Church of England. Her poem was printed with different music in the 1905 songbook but has been included in every book to the present.

The first two lines were identified as the refrain. Singing the refrain after each verse is normal but makes a long song. Instructions for a shortened version were suggested. The music leader could direct the children to sing the refrain, then all four verses one after the other, and end with the refrain.

See also **Alexander**: *Hymns*, He is Risen, 199 (words); Once in Royal David's City, 205 (words); There Is a Green Hill Far Away, 194 (words).

BEAUTY EVERYWHERE, 232

Words: Matilda Watts Cahoon (1881–1973) LDS
Music: Mildred Tanner Pettit (1895–1977) LDS

President Gordon B. Hinckley paid tribute to **Matilda Cahoon** in a meeting at the Hymn Celebration in the Assembly Hall in 1985. He said, "She somehow coaxed a tune out of me as a part of the boy's chorus in junior high school. She was a great and delightful and lovely teacher."[160] She taught in the public schools for thirty-nine years, was the first woman delegate to the state legislature from Salt Lake County, and served from 1913–1939 on the Primary general board. Her poem was set to music by a Primary co-worker, Sister Pettit, and has appeared in every Primary songbook since 1920.

Mildred Pettit had ancestors who were Mayflower pilgrims, and some who were original Utah pioneers. She studied piano, pipe organ, and composition at the McCune School of Music and also attended the Latter-day Saints College in Salt Lake City. Sister Pettit taught school and then married a medical school graduate. She served for thirty-five years in the Primary, with four of those years on the Primary general board. During that time, she wrote many programs and songs for children. She has composed 145 musical selections.

See also **Cahoon**: *Hymns*, The Light Divine, 305 (words).

See also **Pettit**: Father, I Will Reverent Be, 29 (music); I Am a Child of God, 2 (music); Mother Dear, 206 (music); *Hymns*, The Light Divine, 305 (music).

THE WORLD IS SO LOVELY, 233

Words and music: Moiselle Renstrom (1889–1956) LDS

Moiselle Renstrom was a gifted teacher and had the ability of "becoming as a little child." The cover of one of her collections shows her seated at an upright piano, playing and singing with young children seated on the floor all around her. One year before her death, she was asked by the General Church Music Committee to write songs and sermons for Junior Sunday School children, ages three to seven. Many of the thirteen songs written by her and included in this collection resulted from that request. She knew the range for children's voices, wrote so that it was easy to play, taught well with her rhymes, and was doctrinally accurate. Her songbooks, *Merrily We Sing, Musical Adventures*, and *Rhythm Fun*, have been used by early childhood teachers everywhere.[161]

See also **Renstrom**: A Happy Family, 198 (words and music); A Happy Helper, 197 (words and music); A Prayer, 22 (words and music); I Am Glad for Many Things, 151 (words and music); I Love to Pray, 25 (words and music); Jesus Loved the Little Children, 59 (words and music); Jesus Said Love Everyone, 61 (words and music); Little Seeds Lie Fast Asleep, 243 (words and music); Once There Was a Snowman, 249 (words and music); Rain Is Falling All Around, 241 (words and music); To Get Quiet, 275 (words and music); Two Little Eyes, 268 (words and music).

BECAUSE GOD LOVES ME, 234

Words and music: Joleen Grant Meredith (1935–) LDS

Joleen Grant Meredith grew up writing music. Sometimes she would come home from grade school at lunchtime to work on her songs. Her grandfather, William Grant, had been sent to settle American Fork, Utah, and to bring music to the people there. Sister Meredith encourages children to be sure to put their musical ideas down on paper. She served as a member of the Young Women's General Board and has written piano solos, choral works, children's songs, and hymns.

See also **Meredith**: *Hymns*, Where Can I Turn for Peace?, 129 (music).

THE WORLD IS SO BIG, 235

Words: Beverly Searle Spencer (1921–1999) LDS
Music: K. Newell Dayley (1939–) LDS

Beverly Searle Spencer earned a degree in secondary education with majors in physical education and speech. After teaching in junior high schools, she qualified in early childhood education and taught in the Head Start program. She used her writing skills as requested by the Sunday School and Primary general boards, and assisted with programs and presentations.

Author's Note: My husband worked in the same company as her husband, Harold, and we enjoyed many company parties together. Beverly

PART THREE

had beautiful white hair, and spoke and dressed in a refined and dignified manner. She was very modest about her writing contributions.

K. Newell Dayley served as a member of the Brigham Young University Music Faculty and also the General Music Committee of the Church. Brother Dayley is an excellent trumpet player and became chairman of the Brigham Young University Music Department. He composed the music for the musicals *III Nephi* and *Kirtland* and the soundtrack of the show at the Polynesian Cultural Center in Hawaii. He said, "I have a deep love for children's music and feel that some of our most important work ought to be focused in that direction."[162]

See also **Dayley**: Every Star Is Different, 142 (music); Home, 192 (music); Hum Your Favorite Hymn, 152 (music); I Feel My Savior's Love, 74 (words and music); *Hymns*, Lord, I Would Follow Thee, 220 (music).

"GIVE," SAID THE LITTLE STREAM, 236

Words: Fanny J. Crosby (1820–1915)
Music: William B. Bradbury (1816–1868) arranged

What word is missing in this sentence from the song? "I'm small, I know, but wherever I go the _____ grow greener still." If you said "grass," you are wrong! The song has obviously been taught by rote rather than by looking at the words, as this is not a word change. Every printing, including the 1920 songbook edition, says "fields." So where did "grass" come from? Perhaps we have been influenced by the saying "the grass is greener on the other side."

The 1979 edition of the *Guinness Book of World Records* lists the author, **Fanny Crosby,** as the world's most prolific hymnist. Although she had been blind almost from birth, she is credited with over 8,500 hymns, songs, and poems. Her talent was at first used to write popular song lyrics, such as "There's Music in the Air." But at age forty-four she began writing religious verse and completed over eight thousand religious poems. She married a blind musician, Alexander Van Alstyne, and some of her credit lines are Mrs. Frances Jane Van Alstyne.

William Batchelder Bradbury was born in Maine. He studied at the Boston Academy of Music, in New York, and also Leipzig, Germany. He held the position of organist at the Baptist Temple while in New York, and gave lessons in voice and piano. Mr. Bradbury taught free singing classes for children and was a popular conductor of musical festivals. He manufactured and sold pianos the last ten years of his life.

See also **Crosby**: *Hymns*, Behold! A Royal Army, 251 (words).

STORIES OF THE CHILDREN'S SONGBOOK

See also **Bradbury:** *Hymns,* Come, All Ye Saints Who Dwell on Earth, 65 (music); God Moves in a Mysterious Way, 285 (music); Sweet Hour of Prayer, 142 (music); We Are All Enlisted, 250 (music).

THE PROPHET SAID TO PLANT A GARDEN, 237

Words and music: Mary Jane McAllister Davis (1925–1988) LDS

Mary Jane McAllister Davis attended East High School and the University of Utah in Salt Lake City. She was a gentle and gifted writer who used her talents to write stories and poems for children. Sometimes she made her poems into songs. Even when she was bed-ridden with crippling rheumatoid arthritis, she continued to write. She would create the ideas for programs and musicals, and someone would write them down for her. When her ward Primary built a float for the Days of '47 Children's Parade, the leaders asked her to write a song for the children to sing while they walked in the parade. Mary Jane wrote "The Prophet Said to Plant a Garden" based on President Kimball's instruction for members to plant gardens. A small tractor pulled a "garden" float and the children walked behind dressed as vegetables and singing the song. The *Friend* published the song in 1982, and then it was selected for the *Children's Songbook.*

SPRINGTIME IS COMING, 238

Words: Fanny Giralda Pheatt
Music: Alsatian Folk Tune

The poem "Springtime Is Coming" appeared as a song set to a folk tune in *Sing a Song* of *The World of Music* series, published by Silver, Burdett & Ginn, Inc., in 1936. There is no biographical information available.

BECAUSE IT'S SPRING, 239

Words and music: Faye Glover Petersen (1914–2009)

Faye Glover Petersen was born in Midvale, Utah. She studied piano and voice even though she claimed to be a tomboy. She grew up on a farm and loved to climb trees. Sister Petersen spent one year in New York studying, and then worked at the Utah State School Board Office in youth corrections, and also Zion's Bank. She enjoys traveling and learning about different cultures.

The first line originally said, "Why is the sky so blue today? Why is the robin's song so gay?" Children may not know that the dictionary

PART THREE

definition of "gay" is merry, bright, and cheerful. The additional inference today required a word change, and so it became "clear" and "dear."

See also **Petersen**: When I Go to Church, 157 (words and music).

IN THE LEAFY TREETOPS, 240

Words and music: anonymous

No credits have been given for this favorite Primary song. The 1983 survey ranked the song number twenty-four, and it has been in Primary songbooks since 1939. The original title was "How Do You Do."

BIRDS IN THE TREE, 241

Words: Glenna Tate Holbrook (1925–) LDS
Music: Marjorie Castleton Kjar (1927–) LDS

Glenna Tate Holbrook wrote her first poem while serving a mission in the Southern States. She continued her writing with song lyrics, roadshows, poems, and an operetta. She lived in the same ward with Sister Kjar, and they worked together to write songs which were published in *Songs to Sing for Latter-day Saint Children*. The songbook included "Birds in the Tree" and "Stand Up."

Marjorie Castleton Kjar, the composer, loves to have her family, including her grandchildren, sing together. She believes that music can bring happiness to the soul. Sister Kjar teaches piano "to help children prepare to serve in the Church as musicians."[163] She received a music degree from the University of Utah, and served for five years on the Primary general board. Her advice to Church music directors and pianists is "to prepare ahead by learning the gospel messages of the songs. I strongly feel that the music director is her [own] best visual aid."[164] She and her husband also presided over a mission in New Zealand.

See also **Holbrook**: Stand Up, 278 (words).

See also **Kjar**: Where Love Is, 138; Come with Me to Primary, 255 (words and music); We Welcome You, 256 (music); Stand Up, 278 (music).

RAIN IS FALLING ALL AROUND, 241

Words and music: Moiselle Renstrom (1889–1956) LDS

With imaginative alternate words, this song can be relevant to any season. It can also be a rest song such as "Matt is stretching, or jumping, or dancing." The words can be a positive reinforcement, such as "We are quiet; we can tiptoe; we are happy." Children can give ideas that could be sung, which extends both the children and the use of the song.

Moiselle Renstrom wrote both words and music to thirteen songs included in this collection. She was born in Huntsville, Utah, and taught school in Salt Lake, Weber, and Davis Counties. Sister Renstrom was a gifted teacher and her volumes for little children encourage them to pretend and move with the music, such as this action song and "Once There Was a Snowman." As we were evaluating songs, we noticed that her work required no changes. She knew the range for children's voices, wrote so that it was easy to play, taught well with her rhymes, and was doctrinally accurate. Her songbooks, *Merrily We Sing*, *Musical Adventures*, and *Rhythm Fun* have been used by early childhood teachers everywhere.

See also **Renstrom**: A Happy Family, 198 (words and music); A Happy Helper, 197 (words and music); A Prayer, 22 (words and music); I Am Glad for Many Things, 151 (words and music); I Love to Pray, 25 (words and music); Jesus Loved the Little Children, 59 (words and music); Jesus Said Love Everyone, 61 (words and music); Little Seeds Lie Fast Asleep, 243 (words and music); Once There Was a Snowman, 249 (words and music); The World Is So Lovely, 233 (words and music); To Get Quiet, 275 (words and music); Two Little Eyes, 268 (words and music).

POPCORN POPPING, 242

Words and music: Georgia W. Bello (1924–2007) LDS
Arrangement: Betty Lou Cooney (1924–2013) LDS
One spring when the orchards in Magna, Utah, were blossoming, **Georgia W. Bello's** four-year-old son said, "Oh, look, Mother . . . popcorn's popping on the apricot tree!" In the springtime some years later, Sister Bello looked out her window and saw the apricot blossoms. Her son's words came back to her, and she wrote the song that has since become the number one favorite of Primary children. She did not have a piano at the time and used her daughter's toy piano to find the melody—that is why it is all on white keys. She said, "I attribute to inspiration the words that came to mind after six years: 'popcorn's popping on the apricot tree.' I wrote the music and words in half an hour. I still feel to this day that this was a special gift."[165]

Sister Bello said she is a Church-trained musician. She developed her talents as she served in Church callings. She was a Primary music leader and asked her friend, **Betty Lou Packard Cooney**, to write down

PART THREE

the melody and make a left hand so that she could teach the song to the children of her ward. Sister Cooney taught music in secondary schools, and singing and conducting seminars. The song has been published in many other collections for school children and was simplified for the *Children's Songbook*.[166]

LITTLE SEEDS LIE FAST ASLEEP, 243

Words and music: Moiselle Renstrom (1889–1956) LDS

Moiselle Renstrom was born in Huntsville, Utah, and taught school in Salt Lake, Weber, and Davis Counties. Sister Renstrom was a teacher who had the gift of "becoming as a little child." She was thrilled by new ideas and discoveries by her students and shared their enjoyment of learning. Many of her songs encourage pretending and movement as this one does. She wrote both words and music to thirteen songs included in this collection, many of them at the request of the Deseret Sunday School Music Committee. She knew the range for children's voices, wrote so that it was easy to play, taught well with her rhymes, and was doctrinally accurate. Her songbooks, *Merrily We Sing*, *Musical Adventures*, and *Rhythm Fun* have been used by early childhood teachers everywhere.[167]

See also **Renstrom**: A Happy Family, 198 (words and music); A Happy Helper, 197 (words and music); A Prayer, 22 (words and music); I Am Glad for Many Things, 151 (words and music); I Love to Pray, 25 (words and music); Jesus Loved the Little Children, 59 (words and music); Jesus Said Love Everyone, 61 (words and music); Once There Was a Snowman, 249 (words and music); Rain Is Falling All Around, 241 (words and music); The World Is So Lovely, 233 (words and music); To Get Quiet, 275 (words and music); Two Little Eyes, 268 (words and music).

LITTLE PURPLE PANSIES, 244

Words: anonymous
Music: Joseph Ballantyne (1868–1944) LDS

Joseph Ballantyne was born in Ogden Valley, Utah, the son of Richard Ballantyne, the founder of the Sunday School of the Church. He studied music in New York and with musicians from Chicago, New York, London, and Paris. He directed the Ogden Tabernacle Choir and then chaired the music committee for the Deseret Sunday School Board. During this time he wrote many children's songs. When he moved to

Long Beach, California, he directed the Los Angeles Stake choir and the choir at St. Anthony's Church. He also taught private voice lessons.

There was some question as to whether "you and *I*" was correct in the last line, or whether it should be "you and *me*." But right or wrong, the song could not be changed—it simply has to rhyme with the message of the song which is to "try, try, try" to make the place where we are happy. The accompaniment was lightened to match the mood of the song. This lilting tune is timeless and attracts one generation after another.

A big basketball player came to his piano lesson and saw the new Primary songbook on the music stand. Gently he picked up the book and asked, "Is 'Little Purple Pansies' in this book?" "Why, yes it is," his surprised teacher answered. The young man replied, "I've heard my mother sing it, but I've never seen it before."[168]

See also **Ballantyne:** Jesus Once Was a Little Child, 55 (music); Oh, Hush Thee, My Baby, 48 (words and music); Shine On, 144 (words and music); Stand for the Right, 159 (words and music).

OH, WHAT DO YOU DO IN THE SUMMERTIME? 245

Words and music: Dorothy S. Andersen (1927–) LDS

Dorothy S. Andersen played a pump organ for Sunday School when she was only ten. She has an MA in English, a secondary education certificate, and an MM in musical composition from the University of Utah. She has taught in public schools and at Salt Lake Community College, Westminster College, and the University of Utah. She has written instrumental and choral works and musical skits, and was first place in the 1975 Relief Society music competition with her song "The Spirit of Our Father." Sister Andersen said, "The most important things about music are, first, to enjoy it, and second to share it with others. Music seems to be the most direct and natural expression of the heart about the things that matter most, so it is not surprising that we express our love for the Lord, our reverence for him, and our gratitude and praises to him, through music."[169]

Alternate words could be suggested by the children for what they do in the wintertime.

IT'S AUTUMNTIME, 246

Words and music: Rita Mae Olsen (1932–) LDS
Arrangement: Vanja Y. Watkins (1938–) LDS

PART THREE

Rita Mae Olsen said, "I wanted to emphasize the beauty of nature in the fall as being part of God's creation. I wanted the children to notice the autumn colors and the beautiful time of year."[170] She was inspired by the beautiful leaves around her home. Sister Olsen has been a schoolteacher and taught organ and piano lessons. She plays the organ at the Ogden Temple. She feels, "Beautiful music is inspirational, uplifting, and delightful. Whenever I am depressed or down, it lifts my spirit and brings joy back into my life. . . . Music is an international language."[171]

Vanja (VON-yuh) **Yorgason Watkins** served as Primary general board music chairman and then as a member of the General Church Music Committee. Sister Watkins said that when this song was submitted to the *Friend*, it had words and melody only. One of her first assignments on the Primary general board was to write an accompaniment for the song. She wrote the sound of leaves falling down in three places in the accompaniment.

See also **Watkins**: Easter Hosanna, 68 (music); Families Can Be Together Forever, 188 (music); For Thy Bounteous Blessings, 21 (arrangement); I Want to Be Reverent, 28 (music); I Will Be Valiant, 162 (words and music); I Will Follow God's Plan, 164 (words and music); Latter-day Prophets, 134 (music); Thank Thee for Everything, 10 (words); Thank Thee for Everything, 10 (words); The Articles of Faith, 122–132 (words); The Sacrament, 72 (words and music); The Things I Do, 170 (music); This Is My Beloved Son, 76 (music); To Be a Pioneer, 218 (arrangement); Truth from Elijah, 90 (words and music); *Hymns*, Families Can Be Together Forever, 300 (music); Press Forward Saints, 81 (music).

AUTUMN DAY, 247

Words and music: Grace Wilbur Conant (1858–1948)

Composer and musical editor **Grace Wilbur Conant** studied piano, harmony, and composition in Boston and Paris. Her kindergarten and school part-songs were published in magazines and periodicals. She compiled and edited *Songs for Little People* in 1905. Several songs in the children's music resources of the Church are from this source. She also edited the musical department of *Kindergarten Review*.

Grace Conant's songs were also published under the pen name **A. B. Posonby**. Songs by A. B. Posonby were published in a songbook by the Congregational Sunday School and Publishing Society in the early 1900s, and also in *Songs for Little Children*, 1905, by the Pilgrim Press.

STORIES OF THE CHILDREN'S SONGBOOK

This song appeared in 1939 in *The Primary Songbook* and also *Sing With Me,* 1969.

FALLING SNOW, 248

Words and music: Lois Lunt Metz; alt. (1906–2004) LDS

Lois Lunt Metz missed the snow when she moved to California from her home state of Utah, and wrote this song for children everywhere. She taught elementary, junior, and high school and prepared operettas and plays with her students. Sister Metz has published five books of songs she has written for children, and contributed poems, articles, and songs in children's magazines.

The imaginative, active second part of the original song was cut for this collection so that the song would be used as a "quiet" winter song.

ONCE THERE WAS A SNOWMAN, 249

Words and music: Moiselle Renstrom (1889–1956) LDS

According to the 1983 survey, "Once There Was a Snowman" was one of the top twenty-five Primary song favorites. And it is a favorite even in Tahiti where there is no snow! **K. Moiselle Renstrom** wrote many songs, which encouraged children to pretend and move with the music. She was thrilled by the new ideas and discoveries of her students and shared their enjoyment of learning. Although the teacher, she had the gift of "becoming as a little child." Three of her books of songs include *Rhythm Fun, Merrily We Sing,* and *Musical Adventure.* These volumes have been used throughout the world.

Thirteen of Sister Renstrom's many songs are included in the *Children's Songbook.* Few changes were needed in her songs as she wrote simply, in the right range for children's voices, and was doctrinally accurate. She was born in Huntsville, Utah, and taught school in Salt Lake, Weber, and Davis Counties.[172]

See also **Renstrom**: A Happy Family, 198 (words and music); A Happy Helper, 197 (words and music); A Prayer, 22 (words and music); I Am Glad for Many Things, 151 (words and music); I Love to Pray, 25 (words and music); Jesus Loved the Little Children, 59 (words and music); Jesus Said Love Everyone, 61 (words and music); Little Seeds Lie Fast Asleep, 243 (words and music); Rain Is Falling All Around, 241 (words and music); The World Is So Lovely, 233 (words and music); To Get Quiet, 275 (words and music); Two Little Eyes, 268 (words and music).

PART THREE

Fun and Activity

"The world's a very happy place, where every child should dance and sing." [173]
—Charles Lamb (1775–1832), English essayist and critic, and Mary Lamb (1764–1847) his sister and collaborator.

In this section, there are songs about Primary and friendship, songs with actions, and birthday songs. Look at the two-page picture and see if you can tell what activity song the children are singing. The children are touching their heads, shoulders, knees, and toes. One little boy is not paying attention. He will probably be behind when they do the actions very fast!

LIFT UP YOUR VOICE AND SING, 252

Words and music: Richard C. Berg (1911–)

Richard C. Berg takes great pleasure in hearing large festival choruses, and he likes to hear classrooms of children singing. He said the song he wrote expresses his feelings about the joys of singing to show gratitude for the blessings of living. Dr. Berg is a music educator. He received his doctorate degree from Columbia University and then served as the director of music education for public schools in four states: Maryland, Massachusetts, New York, and Missouri. He has been a professor of music at the University of Missouri and Western Oregon State College.

It is good musicianship to do something different with repetitions, such as the three times the phrase, "Lift up your voice" is sung on the last line. Dynamic markings were added to support the natural crescendo that concludes the song.

SING A SONG, 253

Words and music: Ingrid Sawatzki Gordon (1949–) LDS

Ingrid Gordon is a beautician and a vocalist. She loves directing children's music, and learned how to do it from her Primary music director.

Author's Note: One day when Ingrid was cutting my hair, she told me how much fun she had helping with music at her children's elementary school. She had wanted to begin her lesson with a song about singing—something that the children could hear once and easily join in. As she thought about what she wanted, a little idea popped into her mind and she taught it to the children. She asked me if I could write it down and make an accompaniment. When she sang it to me, I realized that it could be sung as a round. Because we needed rounds to involve older children, I submitted it to the committee and it was approved. To her surprise, Ingrid is now a composer! Many successful songs have been written this way—by pondering a particular need for a particular group of children for a particular occasion.

FUN TO DO, 253

Words: Rebecca Stevens
Music: Cecilia Johns
Unfortunately, no biographical information is available on either **Rebecca Stevens** or **Cecilia Johns**. The song was printed in *Sing With Me,* and the copyright was 1963 by DC Heath and Company. The Primary survey placed this song number twenty-five on the list of children's favorites. This song may provide the first creative writing experience for many children. Being asked to think of something fun to do, and then singing about it, gives a feeling of competence. As children realize they are capable they develop intrinsic motivation, or self-worth. One success transfers into the courage to try the next experience.

HELLO, FRIENDS! 254

Words and music: Wilma Boyle Bunker (1910–1992) LDS
Wilma Bunker was a high school teacher and taught piano lessons for sixty-three years. She served on the Primary general board for eight years, was president of the National League of American Pen Women, and in 1962 received a Distinguished Service Award from the Brigham Young University Alumni Association.

See also **Bunker**: I Will Try to Be Reverent, 28 (words and music).

OUR DOOR IS ALWAYS OPEN, 254

Words: anonymous
Music: French folk tune; arrangement
The rhythm of the penultimate (next to last) measure was adjusted to match the natural word accents. Quarter two eighths was changed to eighth quarter eighth to match the way you would speak the words

PART THREE

"passes along." It is unfortunate that we cannot acknowledge either an author or a composer.

COME WITH ME TO PRIMARY, 255

Words and music: Patricia Critchlow Maughan (1926–1980) LDS
Words and music: Marjorie Castleton Kjar (1927–) LDS

Pat Maughan taught music in the Salt Lake and Davis School Districts, and was a member of the Tabernacle Choir and the Primary general board. She also taught private voice, and performed as a soloist with Utah Opera Theater and the University Civic Chorale. As a member of the Primary music committee, she directed a children's chorus in the Tabernacle.

Marjorie Kjar loves to have her family, including her grandchildren, sing together. She believes that music can bring happiness to the soul. Sister Kjar teaches piano "to help children prepare to serve in the Church as musicians."[174] She received a music degree from the University of Utah, and served for five years on the Primary general board. She and her husband also presided over a mission in New Zealand. Her advice to music directors and pianists of the Church is "to prepare ahead by learning the gospel messages of the songs." She said, "I strongly feel that the music director is her [own] best visual aid."[175]

See also **Kjar**: Where Love Is, 138 (music); Birds in the Tree, 241 (music); We Welcome You, 256 (music); Stand Up, 278 (music).

WE WELCOME YOU, 256

Words: Ruth Muir Gardner (1927–1999) LDS and Lois Coombs Sprunt (1930–) LDS
Music: Marjorie Castleton Kjar (1927–) LDS

There are two copyright dates on the words of this song. It was first published in 1978 as "A Happy Birthday to the Primary" to celebrate Primary's centennial year. Three Primary general board members collaborated to write the song, which gave a little taste of the things that were taught in the first Primary and commemorated the number of years since it began.

Some committee members felt the song was not needed because it would only be used once a year and that one of the birthday songs could be used instead. On the other hand, this song could motivate leaders to talk about the founding of Primary by Aurelia Rogers in the Farmington

Utah Rock Chapel (note the cover illustration) and how Primary has grown.

In an attempt to make the song more versatile, the author, Ruth Gardner, was asked to write additional words which could be sung as a welcome song, and then the original words could be used as "alternate" for celebrating the August 25 birthday of Primary. The first part of the song can now stand alone and could be sung when a new child moves into the ward, the nursery children come into Primary, or the Bishop visits! Because of the changes, the song also has a 1987 copyright.

Author's Note: I was glad we saved a bit of history.

Ruth Muir Gardner loves to do crossword puzzles. She was a high school English and business teacher, and taught piano in her home. While serving on the Primary general board, she was music chairman, and presented workshops at the Brigham Young University Church Music Workshops. Even after her husband suffered a stroke, they were willing to serve a mission to Florida.

Lois Coombs Sprunt taught elementary school and then served an Eastern States mission. For five years she served on the Primary general board and was a member of the Child Correlation Review Committee. She and her husband have nine children.

Marjorie Castleton Kjar believes that music can bring happiness to the soul. Sister Kjar teaches piano "to help children prepare to serve in the Church as musicians."[176] She received a music degree from the University of Utah, and served for five years on the Primary general board. She and her husband also presided over a mission in New Zealand.

See also **Gardner**, Ruth: Families Can Be Together Forever, 188 (words); Go the Second Mile, 167 (words and music); I Believe in Being Honest, 149 (words); To Be a Pioneer, 218 (words and music); *Hymns*, Families Can Be Together Forever, 300 (words); Go Forth With Faith, 263 (words).

See also **Kjar**: Where Love Is, 138 (music); Birds in the Tree, 241 (music); Come With Me To Primary, 255 (words and music); Stand Up, 278 (music).

OUR PRIMARY COLORS, 258

Words and music: Marzelle Mangum (1914–2003) LDS

The 1985 Primary Handbook stated that the Primary colors are red, yellow, and blue, and that blue represented "truth." The song said "blue is for purity in thought and deed." Inasmuch as "truth" is probably more concrete to children, the song was changed to match the handbook. One scripture reference is given for each symbol. The meter was changed from three beats to six beats per measure, which allows the conductor to direct two beats per measure for a happy lilt.

Marzelle Jesperson Mangum was the oldest of seven children. During the depression, she was attending Brigham Young University. When her father became unemployed, she left school to help support the family. Sister Mangum taught piano for thirty years. She has membership in many music associations and served in the American Red Cross. Sister Mangum didn't think she wanted her birthday year printed in the *Children's Songbook* where everyone could figure out her age. So it was not published until after she passed away. However, it does give a bit of history to read the date when the writer lived.

WE'RE ALL TOGETHER AGAIN, 259

Words: traditional; adapted
Music: Satis N. Coleman (1878–1971)

Satis Narrona Coleman was a music educator and earned her MA from Columbia University. She was also an author and editor, and in 1922 published *Singing Time, Songs for Nursery and School,* and *Creative Music for Children.* These books have had a wide influence in music education. Training was combined in dancing, singing, poetry, and the making and playing of instruments. Ms. Coleman served as national chairman for the music committee for the Association for Childhood Education, and affiliated with the National Educational Association.

HELLO SONG, 260

Words and music: Maurine Benson Ozment (1932–) LDS

Maurine Benson Ozment has a master's degree in Music Education from Utah State University and is an author, accompanist, conductor, and teacher from the preschool to college levels. She said, "In our international church, music is one of the things that remains the same from one culture to the next, building bonds of unity among the members. One can travel the world over and not understand the language at church in a faraway land, but the familiar music of a beloved song can immediately bring feelings of security and belonging to one's heart. Oh, how I love our wonderful Primary songs and the joy they bring to people everywhere!"[177]

Sister Ozment taught elementary school for ten years and private piano for thirty years, including lessons at the college level.

See also **Ozment**: Feliz Cumpleaños, 282 (words and music).

HERE WE ARE TOGETHER, 261

Words: traditional

Music: old tune

The Primary Music Committee and Ad Hoc Committee brainstormed possible alternate phrases to extend the use of this action song. The song can be adapted to any relevant weather, holiday, or activity.

FRIENDS ARE FUN, 262

Words and music: Glenn Gordon (1956–) LDS

Glenn Howard Gordon began serving in the Church when he and his parents were baptized. He was Junior Sunday School pianist; ward organist in Newcastle, Australia, when he was fifteen; and assistant stake organist at sixteen. He earned a degree in Fine Arts and Semitic Studies from the University of Sydney, and has done graduate work in Jewish Education and Australian Jewish History. Brother Gordon's happy song was first printed in the *Friend*, Feb. 1981, 48.

WE ARE DIFFERENT, 263

Words and music: Patricia Kelsey Graham (1940–) LDS

Pat Graham was commissioned by Granite School District to write songs on positive values for a curriculum about families. One of the lessons was centered on the uniqueness of each person and was the springboard for writing "We Are Different." When it was suggested that there should be a "lively" song on this topic for the songbook, she simplified the original song and anonymously submitted it to the committee. She felt honored that it was selected.

The song was taught at an interfaith conference on special needs sponsored by the Joliet Illinois Stake. Sister Gretchen Saitzeff, the project leader, said, "The time and effort that went into this conference were staggering, but it was all worth it for the moment of pure joy we experienced when singing that song together. Like the words say, 'I help you and you help me. We learn from problems and we're starting to see. I help you, and you help me, And that's the way it is supposed to be.'"[178]

People may have trouble with the syncopated rhythm and should count out loud and play the song very slowly. She thinks that this is how it is with anything that is different—at first we are uncomfortable with the "unknown," but with time, the differences become the attraction.

For a Relief Society General Women's Conference, Chieko Okazaki asked her to arrange the song as a women's duet.

Author's Note: We added a wood block to emphasize the Latin rhythm, and I secretly wondered if we might be struck by lightning for being so jazzy in the Tabernacle. Sister Okazaki said that was exactly her point—we should not be afraid of differences. The rehearsal was difficult, as the singers could not hear the piano or each other. Finally the sound technicians solved the problem with a speaker set up so we could hear each other. I had been so concerned about the sound problems that I didn't worry about playing. Driving to the prayer meeting before the conference, I suddenly realized that I was going to be playing the piano at a meeting attended by 7,000 people and broadcast via satellite to stakes around the world and recorded for later showings. In the bustle of preparation I had not had time to worry. As I listened to the prayer asking for all participants to be blessed and magnified, my butterflies left and I thought only of how to support the singers. And I also thought how wonderful that my little "jazzy" song could be useful in this way.

Sister Graham served as the chairman of the General Primary Music Committee, which prepared the 1989 *Children's Songbook*, and also originated and wrote the Sharing Time page for the *Friend* for seven years. She co-authored *A Children's Songbook Companion*, a collection of lesson plans for all the songs in the *Children's Songbook*. She has a master's degree in education; has taught elementary school and private piano and organ lessons; and loves to accompany singers and musicians.

See also **Graham**: I Am Like a Star, 163 (words and music); Picture a Christmas, 50 (words and music); The Hearts of the Children, 92 (words and music); The Nativity Song, 52 (words and music).

HAPPY SONG, 264

Words: anonymous

Music: Czech folk song

Part of the charm of the *Children's Songbook* is that it does not sound like the same person wrote all of the songs. Folk tunes and classic melodies are mixed in with the work of lay writers and composers as well as trained musicians and poets. The result is a diverse yet satisfying collection.

BE HAPPY! 265

Words: Alice Jean Cleator (1871–1926)
Music: Arthur Wilton

Alice Cleator was born in England and emigrated to America. She taught school in New York City and wrote other hymn texts.

The earliest copyright on the song "Be Happy!" was 1914. It has been in Primary music resources since 1920. "'Be happy!' sings the little bird" was changed to "Be happy like the little bird." And the second verse was made consistent for the little brook. Everything that is taught in Primary should be true, and this change removes the inference that the bird is able to speak.

IF YOU'RE HAPPY, 266

Words and music: anonymous

Little children can participate with actions even before they find their singing voices. This explains the enduring quality of this anonymous song. The alternate phrases can encourage older children to think of things they do to show that they are happy.

SMILES, 267

Words: Daniel Taylor
Music: anonymous

There is no biographical information about the author, **Daniel Taylor**. His poem has been included as a song in every Primary songbook since 1939. The composer credit for the first printing gave only the initials H.S.L.-E.H. The name remains anonymous. Maybe the composer didn't want anyone to know that they wrote melodies as a hobby; or maybe they were just very shy and humble. Whatever the case, they wrote a favorite.

Author's Note: One of my first visual memories of Primary is watching the music leader turn a paper plate upside down to change it from a frown to a smile. I was entranced with the magic of it. Then, as she suggested, I would feel my mouth to see if I could make the corners go down into a frown and then squeeze up into a smile.

A SMILE IS LIKE THE SUNSHINE, 267

Words: Anna Johnson (1892–1979) LDS
Music: Greitje Terburg Rowley (1927–) LDS

Anna Johnson was a special feature writer for the *Deseret News* and the author of "Hopscotch Valley," a children's column. Many books of her poetry were published, and many of them were set to music for children. She also worked in the office of the YWMIA. One of Sister Johnson's hobbies was collecting dolls from other countries. To her, the dolls represented children everywhere in whom she was interested. The collection was given to the Primary Children's Hospital in Salt Lake City, Utah.

Grietje (GREE-chuh) **Rowley** thinks that the songs we learn in Primary can bring us joy and comfort forever. For over twenty-five years, Sister Rowley played the piano for children at church. When she reads the words of a poem they "sing" to her, and she said that the melody for this poem came very quickly. When she writes songs, she tries to make them easy to sing, easy to play, and easy to remember. She has written musical settings for over one hundred scriptures that are important to her. She writes every day, and says it is more fun than washing dishes.

Sister Rowley served on the General Music Committee. She simplified, transposed, offered helpful suggestions, and proofed the notation of the words, markings and notation of every song in the *Children's Songbook* three times! She would remind us that this book was important to our Father in Heaven and that he would help us to do it in the best way.

See also **Johnson**: An Angel Came to Joseph Smith, 86 (words); I Think the World Is Glorious, 230 (words); Jesus Is Our Loving Friend, 58 (words); My Flag, My Flag, 225 (words); We Bow Our Heads, 25 (words).

See also **Rowley**: Distant Bells, 299 (music); Each Sunday Morning, 290 (music); I Want to Be a Missionary Now, 168 (words and music); Roll Your Hands, 274 (arrangement); Samuel Tells of the Baby Jesus, 36 (music); *Hymns*, Be Thou Humble, 130 (words and music).

TWO LITTLE EYES, 268

Words and music: Moiselle Renstrom (1889–1956) LDS

Moiselle Renstrom wrote both words and music to thirteen songs included in this collection. She was born in Huntsville, Utah, and taught school in Salt Lake, Weber, and Davis Counties. Sister Renstrom was a gifted teacher, and her songs for little children encourage them to pretend and move with the music. She had the gift of "becoming as a little child" and was thrilled by the accomplishments of her students. She knew the range for children's voices, wrote so that it was easy to play, taught well with her rhymes, and was doctrinally accurate. One year before she died, she wrote a number of little songs and sermons for Junior Sunday School children at the request of the General Church Music Committee. Her songbooks, *Merrily We Sing*, *Musical Adventures* and *Rhythm Fun* have been used by early childhood teachers throughout the world.[179]

See also **Renstrom**: A Happy Family, 198 (words and music); A Happy Helper, 197 (words and music); A Prayer, 22 (words and music); I Am Glad for Many Things, 151 (words and music); I Love to Pray, 25 (words and music); Jesus Loved the Little Children, 59 (words and music); Jesus Said Love Everyone, 61 (words and music); Little Seeds Lie Fast Asleep, 243 (words and music); Once There Was a Snowman, 249 (words and music); Rain Is Falling All Around, 241 (words and music); The World Is So Lovely, 233 (words and music); To Get Quiet, 275 (words and music); Two Little Eyes, 268 (words and music).

I HAVE TWO EARS, 269

Words: Georgia Maeser (1893–1972) LDS
Music: A. Laurence Lyon (1934–2006) LDS

The day before her third birthday, **Georgia Maeser** suffered a serious illness that caused permanent injury to her spine. Her physical problems, however, did not keep her from being grateful for her life. She earned a master of arts degree from Columbia University after studying at Brigham Young University and the University of California. She taught for twenty-six years at the Brigham Young University Training School and also filled a mission to the Southern States. The last line of her poem is touching: "I thank my Heavenly Father for making me this way."

Laurence Lyon was born in Holland when his father, T. Edgar Lyon, was mission president. He also served a mission to Holland as a young man. Brother Lyon received a doctorate in composition from Eastman School of Music and has more than one hundred published compositions, many performed by the Tabernacle Choir. Dr. Lyon served on the Sunday School General Board and the General Church Music Committee.

See also **Lyon**: Christmas Bells, 54 (words and music); How Will They Know? 182 (arrangement); Little Pioneer Children, 216 (words and music); We Are Reverent, 27 (music); Whenever I Think about Pioneers, 222 (music); *Hymns*, Each Life That Touches Ours for Good, 293 (music); Saints, Behold How Great Jehovah, 28 (music).

PART THREE

TWO HAPPY FEET, 270

Words: Norma Madsen Thomas (1908–1988) LDS
Music: Barbara Boyer Obray (1927–) LDS

Norman Madsen Thomas was a talented poet even at age ten. She wrote more than two hundred poems, and many of her poems and songs were for her family. Sister Thomas had love and reverence for the house of the Lord. When she served as Primary president in San Diego, she wanted to help her own little children as well as the Primary children learn to be more reverent. The poem she wrote for them was set to music by her friend and Primary co-worker, and the song was used in their ward Primary.

Barbara Boyer Obray grew up in Monrovia, California, and also lived in Phoenix, Arizona. She majored in music at Brigham Young University, and as a grandmother worked to complete her degree in fine arts. She is a member of the Arizona Mormon Songwriters Association and has written songs for beginning pianists.

I WIGGLE, 271

Words: Louise B. Scott (1914–)
Music: Lucille F. Wood (1915–1986)

Louise Binder Scott grew up on a farm in Iowa. She earned her master's degree in education from Boston University and also studied at Yale and the University of Southern California. She was a speech pathologist and audiologist in San Marino School District and associate professor of speech at California State College. She and a colleague, Lucile Wood, collaborated to write *Singing Fun* and *More Singing Fun*. She also wrote *Time for Phonics*, which sold five million copies before revision.

Lucile F. Wood played the family pump organ when she was not quite tall enough to reach the keys. After she took piano lessons, she played for church and at the silent movies in her small town of Deep River, Iowa. She graduated from UCLA and became associate professor of music at California State College in Los Angeles. She became a noted music educator and created multimedia aids for education, as well as publishing *The Bowman Orchestral Library, Meet the Instruments, The Small Musician Series, Symphonic Fantasies, Rhythms to Reading*, and the singing books with Louise Scott.

"My Hands" and "I Wiggle" provide activity and end quietly. They were printed in *Singing Fun*, and were the last two songs to be negotiated for use in the *Children's Songbook*. There was some difficulty obtaining copyright permission for the life of the songbook, and we decided we would pull them from the book if negotiations were not successful. Fortunately for the children, the problems were finally resolved and we received permission to include them.

See also **Scott**: My Hands, 271 (words).
See also **Wood**: My Hands, 271 (music).

I HAVE TWO LITTLE HANDS, 272

Words: Bertha A. Kleinman (1877–1971) LDS
Music: William Frederick Hanson (1887–1969) LDS

Since 1920, this sweet "quiet" song has been included in the Primary songbooks of the Church. The author, **Bertha A. Kleinman,** was a published poet by the age of twelve. Her work has appeared in many magazines and in a book of her poetry, *Through the Years*. She earned a kindergarten teaching degree at Brigham Young University and a secretarial degree from LDS Business College. President Heber J. Grant asked her to write pageants to celebrate the one-hundredth birthday of the Church and of the pioneers arriving in the Salt Lake Valley. Sister Kleinman was awarded the first David O. McKay Humanities Award from Brigham Young University and Poet Laureate of the state of Arizona.

William Frederick Hanson played at dances with his father's orchestra when he was only ten. While serving in the Northern States mission, he was assigned to prepare *The Songs of Zion*, which was widely used by missions and stakes in the Church. He taught school at the Uintah Academy, and after attending the Chicago Musical College, he accepted a position in the music department at Brigham Young University. He composed the music for the Brigham Young University school song, and "Utah, We Love Thee," which was in earlier hymnbooks. With the worldwide growth of the Church, it is no longer included as a hymn, but it is still appropriate to sing in Utah.

"I Have Two Little Hands" has been in Primary songbooks since 1920 and was 23rd in the 1983 survey of favorite Primary songs.

MY HANDS, 273

Words: Louise B. Scott (1914–)
Music: Lucille F. Wood (1915–1986)

Louise Binder Scott grew up on a farm in Iowa. She earned her

PART THREE

master's degree in education from Boston University and also studied at Yale and the University of Southern California. She was a speech pathologist and audiologist in San Marino School District and associate professor of speech at California State College. She and a colleague, Lucile Wood, collaborated to write *Singing Fun* and *More Singing Fun*. She also wrote *Time for Phonics*, which sold five million copies before revision.

Lucile F. Wood played the family pump organ when she was not quite tall enough to reach the keys. After she took piano lessons, she played for church and at the silent movies in her small town of Deep River, Iowa. She graduated from UCLA and became associate professor of music at California State College in Los Angeles. She became a noted music educator and created multimedia aids to education, as well as publishing *The Bowman Orchestral Library, Meet the Instruments, The Small Musician Series, Symphonic Fantasies, Rhythms to Reading,* along with the singing books with Louise Scott.

"My Hands" and "I Wiggle" provide activity and end quietly. They were printed in *Singing Fun*, and were the last two songs to be negotiated for use in the *Children's Songbook*. There was some difficulty obtaining copyright permission for the life of the songbook, and we decided we would pull them from the book if negotiations were not successful. Fortunately for the children, the problems were finally resolved and we received permission to include them.

See also **Scott**: I Wiggle, 271 (words).

See also **Wood**: I Wiggle, 271 (music).

ROLL YOUR HANDS, 274

Words: traditional

Music: old tune; arranged by Grietje Terburg Rowley (1927–) LDS

In 1905, the *Primary Song Book* contained this song entitled "Hand Exercise Song." For the 1989 *Children's Songbook*, the melody was changed in the penultimate (next to last) measure to mirror the first measure. The arranger, **Grietje** (GREE-chuh) **Rowley,** is of Dutch descent. She attended the Oberlin Conservatory of Music, and received a bachelor's degree in music education from the University of Miami. She joined the Church when she was teaching school in Hawaii. Sister Rowley served on the Primary Songbook Ad Hoc Committee and the General Church Music Committee. She was asked to make a simple arrangement of this anonymous tune. The melody was adjusted to conclude with a mirror image of the first two measures.

STORIES OF THE CHILDREN'S SONGBOOK

Sister Rowley has played the piano for children at church for over twenty-five years. She thinks that the songs we learn in Primary can bring us joy and comfort forever. When she writes songs, she tries to make them easy to sing, easy to play, and easy to remember. When she reads the scriptures, they "sing" to her. She has written over one hundred musical settings for scriptures that are important to her. She writes every day, and says it is more fun than washing dishes.

See also **Rowley**: A Smile is Like the Sunshine, 267 (music); Distant Bells, 299 (music); Each Sunday Morning, 290 (music); I Want to Be a Missionary Now, 168 (words and music); Samuel Tells of the Baby Jesus, 36 (music); *Hymns*, Be Thou Humble, 130 (words and music).

HEAD, SHOULDERS, KNEES AND TOES, 275

Words and music: anonymous

A teacher who understood the importance of helping children "get the wiggles out" must have created this perfect rest exercise. The usual way to sing it is to touch the part named. For a challenge, children can be asked to move what they sing about—nod their head, shrug their shoulders, bend their knees, stand tiptoe. This needs to be done slowly and requires focus. Remind the children that it doesn't say to move their mouths!

TO GET QUIET, 275

Words and music: Moiselle Renstrom (1889–1956) LDS

Moiselle Renstrom was born in Huntsville, Utah, and taught school in Salt Lake, Weber, and Davis Counties. A picture of her in a classroom shows the children on the carpet all around a big, tall, upright piano. Her hair is pushed in beautiful finger waves, and she is playing the piano and singing with the children. At the request of the General Church Music Committee, she wrote a number of little songs and sermons for the Sunday School children.

Sister Renstrom wrote both words and music to thirteen songs included in this collection. She was a gifted teacher and knew the range for children's voices, wrote so that it was easy to play, taught well with her rhymes, and was doctrinally accurate. This activity song is from her book *Merrily We Sing*, copyright 1948 by Pioneer Music Press, Inc. This book, along with *Musical Adventures*, and *Rhythm Fun* has been used by early childhood teachers everywhere.[180]

See also **Renstrom**: A Happy Family, 198 (words and music); A

PART THREE

Happy Helper, 197 (words and music); A Prayer, 22 (words and music); I Am Glad for Many Things, 151 (words and music); I Love to Pray, 25 (words and music); Jesus Loved the Little Children, 59 (words and music); Jesus Said Love Everyone, 61 (words and music); Little Seeds Lie Fast Asleep, 243 (words and music); Once There Was a Snowman, 249 (words and music); Rain Is Falling All Around, 241 (words and music); The World Is So Lovely, 233 (words and music); Two Little Eyes, 268 (words and music).

DO AS I'M DOING, 276

Words: anonymous
Music: folk style
For children, a change is as good as a rest. This "rest" song requires children to follow the leader or to be the leader and think of the activity to imitate. The action song was number 15 on the 1983 survey of the use of Primary songs—a real favorite of the children.

HINGES, 277

Words: Aileen Fisher (1906–2002)
Music: Jeanne P. Lawler (1924–) LDS

Aileen Fisher received a degree in journalism from the University of Missouri and became director of the Women's National Journalistic Register based in Chicago. When she became a freelance writer, she settled in Boulder, Colorado. Her work includes children's books, nature-verse picture books, collections of poems for children, non-fiction work, plays, and adaptations. She received many awards, including National Council of Teachers of English Award for Excellence in Poetry; and Golden Spur, Western Writers of America Award. She contributed to *Child Life*, *Jack and Jill*, and *Story Parade*.

Jeanne P. Lawler thinks music leaders should "teach with enthusiasm and sing more and talk less. Children will remember thoughts set to music longer than conversation."[181] Using the words of Aileen Fisher, she created a favorite activity song, which has a melody similar to the folk song, "Sweet Betsy of Pike."

Sister Lawler served in the U.S. Coast Guard and then received an associate degree in music from Glendale CA College. She and her daughter joined the Church and moved to Provo, Utah. To fulfill part of the requirements for her Brigham Young University degree (which she completed at age fifty-seven), she wrote "Sing Unto the Lord," a musical based on Isaiah. She has served proselyting and temple missions.

See also **Lawler**: Family History—I Am Doing It, 94 (words and music); I Often Go Walking, 202 (music); The Holy Ghost, 105 (words and music); When Jesus Christ Was Baptized, 102 (words and music).

STAND UP, 278

Words: Glenna Tate Holbrook (1925–) LDS
Music: Marjorie Castleton Kjar (1927–) LDS

Glenna Tate Holbrook wrote her first poem while serving a mission in the Southern States. She continued her writing with song lyrics, road shows, poems, and an operetta. She lived in the same ward with Sister Kjar, and they worked together to write songs which were published in *Songs to Sing for Latter-day Saint Children*. The songbook included "Birds in the Tree" and "Stand Up."

When this song was first printed, the melody began g-g-b-g and continued with the same motif. Later the suggestion was made to have the melody follow the word "up," and so the melody in *Activity Songs and Verses* was revised to g-g-g-b. At the request of the composer, the melody was returned to the original g-g-b-g.

Marjorie Castleton Kjar, the composer, loves to have her family, including her grandchildren, sing together. She believes that music can bring happiness to the soul. Sister Kjar teaches piano "to help children prepare to serve in the Church as musicians."[182] She received a music degree from the University of Utah, and served for five years on the Primary general board. Her advice to music directors and pianists of the Church is "to prepare ahead by learning the gospel messages of the songs. I strongly feel that the music director is her own best visual aid."[183] She and her husband also presided over a mission in New Zealand.

See also **Holbrook**: Birds in the Tree, 241 (words).

See also **Kjar**: Where Love Is, 138 (music); Birds in the Tree, 241 (music); Come with Me to Primary, 255 (words and music); We Welcome You, 256 (music).

OH, HOW WE LOVE TO STAND, 279

Words and music: Olga Carlson Brown (1894–1987) LDS

Olga Brown was born in Logan, Utah and after graduating from the University of Utah and teaching in elementary schools, she returned to teach at Utah State University. From 1940–1964 she was a member of the Primary general board. She was executive secretary and director for the Salt Lake City Girl Scouts, and then served on the national staff.

The original title and first line was "Jenny Lou Loves to Stand" and was changed so that it was for boys, too. The artwork on this page was the sample Brother Hull submitted when we were selecting the artists for the *Children's Songbook*.

HEALTHY, WEALTHY, AND WISE, 280

Words: Benjamin Franklin (1706–1790)
Music: Moravian folk tune, arranged

Benjamin Franklin was born in Boston, Massachusetts, and is remembered as one of the founding fathers of the United States. Among his inventions were the Franklin stove and the discovery of electricity through his kite and key experiment. He was a printer and wrote many memorable sayings, including the words used for this song. The wit and wisdom he is known for served him well as an author and a diplomat.

The accompaniment evolved from chord symbols to a vamp, and finally to a staccato pattern. This was a musical refinement that Grietje Rowley added to the song but declined credit.

THE WISE MAN AND THE FOOLISH MAN, 281

Words and music: Southern folk song

The words are based on the parable in Matthew that Jesus told about the result of obeying or disobeying the counsel of the Lord. All the verses were included within the staff to show how they should fit with the rhythm.

The melody of the song is now in public domain, which means that it can be printed and recorded without a fee to the first person who claimed a written version of the song. Suggestions are given for actions, which is an important reason that the song is included. Children learn through movement, and a change of pace is needed to keep them actively involved. No one knows who first put actions to the song, and there are many ways that could be successful.

FELIZ CUMPLEANOS, 282

Words and music: Maurine Benson Ozment (1932–) LDS

Maurine Ozment has a master's degree in music education from Utah State University. She is an author, accompanist, conductor, and teacher from the pre-school to college levels. She said, "In our international church, music is one of the things that remains the same from one culture to the next, building bonds of unity among the members. One can travel the world over and not understand the language at church in a faraway land, but the familiar music of a beloved song can immediately bring feelings of security and belonging to one's heart. Oh, how I love our wonderful Primary songs and the joy they bring to people everywhere!"[184]

The expansion of the Church prompted the need for another verse that could include non-European countries. The Church Translation Department provided the words "Happy Birthday" in 18 major languages, and included the phonetic pronunciation and accent markings. The possibilities were based on the number of syllables and where the natural accents could match the music accents.

Author's Note: I have a new appreciation for anyone who translates songs into another language—it is difficult to work inside such limits. This was definitely one of the most unusual writing challenges I ever attempted. Finally, with only three note adjustments for additional syllables, I was able to fit Samoan, Japanese, and Korean into a second verse!

The author gave permission to add the additional verse, as well as to use the flat symbols as needed on line three rather than showing a key change. Perhaps the new verse could be sung to wish a child from one of those cultures a happy birthday in the language of their family.

YOUR HAPPY BIRTHDAY, 283

Words and music: Charlene Anderson Newell (1938–) LDS

Charlene Newell is the mother of twelve children. She loves the arts, spiritual education, children, and family. She graduated from Brigham Young University and also studied at the University of Utah, BYU–Hawaii, and the New England Conservatory of Music. Her music has been published in the *Friend,* and she won the 1977 Relief Society song contest. Sister Newell's music has been performed in the Tabernacle and at the dedication of the Nauvoo Monument to Women. She is an outstanding pianist and has taught private voice and organ lessons and music in Utah's Granite School District.

See also **Newell**, Charlene: He Died That We Might Live Again, 65 (music); Little Jesus, 39 (music); The Commandments, 112 (music); *Hymns,* A Key Was Turned in Latter Days, 310 (music).

PART THREE

HAPPY, HAPPY BIRTHDAY, 284

Words and music: Mildred E. Millett McNees (1925–2006) LDS

Mildred Millett NcNees said, "I'm grateful for the beautiful gift of music that God has given us to uplift and edify us in numerous ways."[185] When she was young she wanted piano lessons, but her father had died and there was no money. Luckily, a generous grade-school teacher taught her to play. She became an accompanist in church and school and later became a dancer through the high school dance program. She taught ballet lessons and piano lessons after she married. She realized the power Primary songs have on the lives of children when she was asked to be the Primary chorister. The birthday song she composed is a favorite and ranked number eight in the 1983 survey of Primary songs.

HAVE A VERY HAPPY BIRTHDAY! 284

Words: Mabel Jones Gabbott (1910–2004) LDS
Music: Michael Finlinson Moody (1941–) LDS

Mabel Jones Gabbott, the author, has worked on the staffs of the Church magazines and as a member of the YWMIA General Board and the General Church Music Committee. She chaired the Hymnbook Text Committee for the 1985 hymnbook. Sister Gabbott was a very small lady with a very large talent for writing, and has written the words for sixteen Primary songs and four hymns. She lived in Bountiful, Utah, and grew roses and cherries. She said, "I love to hear children sing."[186] Her lyrics have been set to music by many LDS composers, including Crawford Gates, Robert Cundick, Darwin Wolford, Robert Manookin, Nora Hogan, Lynn Lund, and Michael Moody.

Michael Finlinson Moody used the same tune for two of Sister Gabbott's poems, "Have a Very Happy Birthday" and "Have a Very Merry Christmas." Brother Moody used the same melody and meter but cleverly shifted the musical accent—that is, one poem begins on the upbeat and the other on the downbeat. This creates a feeling of familiarity but not of sameness and is the mark of a creative mind.

Dr. Moody earned his bachelor's and master's degrees in music theory and composition from Brigham Young University and a doctorate in church music from the University of Southern California. He became executive secretary and then chairman of the Church Music Department and directed the production of the 1985 hymnbook. He guided the Primary in every phase of the *Children's Songbook* preparation and at the

STORIES OF THE CHILDREN'S SONGBOOK

same time served as bishop and then stake president in Woods Cross, Utah. With his wife, Maria, he served as mission president in Haiti, and they are now music missionaries in Jerusalem.

See also **Gabbott**: Baptism, 100 (words); Before I Take the Sacrament, 73 (words); Did Jesus Really Live Again?, 64 (words); Father Up Above, 23 (words); Had I Been a Child, 80 (words); Have a Very Merry Christmas!, 51 (words); He Sent His Son, 34 (words); My Country, 224 (words); Samuel Tells of the Baby Jesus, 36 (words); Sleep, Little Jesus, 47 (words); The Family, 194 (words); There Was Starlight on the Hillside, 40 (words); To Think about Jesus, 71 (words); We Are Reverent, 27 (words); Who Is the Child, 46 (words); *Hymns*, In Humility, Our Savior, 172 (words); Lord, Accept Into Thy Kingdom, 236 (words); Rejoice, Ye Saints of Latter Days, 290 (words); We Have Partaken of Thy Love, 155 (words).

See also **Moody**: Faith, 96 (music); Have a Very Merry Christmas!, 51 (music); He Sent His Son, 34 (music); Sleep, Little Jesus, 47 (music); Teacher, Do You Love Me? 178 (words and music); There Was Starlight on the Hillside, 40 (music); Who Is the Child?, 46 (music); *Hymns*, Testimony, 137 (music).

YOU'VE HAD A BIRTHDAY, 285

Words and music: Barbara A. McConochie (1940–) LDS

Barbara McConochie began teaching piano at thirteen, the same year she was called to be ward organist. After graduating from college, she taught high school English and now has raised nine children. When she sent in her revised arrangement of "Keep the Commandments," she included a copy of a birthday round she had written for the children in her stake. It had just been determined not to include the traditional "Happy Birthday to You" in the songbook because the royalty fee had increased substantially since the contract for its use in the Nursery Manual. Sister McConochie's song was appealing and had the advantage of being used as a round, plus it fit in the exact space planned for the other song! It seemed more than a coincidence it came to our attention just when it did.

Sister McConochie had been serving on a Primary stake board when she received a request from a ward chorister to write a new birthday song. Her response came with a variety of suggestions. She said "You've Had a Birthday" can be sung (1) as a round, (2) with a group of children singing an ostinato (repeated pattern) on the words "happy birthday, happy

PART THREE

birthday" sung on F, F, high C, high C, on even quarter notes throughout the song, or (3) as an echo—boys sing two measures, girls repeat softly, continue with each additional two measures. Creative people always think of more than one way to do something!

See also **McConochie**: Keep the Commandments, 146 (words, music, obbligato); *Hymns*, Keep the Commandments, 303 (words, music).

STORIES OF THE CHILDREN'S SONGBOOK

Prelude Music

"Music is the greatest gift, indeed it is divine.
It puts to flight all sad thoughts." [187]
—Martin Luther (1483–1546),
Father of the Reformation

Thirteen classic piano selections are arranged by key so that you can play smoothly from one page to another. Six pieces are in the key of G major, three in C major, and four in F major. Darwin Wolford made simplifications of pieces he thought would be appropriate, and they were submitted for the voting process. The thirteen selected preludes are a collection from some of the greatest composers, including Tchaikovsky, Schubert, Mendelssohn, and Bach. Also included are several appropriate and beautiful selections written in our day by Brother Wolford and Sister Rowley.

IMPROMPTU, 288

Music: Franz Schubert (1797–1828) arrangement

Schubert was a child prodigy born in Vienna, Austria. He played the viola in his family string quartet and studied organ and theory. He won a scholarship to the Imperial Court Chapel Choir when he was eleven, and after his voice changed, he spent several years teaching with his father, who was a schoolmaster. He devoted most of his time to composing symphonies, string quartets, and his unique *Lieder*, which were romantic songs based on poems.

In a café one evening, he read aloud the words of a poem by Shakespeare which begins, "Hark, hark, the lark." A melody came to his mind and Franz wanted to write it down, but had no paper. A friend gave him a menu and scratched some music staves on the back of it. In the candlelight, the young composer wrote rapidly. He and his friends gathered around a piano later that night, and his new composition was sung for the first time—one of the most beautiful songs of the nineteenth century.

Schubert gave up teaching and lived in poverty because he lacked the ability to promote himself and his works. He said, "It sometimes seems to me as if I did not belong to this world at all."[188] He acknowledged that his talent was God-given, and shared it with a group of friends who called themselves the Schubertians. They enjoyed many evenings together playing games, dancing to his music, and singing his beautiful melodies. He wrote over 600 songs, as many as four in a day. Some favorites are "Serenade," "Ave Maria," and "Who Is Sylvia?" It is said that he slept with his glasses on so that he wouldn't have to look for them to begin composing in the morning. One close friend wrote, "Schubert had a devout nature and believed firmly in God and the immortality of the soul. His religious sense is also clearly expressed in many of his songs. At the time when he was in want he in no way lost courage, and if, at times, he had more than he needed he willingly shared it with others who appealed to him for alms."[189] He died of a fever diagnosed as typhus, the disease common in the city slums. He was only 31, and sadly, became popular only after his death. As he had wished, he was buried close to his hero, Ludwig van Beethoven. The beautiful melody and accompaniment of Schubert's "Impromptu" was simplified for the *Children's Songbook*.

See also **Schubert**: Andante, 294 (music); God is Watching Over All, 229 (music).

TO A WILD ROSE, 289

Music: Edward MacDowell (1861–1908) arrangement

Edward MacDowell's father was a successful businessman, which made it possible for his mother to take him to Paris. He studied with Marmontel, the teacher of Claude Debussy. MacDowell became head of the Darmstadt Conservatory piano department, and married one of his promising piano students. When he returned to the United States, he became the most important American composer of his time. Many of his works were composed in a cabin in the woods outside of Peterborough, New Hampshire. After a walk in the woods one morning, he dashed off a short piano piece. His wife found it crumpled on the floor, and rescued "To a Wild Rose," the most famous of his *Woodland Sketches*. Edward again traveled to Europe and visited the acclaimed 75-year-old Liszt, who arranged performances for him and helped to get his work published. MacDowell was appointed head of the Columbia University music department. After a nervous breakdown and declining health, he retreated to his woodland cabin. His wife made the property into the *MacDowell Colony* after his death and invited other composers, writers, and artists to compose, write, or paint in the peaceful setting.

EACH SUNDAY MORNING, 290

Music: Grietje Terburg Rowley (1927–) LDS

Grietje (GREE-chuh) **Rowley** played the piano for children in the Church for over twenty-five years. She composed many prelude pieces that have the same simply beautiful sound as the Primary songs. It was her idea to arrange the songs by key so that you could play from one page to the other without needing to modulate. She simplified, transposed, offered helpful suggestions, and proofed the notation of the words, markings, and notation of every song in the songbook *three* times!

Author's Note: Often when I was discouraged, she would remind me that this book was important to our Father in Heaven and that he would help us to do it in the best way.

Sister Rowley thinks that the songs we learn in Primary can bring us joy and comfort forever. When she writes songs, she tries to make them easy to sing, easy to play, and easy to remember. She has written over one hundred scripture melodies, making musical arrangements for scriptures that are important to her. She writes every day, and says it is more fun than washing dishes. Because of her contribution to the preparation of the *Children's Songbook*, we chose two of her preludes and put them next to MacDowell and Mozart.

See also **Rowley**: A Smile is Like the Sunshine, 267 (music); Distant Bells, 299 (music); I Want to Be a Missionary Now, 168 (words and music); Roll Your Hands, 274 (arrangement); Samuel Tells of the Baby Jesus, 36 (music); *Hymns*, Be Thou Humble, 130 (words and music).

IN QUIETUDE, 291

Music: Darwin Wolford (1936–) LDS

Darwin Wolford was a music professor at BYU–Idaho. He served on the 1985 Hymnbook Committee and was released about the time we were ready to implement changes needed for the Primary songs.

Author's Note: I asked Brother Moody if it would be possible to have Dr. Wolford's help, but he said he thought he deserved a rest and to think of someone else who could serve. Several months went by and I still felt the need for Brother Wolford's editing expertise. Later, Brother Wolford told me that one night after family prayer, his wife, Julie, said she had the feeling that Darwin would be involved in the children's songbook. He said to his wife that he didn't think so—he was "recuperating" from the hymnbook, and besides he had not been asked. By the time Brother Moody finally

PART THREE

agreed to at least inquire if Brother Wolford might help us, the thought had grown in his mind and he felt, as I did, that he was the one to do it. It was a monumental time commitment, with no recognition, and so I am especially pleased to acknowledge his years of service on the project. Batches of songs would be mailed to him with suggestions, and he was always able to fill the need. The musical standard of the book can be credited to his careful scrutiny and advice. We are very much in his debt.

See also **Wolford**: Beautiful Savior, 62 (arrangement); Had I Been a Child, 80 (music); I Am a Child of God, 2 (arrangement); I Have a Family Tree, 199 (music); Keep the Commandments, 146 (arrangement); Mary's Lullaby, 44 (arrangement); Our Chapel Is a Sacred Place, 30 (music); Stars Were Gleaming, 37 (arrangement); Supplication, 297 (music); Teach Me to Walk in the Light, 177 (obbligato); Thanks to Thee, 6 (music); The Lord Gave Me a Temple, 153 (music); *Hymns*, Sons of Michael, He Approaches, 51 (music); We Listen to a Prophet's Voice, 22 (music).

LOVING SHEPHERD, 292

Music: Louis Gottschalk (1829–1869) arranged

Louis Moreau Gottschalk was born in New Orleans of French parents. He studied piano at the age of three and at six was substitute organist for a church. His socially prominent family sent him to Paris to study with Hector Berlioz when he was thirteen. Gottschalk was the first American pianist to tour Europe and achieve an international reputation. Frederic Chopin predicted he would become a "king of pianists." Gottschalk was widely known as a conductor and composer and used Creole and Caribbean folk melodies in his compositions. Most of his concerts included "Le Banjo," "Ojos Creollos," and "Last Hope." He wrote during the romantic musical period. The appealing melody for "The Last Hope" has been paired with many hymn texts, and appears in the 1909 *Deseret Sunday School Songs* with Annie Pinnock Malin's text, "God, Our Father, Hear Us Pray."

See also **Gottschalk**: *Hymns*, God, Our Father, Hear Us Pray, 170 (music).

MORNING PRAYER, 292

Music: Peter Ilyich Tchaikovsky (1840–1890) arranged

Piotr Ilyich Tchaikovsky (Americanized spelling Tschaikowsky) is best known to children for his beloved *Nutcracker Suite* ballet music.

STORIES OF THE CHILDREN'S SONGBOOK

Album for the Young is piano music about children, but not necessarily for children to perform because of the musical demands. It includes titles such as "The Hobby Horse," "The Sick Doll," and "Morning Prayer." His emotional music appeals directly to the heart.

Peter had a fragile temperament and never got over the death of his mother when he was only 14. His father was a mining engineer and encouraged him to study law in St. Petersburg, Russia, which he did. He worked in the ministry of justice and despised the job, resigning to become a music professor at the Moscow Conservatory. His first compositions were not well received—Piano Concerto No. 1 was rejected as unplayable, and *Swan Lake* ballet was considered a failure. The best known of his early work is the Fantasy Overture to *Romeo and Juliet*. After an unhappy marriage and a nervous breakdown, he gave up teaching and concentrated on composing. A wealthy widow gave him a handsome annual income so that he could continue writing. The *1812 Overture,* celebrating the defeat of Napoleon in Russia, and *Sleeping Beauty* ballet are two of his many works which have become favorites in the Romantic repertoire. Tchaikovsky is revered as one of the greatest symphonic composers.

MY HEART EVER FAITHFUL, 293

Music: Johann Sebastian Bach (1685–1750) arranged

Seven generations of Bachs were professional musicians, but they were not famous in their own lifetimes. **Johann Sebastian Bach** studied harpsichord, organ, clavichord, and violin from other family members. He was orphaned at age nine, and he and his brother, Josef, went to live with an older brother, Christoph, and his wife. Johann became a choirboy at St. Michael's Church in Lüneberg and loved music so much that he walked up to thirty miles to hear famous musicians perform. He married Maria Barbara, who bore him seven children. A prestigious post as organist to Duke Wilhelm Ernst was granted to him, and Bach began composing in earnest. He then became *Capellmeiste*r of the court of Prince Leopold and wrote the famous "Brandenburg Concertos" plus two collections of preludes and fugues for keyboard called *The Well-Tempered Clavier.* When Maria died, he married Anna Magdalena and she bore him 13 more children. He taught all of his children music lessons, but only nine lived to be adults. Bach's wife and his older children helped him copy music for different instruments and for his students.

Bach was from first to last a church musician. He became the Cantor at Leipzig's Thomas School and worked there the rest of his life. He was enormously productive, composing nearly three hundred church cantatas and the *St. Matthew Passion*. When asked the secret of his genius, he modestly replied, "I was made to work; if you are equally industrious you will be equally successful." He told a student, "Just practice diligently, and it will go very well. You have five fingers on each hand just as healthy as mine."[190] Because he was a master of counterpoint and harmony, the rules of composition evolved from the study of his music. He often signed his manuscripts "S.D.G"—Soli De Gloria, "To God alone, the glory." In the margin of his Bible at 2 Chronicles 5:13 he wrote, "Where there is devotional music, God is always at hand with his gracious presence."[191] His eyes began failing, and by his death he was completely blind. He was buried in an unmarked grave.

During his lifetime, Bach was known more for his excellent organ playing than for composing. Years after his death, Felix Mendelssohn arranged for Bach's music to be performed, collected, and published into sixty volumes of compositions. Johann Bach was the conclusion to the Baroque period, and one of the greatest creative geniuses in human history.

ANDANTE, 294

Music: Franz Schubert (1797–1828) arranged

Franz Schubert was a child prodigy born in Vienna, Austria. He played the viola in his family's string quartet and studied organ and theory. He won a scholarship to the Imperial Court Chapel Choir when he was eleven, and after his voice changed he spent several years teaching with his father, who was a schoolmaster. He devoted most of his time to composing symphonies, string quartets, and his unique *Lieder*, which were romantic songs based on poems.

In a café one evening, Schubert read aloud a poem by Shakespeare which begins, "Hark, hark, the lark." A melody came to his mind and Franz wanted to write it down but had no paper. A friend gave him a menu and scratched some music staves on the back of it. In the candlelight, the young composer wrote rapidly. He and his friends gathered around a piano later that night, and his new composition was sung for the first time—one of the most beautiful songs of the nineteenth century.

Schubert gave up teaching to compose. He lived in poverty because he lacked the ability to promote himself and his works. He said, "It sometimes seems to me as if I did not belong to this world at all."[192] He acknowledged that his talent was God-given, and shared it with a group of friends who called themselves the "Schubertians." They enjoyed many evenings together playing games, dancing to his music, and singing his beautiful melodies. He wrote over six hundred songs—as many as four in a day. Some favorites are "Serenade," "Ave Maria," and "Who Is Sylvia?" It is said that he slept with his glasses on so that he wouldn't have to look for them to begin composing in the morning. One close friend wrote, "Schubert had a devout nature and believed firmly in God and the immortality of the soul. His religious sense is also clearly expressed in many of his songs. At the time when he was in want he in no way lost courage, and if, at times, he had more than he needed he willingly shared it with others who appealed to him for alms."[193] He died of a fever diagnosed as typhus, the disease common in the city slums. He was only 31 and sadly, his music did not become popular until after his death. As he had wished, he was buried close to his hero, Ludwig van Beethoven.

The melodious "Andante" by Schubert was simplified for the *Children's Songbook*.

See also **Schubert**: God is Watching Over All, 229 (music); Impromptu, 288 (music).

O REST IN THE LORD, 295

Music: Felix Mendelssohn (1809–1847) arranged

Felix Mendelssohn is considered one of the great German pianists, composers and conductors. The name "Felix" in Latin means "happy man" and he lived his life optimistically expecting to be successful. He grew up in a refined and cultured family with choir and orchestral concerts in their home. At the age of nine he began performing with his older sister, Fanny. When people would compliment him on his playing, he would say, "You should hear my sister!"[194]

Felix performed public concerts and composed symphonies and operas when only eleven years old. He wrote many "songs without words" for friends, and often would enclose one in a birthday card or letter. He and Fanny performed his piano duet, "Overture to A Midsummer Night's Dream," at a Sunday evening gathering for friends. Years later, when the Shakespearean play had been translated into German, King Wilhelm requested that Felix write music for the entire story. "The Wedding March" from *A Midsummer Night's Dream* has been played at weddings all over the world. Mendelssohn conducted his own works in Germany and England, including his Oratorio, *Elijah*. "O Rest in the

Lord" is from this well-received Oratorio. Mendelssohn opened his own conservatory in 1843 and continued to travel and perform. As a boy, he had been spellbound by the Bach *St. Matthew Passion*, and with his influence he initiated, after decades of obscurity, the "Bach revival."

Mendelssohn believed in divine inspiration but combined it with a strong work ethic. He said, "I know perfectly well that no musician can make his thoughts or his talents different to what Heaven has made them; but I also know that if Heaven had given him good ones, he must also be able to develop them properly."[195] In 1847, his sister died as she was practicing one of his compositions. The great shock of her death caused him to lose consciousness and fall, rupturing a blood vessel in his head. He never recovered and died a few months later at the age of thirty-eight. He had been married for ten years and left a widow and five children. His symphonies, chamber and piano music, oratorios, and choral music, particularly "Ave Maria," are the legacy of a happy but disciplined and hard-working man.

See also **Mendelssohn**: If With All Your Hearts, 15 (music); *Hymns*, Cast Thy Burden upon the Lord, 110 (music); Hark! The Herald Angels Sing, 209 (music); O God, the Eternal Father, 175 (music).

AIR FROM ORPHEUS, 296

Music: Christoph W. von Gluck (1714–1787) arranged

Christoph Willibald von Gluck was born in Bavaria. His father worked in forestry and Christoph's musical inclination caused him to leave home and make his way to Prague. He supported himself playing in churches and completed his musical studies there and in Italy. Gluck wrote operas in the Italian tradition, but as he began to give greater unity to text and music, he reformed the traditional style of opera. He also wrote for orchestra, chamber music, ballet, choral, and songs during the classical period.

"Air from Orpheus" is a piano reduction from the opera, *Orfeo ed Euridice* which he composed in 1762. *Iphigenie en Tauride* (1779) is considered his masterpiece.

SUPPLICATION, 297

Darwin Wolford was a music professor at BYU–Idaho and holds a PhD in organ and composition. He is widely published, and his works have been performed by the Mormon Tabernacle Choir and the Utah Symphony. He served on the General Church Music Committee and the

1985 Hymnbook Executive Committee. We are very much indebted to him for his expertise in simplifying and refining the songs for the 1989 *Children's Songbook*. It was a monumental time commitment with no recognition, yet he gave cheerful service on the project. Batches of songs would be mailed to him with suggestions, and he was always able to fill the need. The high musical standard of the book can be credited to his careful scrutiny and advice.

See also **Wolford**: Beautiful Savior, 62 (arrangement); Had I Been a Child, 80 (music); I Am a Child of God, 2 (arrangement); I Have a Family Tree, 199 (music); In Quietude, 291 (music); Keep the Commandments, 146 (arrangement); Mary's Lullaby, 44 (arrangement); Our Chapel Is a Sacred Place, 30 (music); Stars Were Gleaming, 37 (arrangement); Teach Me to Walk in the Light, 177(obbligato); Thanks to Thee, 6 (music); The Lord Gave Me a Temple, 153 (music); *Hymns*, Sons of Michael, He Approaches, 51 (music); We Listen to a Prophet's Voice, 22 (music).

PRELUDE IN F, 298

Music: Wolfgang Amadeus Mozart (1765–1791) arranged

Mozart was a boy-genius. He picked up his father Leopold's violin and was able to play without any instruction. Leopold was a fine musician in Salzburg, Austria, and when Wolfgang was four years old, he gave him piano lessons. Little Mozart composed his own pieces when he was five, and many are in books that piano students study today. His older sister, Nannerl, called him "Wolfie" and they gave concerts together, often for royalty. He was a concert pianist, an organist, a conductor, and a composer. Unfortunately, he never received a well-paid position, and struggled constantly against poverty. Mozart believed his talent was a gift from God. He said, "God is ever before my eyes. I realize His omnipotence and I fear His anger; but I also recognize His love, His compassion, and His tenderness towards His creatures."[196] Mozart's motivation to compose was internal, and not dependent on the praise or recompense of others. He wrote in a letter, "Let us put our trust in God and console ourselves with the thought that all is well, if it is in accordance with the will of the Almighty, as He knows best what is profitable and beneficial to our temporal happiness and our eternal salvation."[197]

Mozart had enormous energy for composing. He worked out the ideas in his mind, and then wrote as though by dictation—never changing any of the notes he had written. His barber complained about the difficulty of dressing Mozart's hair, as he would dash to the keyboard as ideas came, leaving the barber to run after him. Once, when he had no money to give a beggar, he took the man to a coffeehouse and quickly wrote a Minuet and Trio, which he gave to the man with a letter to a publisher. The beggar received five guineas as a result.

Mozart's health, which had always been fragile, caused an early death at the age of thirty-five. He had written more than six hundred works including church requiems, operas, symphonies, concertos, sonatas, and chamber and choral pieces. During the suffering of his last year he was working on a requiem, and sang dictation for it the night before he died.

See also **Mozart**: I Pledge Myself to Love the Right, 161 (music).

DISTANT BELLS, 299

Music: Grietje Terburg Rowley LDS (1927–)

Grietje (GREE-chuh) **Rowley** played the piano for children in church for over twenty-five years. During that time, she composed many prelude pieces with the same simple and beautiful sound as the Primary songs. Because of her contribution to the preparation of the *Children's Songbook*, two of her preludes were selected and placed next to MacDowell and Mozart. It was Sister Rowley's idea to arrange the preludes by key so that you could play from one page to the other without needing to modulate. She simplified, transposed, offered helpful suggestions, and proofed the notation of the words, markings, and notation of every song in the songbook *three* times!

Author's Note: Often when I was discouraged, she would remind me that this book was important to our Father in Heaven and that he would help us to do it in the best way.

Sister Rowley thinks that the songs we learn in Primary can bring us joy and comfort forever. When she writes songs, she tries to make them easy to sing, easy to play, and easy to remember. She has written over one hundred scripture melodies, making musical arrangements for scriptures that are important to her. She writes every day and says it is more fun than washing dishes.

See also **Rowley**: A Smile is Like the Sunshine, 267 (music); Each Sunday Morning, 290 (music); I Want to Be a Missionary Now, 168 (words and music); Roll Your Hands, 274 (arrangement); Samuel Tells of the Baby Jesus, 36 (music); *Hymns*, Be Thou Humble, 130 (words and music).

Notes

1. Marion G. Romney, *Friend*, Sept. 1971, 13.
2. Smith and Carlson, *The Gift of Music*, 260.
3. *Ensign*, Oct. 1936, 111.
4. *Friend*, Oct. 1984, 14.
5. *Friend*, Oct. 1984, 14.
6. *LDS Church News*, Apr. 1, 1978.
7. Pers. Comm., 1990.
8. Daryl Van Dam Hoole, pers. comm., 12 Feb. 2004.
9. Cannon, *Our Children's Songs*, 278.
10. *Friend*, Oct. 1985, 15.
11. Pers. comm., May 2006.
12. Perry, *Songs From My Heart*, 59.
13. Diane Bastian, pers. comm.
14. Cannon, *Our Children's Songs*, 341.
15. *Friend*, Oct. 1986, 45.
16. Pers. comm., May 2006.
17. Pers. comm.
18. *Friend*, Oct. 1985, 14.
19. Ibid., 1986, 45.
20. *Friend*, Oct. 1984, 15.
21. Ibid.
22. Ibid., 1985, 14.
23. Cannon, *Our Children's Songs*, 27.
24. Pers. comm., May 2006.
25. *Friend*, Oct. 1985, 14.
26. Ibid.
27. Ibid., 15.
28. Ibid., 14.
29. Ibid., 1986, 45.
30. Cannon, *Our Children's Songs*, 258.
31. Ibid., 258.
32. Ibid., 325.
33. *Friend*, Oct. 1985, 14.
34. Ibid., 15.
35. Ibid., 1986, 44.
36. Ibid., 1985, 15.
37. Ibid.
38. Ibid., 14.
39. Ibid., 15.
40. Cannon, *Our Children's Songs*, 36.
41. *Friend*, Oct. 1986, 45.
42. Ibid., Oct. 1985, 14.
43. Diane Cahoon, pers. comm., Nov. 1990.
44. Pers. comm., May 2006.
45. Cannon, *Our Children's Songs*, 239.
46. Ibid.
47. Pers. comm., May 2006.
48. *Friend*, Oct. 1985, 14.
49. Cannon, *Our Children's Songs*, 339.
50. Ibid., 289.
51. Ibid., 236.
52. Pers. comm, May 2006.
53. Perry, *Songs from My Heart*, 36.
54. *Friend*, Oct. 1985, 14.
55. Cannon, *Our Children's Songs*, 253.
56. *Ensign*, May 1986, 45.
57. *Friend*, Oct. 1984, 15.
58. Cannon, *Our Children's Songs*, 281.
59. Ibid., 227, 281.
60. Ibid., 153, 306.
61. Ibid., 153.
62. Ibid., 281.
63. Ibid.
64. Ibid., 58.
65. Ibid., 309.
66. *Friend*, Oct. 1985, 14.
67. Cannon, *Our Children's Songs*, 53, 304.
68. *Friend*, Oct. 1985, 15.
69. Ibid., 14.
70. Cannon, *Our Children's Songs*, 309.
71. Ibid., 256.

PART THREE

72 Ibid., 322.
73 Ibid., 309.
74 Ibid., 277.
75 Ibid., 175.
76 Ibid., 290.
77 *Children's Songbook,* preface, iii.
78 Cannon, *Our Children's Songs,* 276.
79 Ibid., 54.
80 *Friend,* Oct. 2006, 40.
81 Ibid., 1984, 14.
82 Cannon, *Our Children's Songs,* 283.
83 Ibid., 299.
84 Pers. comm., May 2006.
85 Cannon, *Our Children's Songs,* 329, 128.
86 Pers. comm., May 2006.
87 *Friend,* Oct. 1985, 15.
88 Ibid.
89 Pers. comm.
90 *Friend,* Oct. 1986, 45.
91 Ibid., 45; quote from music spotlight.
92 Pers. comm.
93 Cannon, *Our Children's Songs,* 289.
94 *Friend,* Oct. 1984, 15.
95 Cannon, *Our Children's Songs,* 315.
96 Ibid., 107.
97 *Friend,* Oct. 1984, 14.
98 Ibid., 1985, 15.
99 Cannon, *Our Children's Songs,* 115.
100 *Friend,* Oct. 1985, 14.
101 Cannon, *Our Children's Songs,* 289.
102 Perry, *Songs from My Heart,* 95.
103 *Friend,* Oct. 1984, 15.
104 Cannon, *Our Children's Songs,* 336.
105 *Friend,* Oct. 1984, 15.
106 Kavanaugh, *The Spiritual Lives of Great Composers,* 29, 32.
107 Cannon, *Our Children's Songs,* 108.
108 Pers. comm., May 2006.
109 *Ensign,* Oct. 2003, 64–65.
110 Pers. comm., 12 Apr. 2005.
111 Ibid., May 2006.
112 Ibid.
113 *Friend,* Oct. 1986, 44.
114 Ibid.
115 Cannon, *Our Children's Songs,* 91.
116 Ibid., 230.
117 *Friend,* Oct. 1984, 15; also *A Children's Songbook Companion,* 200.
118 *Friend,* Oct. 1985, 15.
119 Cannon, *Our Children's Songs,* 276.
120 Ibid., 80.
121 *Hymns,* preface, ix–x.
122 Pers. Comm., May, 2006.
123 Cannon, *Our Children's Songs,* 49.
124 Ibid., 332.
125 Perry, *Songs from My Heart,* 38.
126 Cannon, *Our Children's Songs,* 322.
127 Ibid., 289.
128 Ibid., 213.
129 *Friend,* Oct. 1985, 14.
130 Ibid.
131 Ibid.
132 Ibid.
133 Ibid., 1986, 45.
134 Cannon, *Our Children's Songs,* 346.
135 Ibid., 98.
136 Ibid., 312.
137 Ibid., 309.
138 Ibid., 141.
139 Ibid., 310.
140 Ibid., 271.
141 Ibid., 143.
142 *Complete Poetical Works of James Whitcomb Riley,* 339, available from Litfinder.com.

143 Pers. comm. with her daughter, May 2006.
144 *Friend,* Oct. 1984, 14.
145 Ibid.; Pers. comm. from her daughter, Sister Clauson, May 2006.
146 Cannon, *Our Children's Songs,* 306–307.
147 Ibid., 162.
148 Ibid., 313–314.
149 Pers. comm., May 2006.
150 Kenney, ed., *Wilford Woodruff's Journal,* 7:367–69.
151 Cannon, *Our Children's Songs,* 142.
152 Ibid., 142.
153 *Friend,* Oct. 1986, 45.
154 *Ensign,* May 1984, 21.
155 BYU Church Music Workshop, 1984, author's notes.
156 *Friend,* Oct. 1984, 15.
157 Kavanaugh, *Spiritual Lives,* 47.
158 Ibid., 45
159 *Friend,* Oct. 1986, 45
160 *LDS Church News,* also my notes
161 *Friend,* Oct. 1985, 14.
162 Cannon, *Our Children's Songs,* 289
163 Pers. comm., *Friend,* Oct. 1986, 45.
164 Cannon, *Our Children's Songs,* 308.
165 Pers. comm.
166 *Friend,* Oct. 1985, 14.
167 Ibid.
168 Carolee Eriksson, teacher, pers. comm.
169 Ibid., 270.
170 Ibid., 119.
171 Ibid.; Cannon, *Our Children's Songs,* 328.
172 *Friend,* Oct. 1985, 14.
173 Pers. comm.
174 *Friend,* Oct. 1986, 45.
175 Cannon, *Our Children's Songs,* 308.
176 Pers. comm., *Friend,* Oct. 1986, 45.
177 Cannon, *Our Children's Songs,* 329.
178 *LDS Church News,* "Stake sponsors interfaith conference on special needs," 25 Oct. 2003.
179 *Friend,* Oct. 1985, 14.
180 Ibid.
181 Cannon, *Our Children's Songs,* 309.
182 *Friend,* Oct. 1986, 45.
183 Cannon, *Our Children's Songs,* 308.
184 Ibid., 329.
185 Ibid., 321.
186 *Friend,* Oct. 1985, 14.
187 Ibid., 1984, 36.
188 Kavanaugh, *Spiritual Lives,* 47.
189 Ibid., 45.
190 Ibid., 16.
191 Ibid., 15.
192 Ibid., 47.
193 Ibid., 45.
194 Montgomery and Hinson, *Stories of the Great Composers,* 19.
195 Kavanaugh, *Spiritual Lives,* 53–54.
196 Ibid., 29.
197 Ibid., 32.

Appendix One

Stories and author/composer information about Primary Songs that are in the Hymnbook but not in the Children's Songbook

GOD'S DAILY CARE, 306 (Hymns)

Words: Marie C. Turk
Music: Willy Reske (1897–1991) LDS

Marie C. Turk was born and lived in Arizona and wrote and published books of poetry. Many of her works were for Lutheran publications and it is thought that she lived into the 1950s.

Most of **Willy Reske's** compositions are large-scale works for organ or choir, and this eight-measure melody may seem almost inconsequential by comparison. He himself remarked, "It is just a 'little ditty,' but if people love it and sing it, that is all that matters." Brother Reske was born in Königsberg, Germany, and after being baptized a Latter-day Saint, he immigrated to the United States. He has composed hundreds of hymns, anthems, and organ pieces during his career of musical performance and composition. He worked for thirty-three years as organist of St. Paul's Evangelical Lutheran Church in New York City.

This short prayer song is a true Primary "gem." It was selected for inclusion in the hymnbook because it appeals to both children and leaders. That was, however, both a compliment and a "death knell" as it is now quite overlooked.

Author's Note: I think we made a mistake by not creating a different arrangement of it and making space for it in the Children's Songbook.

See also **Reske**: *Hymns,* Thy Servants Are Prepared, 261; 329 (music).

IN OUR LOVELY DESERET, 307 (Hymns)

Words: Eliza R. Snow (1804–1887) LDS
Music: George F. Root (1820–1895)

Eliza Roxey Snow used the catchy tune of the popular Civil War song, "Tramp, Tramp, Tramp" to teach many valuable lessons. The marching song had great appeal and was probably the first song written for the children of the Church. President Spencer W. Kimball told of the song's indelible influence on him:

APPENDIX ONE

I remember the song "In Our Lovely Deseret." . . . I can remember how lustily we sang:

> Hark! Hark! Hark! 'tis children's music,
> Children's voices, O, how sweet. . . .

I remember we sang:
> That the children may live long,
> And be beautiful and strong.

I wanted to live a long time and I wanted to be beautiful and strong— but never reached it.
> Tea and coffee and tobacco they despise.

And I learned to despise them. . . . The song goes on:
> Drink no liquor, and they eat
> But a very little meat

[I still don't eat very much meat.]
> They are seeking to be great and good and wise. . . .

And then we'd "Hark! Hark! Hark" again.[1]

Most people think of Eliza R. Snow as the first great poet of the Church. Before she was twenty-one, she had received a prize for a poem she wrote about the deaths of Adams and Jefferson. After joining the Church at age thirty-one, she helped convert her brother, Lorenzo, who became the fifth President of the Church. Besides teaching school in Kirtland and Nauvoo, she was the first secretary and then the second General President of the Relief Society. She also helped organize the Mutual Improvement Association and the Primary. Sister Snow had a watch that belonged to the prophet, Joseph, and when she would visit Primaries, she would tell the children about him and let them hold his watch.

George F. Root was a native of Massachusetts and is most famous for his Civil War songs, such as "Tramp, Tramp, Tramp" and "The Battle Cry of Freedom." In addition to his original words and Sister Snow's poem, the melody of the chorus has also been used with the words "Jesus Loves the Little Children." Mr. Root taught at music schools in New York and Boston, and became one of America's best-known composers of popular music, including hymns, ballads, and sentimental songs.

See also **Root**: *Hymns*, Hark, All Ye Nations! 264 (music); School Thy Feelings, 336 (music).

See also **Snow**: *Hymns* (words only), Again We Meet Around the Board,

APPENDIX ONE

186; Awake, Ye Saints of God, Awake! 17; Behold the Great Redeemer Die, 191; Great Is the Lord, 77; How Great the Wisdom and the Love, 195; In Our Lovely Deseret, 307; O My Father, 292; The Time Is Far Spent, 266; Though Deepening Trials, 122; Truth Reflects upon Our Senses, 273.

THE LIGHT DIVINE, 305 (Hymns)

Words: Matilda Watts Cahoon (1881–1973) LDS
Music: Mildred Tanner Pettit (1895–1977) LDS

"The Light Divine" was printed in *The Primary Song Book* in 1939, and remained in Primary songbook collections until 1985 when it was included in the hymnbook. Now it is enjoyed by new members as well as those who sang the song in their Primary days.

At the Hymn Celebration in the Assembly Hall in 1985, President Gordon B. Hinckley paid tribute to **Matilda Watts Cahoon**. He said, "She somehow coaxed a tune out of me as a part of the boy's chorus in junior high school. She was a great and delightful and lovely teacher."[2] She taught in the public schools for thirty-nine years, was the first woman delegate to the state legislature from Salt Lake County, and served from 1913–1939 on the Primary general board.

Mildred Tanner Pettit was a descendant of original Utah pioneers. She studied piano, pipe organ and composition at the McCune School of Music and also attended the Latter-day Saints College in Salt Lake City. After teaching school, she married William A. Pettit, a medical school graduate. For thirty-five years she served in the Primary, with four of those years on the Primary general board. During that time, she wrote many programs and 145 songs for children. When she was composing the music for "The Light Divine," she thought the melody of the last line should go up, but finally ended with a firm downward motion on "truth, our guiding star."

See also **Cahoon**: Beauty Everywhere, 232 (words).

See also **Pettit**: Beauty Everywhere, 232 (music); Father, I Will Reverent Be, 29 (music); I Am a Child of God, 2 (music); Mother Dear, 206 (music); Hymns, I Am a Child of God, 301 music).

Notes

1   Spencer W. Kimball, "Strengthening the Family—the Basic Unit of the Church," *Ensign*, May 1978, 47.
2   Gordon B. Hinckley, *LDS Church News*.

Appendix Two

Reviews of the Children's Songbook

A. Responses to the Publication of the 1989 *Children's Songbook*

"I am convinced that this new songbook will be one of the most effective tools the Lord will use in helping the children of the Church fight the evils of Satan. Because Satan so freely uses and abuses music for his good, I am excited to think about our children arming themselves with the teachings of the Gospel that they have learned through music."—Lynn Dayton, mother.

"This songbook is a reflection of the doctrine of the Church. Previous collections promoted "doing good" but without a lot of messages particular to the LDS Church. The book is the epitome of great work, and I hope nothing will dilute the standard that has been set. It promotes the pure, classic sweetness of the singing of children."—Vanja Y. Watkins, composer, music educator.

"In looking at the songbook, I feel as though I have been in the library and come upon a classic—a familiar friend—timeless, but with a new surprise on every page."—Carolee G. Eriksson, music educator, pianist.

"There is a spirit about the book."—Jean Smith, Clinical Psychologist.

B. Ann E. Cannon, "The New *Children's Songbook*," *Ensign*, June 1989, 15 (excerpts)

It's not just for Primary, but for the home and family as well.

Alec is a four-year-old Sunbeam. He likes cartoons, action figures, and hot dogs (always without ketchup, sometimes without the bun). He dislikes shoes and socks and girls—especially girls. He has plenty of muscles that he'll gladly show you—if you beg. Alec also loves to sing Primary songs. Resolutely. Joyfully. And very loudly. His favorite?

"THE GOLDEN PLATES!" he roars.

"The Golden Plates" also happens to be the favorite song of his mother, Annlouise. "Every time we sang that song in Primary when I was a little girl," she remembers, "I used to wonder what the actual golden plates looked like, what they felt like." Annlouise pauses, then smiles. "I was positive that they must have been very heavy for Joseph Smith to carry."

"The Golden Plates," with its familiar lyrics and lilting melody, serves as a link between mother and son, connecting her past with his present. Indeed, many of the best-loved Primary songs—"I Am a Child of God," "Give, Said the Little Stream," "Jesus Wants Me for a Sunbeam"—fill this purpose: they provide a sort of cultural continuity between the Church's children and its adults. "Primary songs," says Michael Moody, chairman of the Church Music Committee, "allow our children to join their voices with the voices of children of earlier times in their expression of the gospel." In addition, says Primary General President Michaelene P. Grassli, "they bring gospel principles into the lives of our children in a joyous way."

And it is for our children that the Church has just published a new Primary songbook. According to Betty Jo Jepsen, first counselor in the Primary General Presidency, the task was undertaken "to consolidate the various existing resources of children's music." Those resources include *Sing with Me*, *More Songs for Children*, *Supplement to More Songs for Children*, *Activity Songs and Verses*, songs published in the *Friend* and the *Ensign*, and songs used in the Primary's annual children's sacrament meeting presentations.

These music resources were reviewed, edited, and compiled—with a new twist. "In the past, songbooks have been published mostly for Primary leaders to use in teaching children," says Pat Graham, a former music chairman of the Primary general board. "Although Primary music leaders and accompanists will continue to teach from this new resource, this book really is for the children."

Appropriately enough, the new book is simply entitled *Children's Songbook*. . . . The preface will begin with "Dear boys and girls," rather than "Dear parents and teachers."

Children of all ages will no doubt be attracted by the songbook's charming, picture-book appearance. Delicate full-color illustrations appear throughout, and two-page spreads introduce each new section. . . . Other attractive features of the new book include pastel-colored borders around each page (songs in the same section sport the same color) and a section in the back called "Using the Songbook." There are also assorted indices of authors and composers, topics, and titles and first lines. . . . While the book's design and illustrations capture the eye, its songs capture the ear—and the heart.

APPENDIX TWO

C. *Children's Songbook* Critique for Hymn Society of America—Hugh D. McKellar

This book is squarely aimed at children already within the household of faith, who require only guidance as they grow in wisdom, stature, and grace. . . . The editors (who are never named) give every indication of genuinely liking and respecting children. They see no harm in grounding young Saints firmly in the fundamentals of their faith, meanwhile exhorting them to behave themselves in church and elsewhere, and to treat other people, even their closest relatives, decently and courteously.

Except for a few classics and folk-airs, most of the lyrics and tunes are the work of living Saints; . . . Melodies unfold gracefully, accompaniments involve enough rhythmical and harmonic sophistications to ensure that a child who grows up on this book will not be lastingly trapped within the confines of one idiom. . . . Perhaps the editors aim at treating children much as the angel in Acts 12 treated the impulsive apostle: coming to him where he was, meeting his immediate need, walking with him through one street—and then, when Peter was fit to carry on without him, departing.[1]

D. The *Children's Songbook* Receives Award of Excellence

The *Children's Songbook* not only presents fine music for the children of the LDS Church, but its appearance and presentation are excellent. The *Children's Songbook* received an award of excellence in book design from the Art Directors of Salt Lake City.[2]

Notes

1   *The Hymn*, vol. 40, no. 4, 38.
2   Cannon, *Our Children's Songs*, preface, viii.

Appendix Three

Children's Songbook *activity pages*

A. Getting Acquainted with the *Children's Songbook*

Here is an activity that will help you get acquainted with the *Children's Songbook*. You can look for the answers by yourself or with your family or friends.

1. What is the purpose of the *Children's Songbook*? (See last paragraph in the preface).
2. What are the names of the sections of the songbook? (See headings on the Contents). Turn to the double-page picture at the beginning of each section by finding the first page of each color.
3. Hum the introduction for "I Am a Child of God" (follow the brackets at the beginning and the end of the song).
4. Look up the scripture references given for "Book of Mormon Stories" (see the lower right-hand corner of the song).
5. Name two songs about missionary work (see topical index under "Missionary").
6. Name three songs by the same composer (see composer/author index).
7. About when was "Beautiful Savior" written? (See lower left-hand corner of the song).
8. How would you conduct "Called to Serve"? (Locate the song number in the alphabetical title index, read the time signature at the beginning of the music, then turn to "Using the Songbook" and find the correct beat pattern). *See also*: "Hymn Hunt" for information about the hymnbook, and a similar activity. Sharing Time Page, *Friend*, Nov. 1985, 22. This was the year the hymnbook was published.

B. *Children's Songbook* Trivia Page

You can become an expert on facts about the *Children's Songbook* by filling in the blanks with the following words (which are in order). Make copies and try this for a family home evening activity. *1989; Children's;*

APPENDIX THREE

500,000; 21; 268; survey; topics; 13; 19; Church; preface; importance; table of contents; topical; cross-referencing; gospel; music; teaching; conducting; accompanying; features; 198; birth; scripture; message; simplified; chord; fingering; verses; alternate; actions; descants; obbligatos; illustrated; sound; 185; cover; section; 8; plan; principles; spiral; pocket edition.

In _____, a new _____ Songbook was published by The Church of Jesus Christ of Latter-day Saints. _____ copies were made on the first printing, and eventually the book was translated into _____ languages. There are _____ songs in the book. They were selected by a _____ and a committee according to _____ needed. There are _____ simple preludes and _____ "new" songs. All other songs were in previous _____ publications.

The _____ explains the _____ of music in our lives. The _____ _____ shows the order of the songs within each section, and the _____ index includes _____. Using the Songbook states the purpose of the book, which is to teach children the _____ through _____. This section also gives tips on _____, _____, and _____ and discusses the _____ of the book.

_____ composers and authors are represented in this volume. Their _____ dates are given at the bottom of the page, along with _____ references that support the _____ of the song.

The songs in this book have been _____ and _____ symbols and _____ have been added to help make them easier to play. Some new _____ have been added, as well as suggestions for _____ words and instructions for _____. Several new _____ and _____ were composed.

The pages are beautifully _____ so that the book looks like the songs _____. There are _____ small pictures, a lovely _____ illustration, and double-page drawings for each _____. The _____ sections of the book tell a story about the _____ of salvation and the _____ we believe in.

The book is available in a hardback _____ binding, or a paperback _____ size edition.

C. How to Make a Melody

(For full text and activity with composer and author pictures, see "Fun with Favorites," Pat Graham, Friend, *Oct. 1984, 14–15.)*

If you were to visit Primary anywhere in the world, you would feel right at home because the boys and girls would be singing the same songs that you sing in your Primary.

A person who writes the lyrics (words, or text) of a song is the author, and his name is printed in the upper left corner of published music.

The person who writes the music for a song is the composer, and his name is in the upper right corner of the printed music. Sometimes a writer and a musician work together to write a song. Other times a composer will use the words of a poem or a scripture for the text of a song. Occasionally the same person writes both the words and the music.

Sometimes a person creates a melody and another person arranges it, or in other words makes an accompaniment. Or an existing melody and accompaniment may be arranged by simplifying it, or adding an alto part, or adding an obbligato for voice or instrument.

D. Music Matching Game

(For full text and activity with composer and author pictures, see "Fun with Favorites," Pat Graham, Friend, *Oct. 1985, 14.)*

Ideas for writing songs can come in many ways. Some Primary songs, such as "Love One Another," begin with a scripture. Sometimes a poem written by one person is given a melody and accompaniment by another person. "He Sent His Son" was written this way. Occasionally a composer or author is asked to write a song to explain or teach a particular principle of the gospel. "I Know My Father Lives" and "Families Can Be Together Forever" are examples of this method.

Songs can also originate with the words of a child—"Popcorn Popping on the Apricot Tree"—or with a teacher and children pretending—"Once There Was a Snowman." Songs may also be about an important experience in the future, the past, or the present—"I Love to See the Temple" and "I Hope They Call Me on a Mission."

E. Music Memory Box Game

(For full text and activity with composer and author pictures, see "Fun with Favorites," Pat Graham, Friend, *Oct. 1986, 44–45.)*

Creating a song is an exciting process. Nearly every person who has written the words or music for a song will say that it was a thrilling experience. Prayer, work, and experimentation combine to make something new. After determining what the subject of a song will be, ideas to express thoughts about the subject are written down. Usually many changes are then made: lines are crossed out, notes altered. When enough of the right

APPENDIX THREE

ideas are present, the new creation usually develops quickly, as though it was "meant to be." This is the moment of inspiration. Heavenly Father blesses people as they pray to Him for help in finding the right combination of ideas.

Appendix Four

Author / Composer Quick Reference

There are one hundred ninety-nine authors and composers who have songs in the *Children's Songbook*. Forty-three of the writers also wrote hymns. One hundred forty-one of them are LDS, a percentage which shows the trend for church members to create songs directed specifically to children. This quick reference includes a complete list of song and hymn titles by author and composer; song and hymn-book page numbers; the appropriate credit line (words, music, words and music, or arrangement); and birth and death dates.

Adams, Lonnie Dobson (1942–) LDS
 I Want to Give the Lord My Tenth, 150 (words and music)
Adams, Marilyn Price (1926–) LDS
 Hum Your Favorite Hymn, 152 (words)
Alexander, Cecil Frances (1818–1895)
 All Things Bright and Beautiful, 231 (words)
 Hymns, He is Risen, 199 (words)
 Hymns, Once in Royal David's City, 205 (words)
 Hymns, There Is a Green Hill Far Away, 194 (words)
Andersen, Dorothy S. (1927–) LDS
 Oh, What Do You Do in the Summertime? 245 (words and music)
Anderson, Thelma McKinnon (1913–1997) LDS
 He Died That We Might Live Again, 65 (words)
Bach, Johann Sebastian (1685–1750)
 My Heart Ever Faithful, 293 (music)
Ballantyne, Dawn Hughes (1932–1995) LDS
 Fathers, 209 (words)
Ballantyne, Joseph (1868–1944) LDS
 Jesus Once Was a Little Child, 55 (music)
 Little Purple Pansies, 244 (music)
 Oh, Hush Thee, My Baby, 48 (words and music)
 Stand for the Right, 159 (words and music)
 Shine On, 144 (words and music)

APPENDIX FOUR

Bassford, William Kipp (1839–1902)
  Can a Little Child like Me? 9 (music)
Bates, Elizabeth Fetzer (1909–1999) LDS
  Book of Mormon Stories, 118 (words and music)
  Pioneer Children Sang as they Walked, 214 (words and music)
Battishill, Jonathan (1738–1801)
  A Song of Thanks, 20 (music)
Beesley, Alvin A. (1873–1940) LDS
  Heavenly Father, Now I Pray, 19 (words and music)
Beesley, Wilford A., Jr. (1927–) LDS
  Thank Thee for Everything, 10 (music)
Bello, Georgia W. (1924–2007) LDS
  Popcorn Popping on the Apricot Tree, 242 (words and music)
Bennett, Wallace F. (1898–1993) LDS
  I Like My Birthdays, 104 (words)
  When We're Helping, 198 (words)
  God of Power, God of Right, 20 *Hymns* (words)
Berg, Richard C. (1911–)
  Lift Up Your Voice and Sing, 252 (words and music)
Black, Carol Baker (1951–) LDS
  Search, Ponder and Pray, 109 (music)
  How Dear to God Are Little Children, 180 (music)
Bourgeous, Polly (1937–) LDS
  Our Chapel is a Sacred Place, 30 (words)
Bradbury, William B. (1816–1868) LDS
  "Give," Said the Little Stream, 236 (music)
  Come, All Ye Saints Who Dwell on Earth, 65 *Hymns* (music)
  God Moves in a Mysterious Way, 285 (music)
  Hymns, Sweet Hour of Prayer, 142 (music)
  Hymns, We Are All Enlisted, 250 (music)
Bradshaw, Merrill (1929–2000) LDS
  The Still, Small Voice, 106 (words and music)
  Listen, Listen, 107 (words and music)
  Hymns, We Will Sing of Zion, 47 (words and music)
Brady, Janeen Jacobs (1934–) LDS
  I Lived in Heaven, 4 (words and music)
Bray, Jo Marie Borgeson (1925–1998) LDS
  Love One Another, 136 (arrangement, obbligato)

APPENDIX FOUR

Brown, Newel Kay (1932–) LDS
   I Hope They Call Me on a Mission, 169 (words and music)
   My Country, 224 (music)
   Hymns, With Songs of Praise, 71 (music)
Brown, Olga Carlson (1894–1987) LDS
   Oh, How We Love to Stand, 279 (words and music)
Bucher, Lester
   For Thy Bounteous Blessings, 21 (words)
Bunker, Wilma Boyle (1910–1992) LDS
   I Will Try to Be Reverent, 28 (words and music)
   Hello, Friends! 254 (words and music)
Cahoon, Matilda Watts (1881–1973) LDS
   Beauty Everywhere, 232 (words)
   Hymns, The Light Divine, 305 (words)
Cameron, John C. (1951–)
   Every Star is Different, 142 (words)
Campbell, Hal K. (1927–) LDS
   The Sacred Grove, 87 (music)
   The Priesthood is Restored, 89 (music)
Campbell, Joan D. (1929–) LDS
   The Sacred Grove, 87 (words)
   The Priesthood is Restored, 89 (words)
Cannon, Tracy Y. (1879–1961) LDS
   I Like My Birthdays, 104 (music)
   Hymns, Come, Let Us Sing an Evening Hymn, 167 (music)
   Hymns, Come, Rejoice, 9 (words and music)
   Hymns, God of Power, God of Right, 20 (music)
   Hymns, How Beautiful Thy Temples, Lord, 288 (music)
   Hymns, Jesus, Mighty King in Zion, 234 (music)
   Hymns, Praise the Lord with Heart and Voice, 73 (words and music)
   Hymns, The Lord Be with Us, 161 (music)
Careless, George (1839–1932) LDS
   I Thank Thee, Dear Father, 7 (music)
   Hymns, Again We Meet Around the Board, 186 (music)
   Hymns, Arise, O Glorious Zion, 40 (music)
   Hymns, Behold the Great Redeemer Die, 191 (music)
   Hymns, He Died! The Great Redeemer Died, 192 (music)
   Hymns, O Lord of Hosts, 178 (music)
   Hymns, O Thou Kind and Gracious Father, 150 (music)

APPENDIX FOUR

Hymns, Prayer Is the Soul's Sincere Desire, 145 (music)
Hymns, The Morning Breaks, 1 (music)
Hymns, Though Deepening Trials, 122 (music)
Carter, Daniel Lyman (1955–) LDS
    The Shepherd's Carol, 40 (words and music)
    A Young Man Prepared, 166 (words and music)
    Hymns, As Now We Take the Sacrament, 169, (music)
Carter, Nancy K. Daines (1935–) LDS
    Book of Mormon Stories, 118 (words optional verses)
Chadwick, Ruth H. (1900–1973) LDS
    Reverence, 27 (words)
Challinor, F. A. (1866–1952)
    Tell Me the Stories of Jesus, 57 (music)
Cleator, Alice Jean (1871–1926)
    Be Happy! 265 (words)
Clinger, Richard (1946–) LDS
    The Family, 194 (music)
Coleman, Satis N. (1878–1961)
    We're All Together Again, 259 (music)
Conant, Grace Wilbur (1848–1948)
    Autumn Day, 247 (words and music)
    God's Love, 97 (music)
Cooney, Betty Lou (1924–2013) LDS
    Popcorn Popping, 242 (arr. music)
Cornwall, J. Spencer (1888–1993) LDS
    The Golden Plates, 86 (music)
    Hymns, Softly Beams the Sacred Dawning, 56 (music)
Crosby, Fanny J. (1820–1915)
    "Give," Said the Little Stream, 236 (words)
    Hymns, Behold! A Royal Army, 251 (words)
Cundick, Robert (1926–) LDS
    To Think about Jesus, 71 (music)
    Hymns, That Easter Morn, 198 (music)
    Hymns, Thy Holy Word, 279 (music)
Darley, Roy M. (1926–) LDS
    I Want to Live the Gospel, 148 (music)
Davidson, Marcia
    Westward Ho! 217 (music)

APPENDIX FOUR

Davis, D. Evan (1923–1979)
    Help Us, O God, to Understand, 73 (words and music)
Davis, Mary Jane McAllister (1925–1988)
    The Prophet Said to Plant a Garden, 237 (words and music)
Dayley, K. Newell (1939–) LDS
    Every Star is Different, 142 (music)
    Home, 192 (music)
    Hum Your Favorite Hymn, 152 (music)
    I Feel My Savior's Love, 74 (words and music)
    The World Is So Big, 235 (music)
    Hymns, Lord, I Would Follow Thee, 220 (music)
Dodge, Mary Mapes (1835–1905)
    Can a Little Child like Me? 9 (words)
Doxey, Joanne Bushman (1932–) LDS
    Seek the Lord Early, 108 (words and music)
    Where Love Is, 138 (words and music)
Excell, Edwin O. (1851–1921)
    Jesus Wants Me for a Sunbeam, 60 (music)
    Hymns, Scatter Sunshine, 230 (music)
    Hymns, Count Your Blessings, 241 (music)
Fisher, Aileen (1906–2002)
    Hinges, 277 (words)
Fox, Luacine Clark (1914–2002) LDS
    Love One Another, 136 (words and music)
    Love One Another, 308 *Hymns* (words and music)
Franklin, Benjamin (1706–1790)
    Healthy, Wealthy, and Wise, 280 (words)
Gabbott, Mabel Jones (1910–2004) LDS
    Baptism, 100 (words)
    Before I Take the Sacrament, 73 (words)
    Did Jesus Really Live Again?, 64 (words)
    Father Up Above, 23 (words)
    Had I Been a Child, 80 (words)
    Have a Very Happy Birthday!, 284 (words)
    Have a Very Merry Christmas!, 51 (words)
    He Sent His Son, 34 (words)
    My Country, 224 (words)
    Samuel Tells of the Baby Jesus, 36 (words)
    Sleep, Little Jesus, 47 (words)

APPENDIX FOUR

The Family, 194 (words)
There Was Starlight on the Hillside, 40 (words)
To Think about Jesus, 71 (words)
We Are Reverent, 27 (words)
Who Is the Child, 46 (words)
Hymns, In Humility, Our Savior, 172 (words)
Hymns, Lord, Accept Into Thy Kingdom, 236 (words)
Hymns, Rejoice, Ye Saints of Latter Days, 290 (words)
Hymns, We Have Partaken of Thy Love, 155 (words)

Gardner, Lyall (1926–2012) LDS
I Believe in Being Honest, 149 (music)
Hymns, Go Forth with Faith, 263 (music)

Gardner, Marvin K. (1951–) LDS
This is My Beloved Son, 76 (words)
Hymns, Press Forward, Saints, 81 (words)
Hymns, Thy Holy Word, 279 (words)

Gardner, Ruth Muir (1927–1999) LDS
Go the Second Mile, 167 (words and music)
Families Can Be Together Forever, 188 (words)
I Believe in Being Honest, 149 (words)
To Be a Pioneer, 218 (words and music)
We Welcome You, 256 (words)
Hymns, Go Forth with Faith, 263 (words)
Hymns, Families Can Be Together Forever, 300 (words)

Gates, Crawford (1921–) LDS
Baptism, 88 (words and music)
On a Golden Springtime, 100 (music)
Hymns, Our Savior's Love, 113 (music)
Hymns, Ring Out, Wild Bells, 215 (music)

Gluck, Christoph W. von (1714–1787)
Air from *Orpheus*, 296 (music)

Gordon, Glenn (1956–) LDS
Friends Are Fun, 262 (words and music)

Gordon, Grace (1873–1956)
Called to Serve, 174 (words)

Gordon, Ingrid Sawatzki (1949–) LDS
Sing a Song, 253 (words and music)

Gottschalk, Louis (1829–1869)
Loving Shepherd, 292 (music)

APPENDIX FOUR

Hymns, God Our Father, Hear Us Pray, 170 (music)
Graham, Patricia Kelsey (1940–) LDS
    I Am Like a Star, 163 (words and music)
    Picture a Christmas, 50 (words and music)
    The Hearts of the Children, 92 (words and music)
    The Nativity Song, 52 (words and music)
    We Are Different, 263 (words and music)
Graham, Rose Thomas (1876–1967) LDS
    The Golden Plates, 86 (words)
Gunn, Carol Graff (1929–) LDS
    Family Night, 195 (words and music)
    My Dad, 211 (words and music)
Hansen, Bill N., Jr. (1952–) LDS
    Nephi's Courage, 120 (words and music)
Hansen, Lisa Tennsmeyer (1958–) LDS
    Nephi's Courage, 120 (words and music)
Hanson, William Frederick (1887–1969) LDS
    I Have Two Little Hands, 272 (music)
Harrison, Thelma J. (1906–1991) LDS
    Quickly I'll Obey, 197 (words)
Haydn, Franz Joseph (1732–1809)
    Thanks to Our Father, 20 (music)
    Hymns, Glorious Things of Thee Are Spoken, 46 (music)
Hiatt, Duane E. (1937–) LDS
    Follow the Prophet, 110 (words and music)
Hill, Chester W. (1912–1997) LDS
    Hosanna, 66 (arr. music)
    Saturday, 196 (arr. music)
Hill, Mildred
    Once Within a Lowly Stable, 41 (words and music)
Hill, Patty Smith (1868–1946)
    Once Within a Lowly Stable, 41 (words and music)
Holbrook, Glenna Tate (1925–) LDS
    Birds in the Tree, 241 (words)
    Stand Up, 278 (words)
Huffman, Laurie (1948–) LDS
    I Feel My Savior's Love, 74 (words)
Hunter, Donnell (1930–) LDS
    The Lord Gave Me a Temple, 153 (words)

APPENDIX FOUR

Jack, Mary R. (1896–1985) LDS
    Thanks to Thee, 6 (words)
Jackson, Beatrice Goff (1943–) LDS
    Faith, 96 (words)
Jensen, Joyce Mills (1936–2002) LDS
    Fathers, 209 (music)
Johns, Cecilia
    Fun to Do, 253 (music)
Johnson, Anna (1892–1979) LDS
    A Smile is Like the Sunshine, 267 (words)
    An Angel Came to Joseph Smith, 86 (words)
    I Think the World Is Glorious, 230 (words)
    Jesus Is Our Loving Friend, 58 (words)
    My Flag, My Flag, 225 (words)
    We Bow Our Heads, 25 (words)
Jolley, Mary Ellen Jex (1926–) LDS
    I Have a Family Tree, 199 (words)
Kaelin, Anne (1917–1995)
    Covered Wagons, 221 (words)
Kaillmark, George (1781–1835)
    The Books in the Old Testament, 114 (music)
    Hymns, Do What Is Right, 237 (music)
Kammeyer, Virginia Maughan (1925–1999) LDS
    On a Golden Springtime, 88 (words)
    Pioneer Children Were Quick to Obey, 215 (words)
Kimball, Maud Belnap (1889–1971) LDS
    Mother Dear, 206 (words)
Kirkell, Miriam H.
    Westward Ho! 217 (words)
Kjar, Marjorie Castleton (1927–) LDS
    Where Love Is, 138 (music)
    Birds in the Tree, 241 (music)
    Come with Me to Primary, 255 (words and music)
    Stand Up, 278 (music)
    We Welcome You, 256 (music)
Kleinman, Bertha A. (1877–1971) LDS
    I Have Two Little Hands, 272 (words)
Lawler, Jeanne P. (1924–) LDS
    Family History—I Am Doing It, 94 (words and music)

Hinges, 277 (music)
I Often Go Walking, 202 (music)
The Holy Ghost, 105 (words and music)
When Jesus Christ Was Baptized, 102 (words and music)
LeeMaster, Vernon J. (1904–2001) LDS
Dearest Mother, I Love You, 206 (words and music)
Lehenbauer, Ruth Benson (1933–LDS)
I'm Glad To Pay a Tithing, 150 (words and music)
Likes, L. Claire (1908–1998) LDS
The Things I Do, 170 (words)
Lloyd, Leah Ashton (1894–1965) LDS
Reverence, 27 (music)
I Think When I Read That Sweet Story, 56 (music)
Lloyd, Sylvia Knight (1933–) LDS
Repentance, 98 (words)
Lowden, Carl Harold (1883–1963)
Tell Me, Dear Lord, 176 (music)
Luch, Phyllis (1937–1995) LDS
I Often Go Walking, 202 (words)
Luke, Jemima (1813–1906)
I Think When I Read That Sweet Story, 56 (words)
Lundberg, Joy Saunders (1936–) LDS
I'm Thankful to Be Me, 11 (words)
Lyon, A. Laurence (1934–2006) LDS
An Angel Came to Joseph Smith, 86 (music)
Christmas Bells, 54 (words and music)
How Will They Know? 185, (arr. music)
I Have Two Ears, 269 (music)
Little Pioneer Children, 216 (words and music)
We Are Reverent, 27 (music)
Whenever I Think about Pioneers, 222 (music)
Hymns, Saints, Behold How Great Jehovah, 28 (music)
Hymns, Each Life That Touches Ours for Good, 293 (music)
MacDowell, Edward (1861–1908)
To A Wild Rose, 289 (music)
Maeser, Georgia (1893–1972) LDS
I Have Two Ears, 269 (words)
Major, Marian (1899–1985)
When Grandpa Comes, 201 (words and music)

APPENDIX FOUR

Mangum, Marzelle (1914–2003) LDS
　Our Primary Colors, 258 (words and music)
Mann, Margaret (1890–1950)
　I Pledge Myself to Love the Right, 161 (words)
Manookin, Robert P. (1918–1997) LDS
　A Prayer Song, 22 (words and music)
　Repentance, 98 (music)
　Our Bishop, 135 (words and music)
　Hymns, Like Ten Thousand Legions Marching, 253 (music)
　Hymns, Rise, Ye Saints, and Temples Enter, 287 (music)
　Hymns, Saints of Zion, 39 (music)
　Hymns, See the Mighty Priesthood Gathered, 325 (music)
　Hymns, Thy Will, O Lord, Be Done, 188 (music)
　Hymns, We Have Partaken of Thy Love, 155 (music)
Matthews, Daphne L. (1917–2014) LDS
　The Books in the Book of Mormon, 119 (words)
Maughan, Patricia Critchlow (1926–1980) LDS
　Come With Me to Primary, 255 (words and music)
McAllister, John Daniel Thompson (1827–1910) LDS
　The Handcart Song, 220 (words and music)
McConochie, Barbara (1940–) LDS
　Keep the Commandments, 146 (words and music)
　You've Had a Birthday, 285 (words and music)
　Hymns, Keep the Commandments, 303 (words and music)
McMaster, Clara Watkins (1904–1997) LDS
　Choose the Right Way, 160 (words and music)
　Kindness Begins With Me, 145 (words and music)
　My Heavenly Father Loves Me, 228 (words and music)
　Remember the Sabbath Day, 155 (words and music)
　Reverently, Quietly, 26 (words and music)
　Teach Me to Walk in the Light, 177 (words and music)
　Hymns, Teach Me to Walk in the Light, 304 (words and music)
McNees, Mildred E. Millett (1925–2006) LDS
　Happy, Happy Birthday, 284 (words and music)
Mendelssohn, Felix (1809–1847)
　If With All Your Hearts, 15 (words and music)
　O Rest in the Lord, 295 (music)
　Hymns, Cast Thy Burden upon the Lord, 110 (music)
　Hymns, Hark! The Herald Angels Sing, 209 (music)

APPENDIX FOUR

   Hymns, O God, the Eternal Father, 175 (music)
M. E. P.
   Tell Me, Dear Lord, 176 (words)
Meredith, Joleen Grant (1935–) LDS
   Because God Loves Me, 234 (words and music)
   Hymns, Where Can I Turn for Peace? 129 (music)
Metz, Lois Lunt (1906–2004) LDS
   Falling Snow, 248 (words and music)
Milne, Jaclyn Thomas (1949–) LDS
   Search, Ponder, and Pray, 109 (words)
   How Dear to God are Little Children, 180 (words)
Milner, Nita Dale (1952–2004) LDS
   When I am Baptized, 103 (words and music)
Miner, Caroline Eyring (1907–1999) LDS
   Home, 192 (words)
Moody, Michael Finlinson (1941–) LDWS
   Faith, 96 (music)
   Have a Very Happy Birthday! 284 (music)
   Have a Very Merry Christmas!, 51 (music)
   He Sent His Son, 34 (music)
   Sleep, Little Jesus, 47 (music)
   Teacher, Do You Love Me? 178 (words and music)
   There Was Starlight on the Hillside, 40 (music)
   Who Is the Child?, 46 (music)
   Hymns, Testimony, 137 (music)
Mozart, Wolfgang Amadeus (1756–1791)
   I Pledge Myself to Love the Right, 161 (music)
   In Quietude, 298 (music)
Murray, James R. (1841–1905)
   Jesus Once Was a Little Child, 55 (words)
   Hymns, Thanks for the Sabbath School, 278 (music)
Newell, Charlene Anderson (1935–) LDS
   Little Jesus, 39 (music)
   He Died That We Might Live Again, 65 (music)
   The Commandments, 112 (music)
   Your Happy Birthday, 283 (words and music)
   Hymns, A Key Was Turned in Latter Days, 310 (music)
Newell, Mark (1961–) LDS
   Little Jesus, 39 (music)

APPENDIX FOUR

Nibley, Reid Neibaur (1923–2008) LDS
    I Know My Father Lives, 5 (words and music)
    I'll Walk With You, 140 (music)
    Hymns, I Know My Father Lives, 302 (words and music)
Nielsen, Patricia Haglund (1936–2009) LDS
    O Hush Thee, My Baby, 48 (ostinato, words and music)
    Quickly I'll Obey, 197 (ostinato, words and music)
Obray, Barbara Boyer (1927–) LDS
    Two Happy Feet, 270 (music)
Ogelvee, Louise M. (abt. 1866–1954)
    This is God's House, 30 (words)
Ogelvee, William G. (1865–1939)
    This is God's House, 30 (music)
Olauson, Maggie (1949–) LDS
    Reverence is Love, 31 (words and music)
Olsen, Rita Mae (1932–) LDS
    It's Autumntime, 246 (words and music)
Ozment, Maurine Benson (1932–) LDS
    Hello Song, 260 (words and music)
    Feliz Cumpleaños, 282 (words and music)
Pace, Cynthia Lord (1955–) LDS
    Latter-day Prophets, 134 (words)
Parker, Judith Wirthlin (1919–2000) LDS
    I Need My Heavenly Father, 18 (words and music)
Parker, W. H. (1845–1929)
    Tell Me the Stories of Jesus, 57 (words)
Payne, I. Reed (1930–) LDS
    When Joseph Went to Bethlehem, 38 (music)
Pearson, Carol Lynn (1939–) LDS
    I'll Walk with You, 140 (words)
Perry, Janice Kapp (1938–) LDS
    A Child's Prayer, 12 (words and music)
    I Love to See the Temple, 95 (words and music)
    I Pray in Faith, 14 (words and music)
    I'm Thankful to Be Me, 11 (music)
    I'm Trying to Be Like Jesus, 78 (words and music)
    Love Is Spoken Here, 190 (words and music)
    Mother, Tell Me the Story, 204 (words and music)
    The Church of Jesus Christ, 77 (words and music)

APPENDIX FOUR

    The Word of Wisdom, 154 (words and music)
    We'll Bring the World His Truth, 172 (words and music)
    Hymns, As Sisters in Zion, 309 (music)
Petersen, Faye Glover (1914–2009)
    When I Go to Church, 157 (words and music)
    Because It's Spring, 239 (words and music)
Peterson, DeVota Mifflin (1910–1996) LDS
    Family Prayer, 189 (words and music)
Pettit, Mildred Tanner (1895–1977) LDS
    Beauty Everywhere, 232 (music)
    Father, I Will Reverent Be, 29 (music)
    I Am a Child of God, 2 (music)
    Mother Dear, 206 (music)
    Hymns, I Am a Child of God, 301 (music)
    Hymns, The Light Divine, 305 (music)
Pheatt, Fanny Giralda
    Springtime Is Coming, 238 (words)
Phelps, William Wines (1792–1872) LDS
    The Books in the New Testament, 116 (music)
    Hymns, Adam-ondi-Ahman, 49 (words)
    Hymns, Come, All Ye Saints of Zion, 38 (words)
    Hymns, Come, All Ye Saints Who Dwell on Earth, 65 (words)
    Hymns, Come, Let Us Sing an Evening Hymn, 167 (words)
    Hymns, Gently Raise the Sacred Strain, 146 (words)
    Hymns, Glorious Things Are Sung of Zion, 48 (words)
    Hymns, If You Could Hie to Kolob, 284 (words)
    Hymns, Joy to the World, 201 (alteration words)
    Hymns, Now Let Us Rejoice, 3 (words)
    Hymns, Now We'll Sing with One Accord, 25 (words)
    Hymns, O God, the Eternal Father, 175 (words)
    Hymns, Praise to the Man, 27 (words)
    Hymns, Redeemer of Israel, 6 (alteration words)
    Hymns, The Spirit of God, 2 (words)
    Hymns, We're Not Ashamed to Own Our Lord, 57 (words)
Pinborough, Jan Underwood (1954–) LDS
    Mary's Lullaby, 44 (words)
    Hymns, A Key Was Turned in Latter Days, 310 (words)
Poorman, Nellie
    God Is Watching Over All, 229 (words)

APPENDIX FOUR

Provost, Della Dalby (1910–1973) LDS
    Whenever I Think About Pioneers, 222 (words)
Randall, Naomi Ward (1908–2001) LDS
    I Am a Child of God, 2 (words)
    I Want to Live the Gospel, 148 (words)
    Hymns, I Am a Child of God, 301 (words)
    Hymns, When Faith Endures, 128 (words)
Randolph, Richard (1911–1969)
    Covered Wagons, 221 (music)
Read, Dorothy Little (1920–) LDS
    The Chapel Doors, 156 (words and music)
Reading, Lucile Cardon (1909–1982)
    The Handcart Song, 220 (words)
Remsen, F.
    Thank Thee Father, 24 (music)
Renstrom, K. Moiselle (1889–1956) LDS
    A Happy Family, 198 (words and music)
    A Happy Helper, 197 (words and music)
    A Prayer, 22 (words and music)
    I Am Glad for Many Things, 151 (words and music)
    I Love to Pray, 25 (words and music)
    Jesus Loved the Little Children, 59 (words and music)
    Jesus Said Love Everyone, 61 (words and music)
    Little Seeds Lie Fast Asleep, 243 (words and music)
    Once There Was a Snowman, 249 (words and music)
    Rain Is Falling All Around, 241 (words and music)
    The World Is So Lovely, 233 (words and music)
    To Get Quiet, 275 (words and music)
    Two Little Eyes, 268 (words and music)
Reynolds, Becky-Lee Hill (1944–) LDS
    Heavenly Father, While I Pray, 23 (words and music)
    My Mother Dear, 203 (words and music)
Riley, Alice C. D. (1867–1955)
    Thank Thee Father, 24 (words)
Robinson, Rita Steele (1920–2011) LDS
    Hosanna, 66 (words and music)
    Saturday, 196 (words and music)
Rodgers, Ralph, Jr. (1936–1990) LDS
    I Feel My Savior's Love, 74 (words)

APPENDIX FOUR

Rowley, Grietje Terburg (1927–) LDS
    A Smile is Like the Sunshine, 267 (music)
    Distant Bells, 299 (music)
    Each Sunday Morning, 290 (music)
    Father, We Thank for the Night, 8 (music)
    I Want to Be a Missionary Now, 168 (words and music)
    Roll Your Hands, 274 (arrangement)
    Samuel Tells of the Baby Jesus, 36 (music)
    Hymns, Be Thou Humble, 130 (words and music)
Ryser, Thelma Johnson (1898–1984) LDS
    Jesus Has Risen, 70 (words and music)
Ryskamp, Peggy Hill (1949–) LDS
    Children All Over the World, 16 (words)
Schreiner, Alexander (1901–1987) LDS
    I Think the World Is Glorious, 230 (music)
    Jesus is Our Loving Friend, 58 (music)
    My Flag, My Flag, 225 (music)
    We Bow Our Heads, 25 (music)
    Hymns, Behold Thy Sons and Daughters, Lord, 238 (music)
    Hymns, God Loved Us, So He Sent His Son, 187 (music)
    Hymns, Holy Temples on Mount Zion, 289 (music)
    Hymns, In Memory of the Crucified, 190 (music)
    Hymns, Lead Me into Life Eternal, 45 (music)
    Hymns, Lord, Accept into Thy Kingdom, 236 (music)
    Hymns, Thy Spirit, Lord, Has Stirred Our Souls, 157 (music)
    Hymns, Truth Eternal, 4 (music)
    Hymns, While of These Emblems We Partake, 174 (music)
Schubert, Franz (1797–1828)
    God Is Watching Over All, 229 (music)
    Impromptu, 288 (music)
    Andante, 294 (music)
Schubring, Julius (1806–1889)
    If with All Your Hearts, 15 (words)
Scott, Louise B. (1914–)
    I Wiggle, 271 (words)
    My Hands, 273 (words)
Seeley, Gladys Ericksen (1899–1985) LDS
    Father Up Above, 23 (music)
    Before I Take the Sacrament, 73 (music)

Shurtleff, Lynn R. (1939–) LDS
  Pioneer Children Were Quick to Obey, 215 (music)
  Hymns, Father, This Hour Has Been One of Joy, 154 (music)
Sleeth, Natalie W. (1930–1992)
  How Will They Know? 182 (words and music)
Smith, Joseph, Jr. (1805–1844) LDS
  The Articles of Faith, 122–132 (words)
Smith, Norma Broadbent (1923–2010) LDS
  Where Love Is, 138 (words)
Smyth, A. C. (1840–1909) LDS
  Dare to Do Right, 158 (arr. music)
  Hymns, Come Along, Come Along, 244 (music)
  Hymns, Come, Thou Glorious Day of Promise, 50 (music)
  Hymns, Joseph Smith's First Prayer, 26 (adapted music)
  Hymns, Zion Stands with Hills Surrounded, 43 (music)
Sorenson, Nonie Nelson (1925–)
  Grandmother, 200 (words and music)
Spencer, Bessie Saunders (1898–1989)
  When Joseph Went to Bethlehem, 38 (words)
Spencer, Beverly Searle (1921–1999) LDS
  The World is So Big, 235 (words)
Sprunt, Lois Coombs (1930–) LDS
  We Welcome You, 256 (words)
Steed, Sharon (1935–) LDS
  A Special Gift is Kindness, 145 (words and music)
Stevens, Rebecca
  Fun to Do, 253 (words)
Stevenson, Robert Louis (1850–1894)
  A Song of Thanks, 20 (words)
Stratton, Beth Groberg (1944–) LDS
  Children All Over the World, 16 (music)
Talbot, Nellie (1874–?)
  Jesus Wants Me for a Sunbeam, 60 (words)
Taylor, Daniel
  Smiles, 267 (words)
Taylor, Elizabeth Cushing
  God's Love, 97 (words)
Taylor, Frances K. (1870–1952) LDS
  Help Me, Dear Father, 99 (words and music)

The Dearest Names, 208 (words and music)
Daddy's Homecoming, 210 (music)
Tchaikovsky, Peter Ilich (1840–1890)
Morning Prayer, 292 (music)
Thayne, Mirla Greenwood (1907–1997) LDS
I Wonder When He Comes Again, 82 (words and music)
Thomas, Norma Madsen (1908–1988) LDS
Two Happy Feet, 270 (words)
Turner, Nancy Byrd (1880–1971)
Stars Were Gleaming, 37 (words)
Twitchell, Royce Campbell (1939–2011) LDS
Did Jesus Really Live Again? 64 (music)
Tyler, Walter G. (1855–1933)
Called to Serve, 174 (music)
Hymns, Behold! A Royal Army, 251 (music)
Hymns, Called to Serve, 249 (music)
Watkins, Vanja Yorgason (1938–) LDS
Easter Hosanna, 68 (music)
Families Can Be Together Forever, 188 (music)
For Thy Bounteous Blessings, 21 (arrangement)
I Want to Be Reverent, 28 (music)
I Will Be Valiant, 162 (words and music)
I Will Follow God's Plan, 164 (words and music)
It's Autumntime, 246 (music)
Latter-day Prophets, 134 (music)
Thank Thee for Everything, 10 (words)
The Articles of Faith, 122–132 (music)
The Sacrament, 72 (words and music)
The Things I Do, 170 (music)
This Is My Beloved Son, 76 (music)
To Be a Pioneer, 218 (arrangement)
Truth from Elijah, 90 (words and music)
Hymns, Families Can Be Together Forever, 300 (music)
Hymns, Press Forward Saints, 81 (music)
Weston, Rebecca J. (1835–1895)
Father, We Thank Thee for the Night, 8 (words)
Wheelwright, Lorin F. (1909–1987) LDS
Beautiful Savior, 207 (words and music)
Hymns, Help Me Teach with Inspiration, 281 (words and music)

    Hymns, O Love That Glorifies the Son, 295 (words and music)
    Hymns, Oh, May My Soul Commune with Thee, 123 (words and music)
White, Marilyn Curtis (1941–) LDS
    Little Jesus, 39 (words)
Wilton, Arthur
    Be Happy! 265 (music)
Wolford, Darwin (1936–) LDS
    Beautiful Savior, 62 (arrangement)
    Had I Been a Child, 80 (music)
    I Am a Child of God, 2 (arrangement)
    I Have a Family Tree, 199 (music)
    In Quietude, 291 (music)
    Keep the Commandments, 146 (arrangement)
    Mary's Lullaby, 44 (arrangement)
    Our Chapel Is a Sacred Place, 30 (music)
    Stars Were Gleaming, 37 (arrangement)
    Supplication, 297 (music)
    Teach Me to Walk in the Light, 177 (obbligato)
    Thanks to Thee, 6 (music)
    The Lord Gave Me a Temple, 153 (music)
    Hymns, Sons of Michael, He Approaches, 51 (music)
    Hymns, We Listen to a Prophet's Voice, 22 (music)
Wood, Lucille F. (1915–1986)
    I Wiggle, 271 (music)
    My Hands, 273 (music)

Appendix Five

Songs Published in The Friend *Since the 1989* Children's Songbook *1988–2006*

Author Note: How to Share New Music

Original compositions can be submitted for the Church Music Contest, or placed on the music website to share with others. Generally, children's songs published in the *Friend* correspond to curriculum being taught in Primary. Brother Moody always suggested that members write for their stewardship and "the cream will rise."

A PROPHET LIVES TODAY (Oct. 2003, 26)
  Words and music: Clive J. Romney
A WONDERFUL FEELING OF LOVE (Jan. 1996, 5)
  Words and music: Harold R. Laycock
A YOUNG BOY NAMED JOSEPH (May 1995, 12–13)
  Words and music: Dean S. Wakefield
ALL THY CHILDREN SHALL BE TAUGHT (Jun. 1994, 5)
  Words and music: Grietje T. Rowley
AS THOUGH I HAD BEEN THERE (May 1998, 12)
  Words and music: Annette W. Dickman
ASK AND YE SHALL RECEIVE (Oct. 1991, 11)
  Words and music: Grietje T. Rowley
AT CONFERENCE TIME (Oct. 1997, 12–13)
  Words: Brad Wilcox
  Music: Steven Perry
BEHOLD YOUR LITTLE ONES (Aug. 1994, 12–13)
  Words: Marvin K. Gardner
  Music: Vanja Y. Watkins
CHRISTMAS LULLABY (Dec. 1994, 12–13)
  Words: Val Camenish Wilcox
  Music: Janice Kapp Perry
COVENANTS ARE PROMISES (Aug. 1999, 38)
  Words: Martin Green, adapted by Penny Moody Allen
  Music: Martin Green
ETERNAL THINGS (Jan. 1993, 12–13)
  Words and music: Ann Kapp Andersen

APPENDIX FIVE

FAITH (Apr. 1990, 22–23)
    Words and music: Susan L. Purves
FATHER IN HEAVEN HEARS ME PRAY (May 1992, 12–13)
    Words and music: Jenny W. Francis
FOLLOW HIS LIGHT (Dec. 1992, 38–39)
    Words and music: Karen Andersen Stephens
GORDON B. HINCKLEY—CONSTANT AS THE NORTH STAR (Jun. 1996, 14–15)
    Words and music: Cheryl Boyer Hansen
HAND IN HAND TOGETHER (May 2001, 44–45)
    Words and music: Janice Kapp Perry
HEROES OF THE SCRIPTURES (Jun. 1998, 14)
    Words: Penny Moody Allen
    Music: Lynn Shurtleff
HOLDING HANDS AROUND THE WORLD (Jul. 2002, 44–45)
    Words and music: Janice Kapp Perry
I CAN BE A MODERN-DAY PIONEER (Jul. 1993, 38)
    Words and music: Barbara A. McConochie
I COME TO THE WATER (Mar. 2000, 46–47)
    Words and music: Janice Kapp Perry
I FEEL THE SPIRIT (Feb. 2004, 15)
    Words and music: Matthew Neeley
I HEARD THE PROPHET (Oct. 2001, 7)
    Words: John V. Pearson
    Music: Janice Kapp Perry
I KNOW THAT JESUS LIVES (Jan. 1991, 42–43)
    Words and music: Lynn S. Lund
I KNOW THAT MY SAVIOR LOVES ME (Oct. 2002, 46–47)
    Words: Tami Jeppson Creamer
    Music: Derena Bell
I LIKE TO LISTEN TO THE PROPHET (Aug. 1997, 12–13)
    Words and music: Ruth B. Gatrell
I LIKE TO LEARN OF JESUS CHRIST (Jan. 1999, 10–11)
    Words: John V. Pearson
    Music: Janice Kapp Perry
I STAND PREPARED (Jan. 1995, 12–13)
    Words and music: Rebecca Smith Adams
I WANT TO BE BAPTIZED (Jul. 2005, 45)
    Words: Gary Croxall
    Music: Kathleen Holyoak

APPENDIX FIVE

I WILL ALWAYS OBEY (Mar. 1996, 36–37)
    Words and music: Janice Kapp Perry
I WILL LOOK UNTO THE LORD IN EVERY THOUGHT (Jan. 1989, 46–47)
    Words: Marvin K. Gardner
    Music: Vanja Y. Watkins
I'LL FOLLOW HIM IN FAITH (Oct. 2002, 24)
    Words and music: Janice Kapp Perry
I'LL SAY NO (Oct. 1989, 34–35)
    Words and music: Rebecca Smith Adams
IF CHRIST SHOULD SPEAK TO ME (Jul. 1995, 5)
    Words and music: Jenny W. Francis
IF I HAD BEEN IN BETHLEHEM (Dec. 1989, 32–33)
    Words and music: Sally DeFord
IF THE SAVIOR STOOD BESIDE ME (Oct. 1993, 14)
    Words and music: Sally DeFord
IN HIS HOLY NAME (Feb. 1996, 12–13)
    Words and music: Rebecca Smith Adams
ISAIAH SAYS (Mar. 1996, 38)
    Words: Penny Moody Allen
    Music: Kenneth Jones
JESUS IS MY FRIEND (Oct. 1992, 5)
    Words and music: Deborah Mayhew
LINE UPON LINE (Jun. 1989, 46)
    Words and music: Nita Dale Milner
LULLABY, LITTLE ONE (Dec. 1999, 8)
    Words and music: Larry A. Allred
MY TESTIMONY GROWS (Apr. 1991, 12–13)
    Words: Mabel Jones Gabbott
    Music: Lynn S. Lund
MY TESTIMONY IS GROWING (Mar. 1994, 36–37)
    Words and music: Kathyrn B. Decker
MY THANKS TODAY (Nov. 1990, 14)
    Words: Anna Johnson
    Music: Nora Hogan
OUR FAMILY PLACE (Jun. 2002, 41)
    Words and music: Matthew Neeley
OUR HOUSE BECOMES A HOME (Jul. 1996, 12–13)
    Words and music: Kathryn B. Decker

APPENDIX FIVE

OUR SAVIOR'S ATONEMENT (Apr. 1997, 12–13)
    Words and music: Ruth D. Ellis
PEACE IS A FEELING (Oct. 1994, 46)
    Words and music: Clive J. Romney
PIONEERS COURAGEOUS (Jul. 1997, 46–47)
    Words: Michaelene P. Grassli
    Music: Janice Kapp Perry
PROPHETS THEN AND NOW (Oct. 1998, 38)
    Words: Penny Moody Allen
    Music: Kenneth Jones
REVERENCE IS A FEELING (Sept. 1996, 5)
    Words and music: Elizabeth Gardner Ricks
SACRED NAMES OF JESUS (Apr. 1998, 35)
    Words: Penny Moody Allen
    Music: Richard Elliott
SAMUEL THE LAMANITE (Dec. 1988, 32–33)
    Words: Mabel Jones Gabbott
    Music: Lynn S. Lund
SCRIPTURE POWER (Oct. 1987, 10–11)
    Words and music: Clive J. Romney
SING OF CHRISTMAS (Dec. 2003, 28)
    Words and music: Vanja Y. Watkins
STUDY THE SCRIPTURES (Jul. 1990, 14)
    Words and music: Kristin H. Cornilles
THANK YOU, NEPHI (Mar. 1992, 14–15)
    Words: Mabel Jones Gabbott
    Music: Lynn S. Lund
THAT NIGHT IN THE STABLE (Dec. 1997, IFC)
    Words: Val Camenish Wilcox
    Music: Janice Kapp Perry
THE BABY JESUS (Dec. 1990, 12–13)
    Words and music: Jo Marie Bergeson Bray
THE BOOK OF MOMON TEACHES ME (Jan. 1988, 47)
    Words: Marvin K. Gardner
    Music: Vanja Y. Watkins
THE BREAD REMINDS ME (Jul. 2000, 40–41)
    Words and music: Clive J. Romney
THE GIFT OF THE HOLY GHOST (Aug. 2005, 24–25)
    Words and music: Annette W. Hickman

APPENDIX FIVE

THE LORD WILL WATCH OVER ME (Jan. 1994, 12–13)
    Words and music: Rebecca Smith Adams
THE SABBATH DAY (Nov. 2004, 27)
    Words: Gary Croxall
    Music: Kathleen Holyoak
THE SCRIPTURES CAN LEAD ME TO JESUS (May 1999, 14–15)
    Words and music: Clive J. Romney
THE SCRIPTURES SAY (Feb. 1999, 11)
    Words: Penelope Moody Allen
    Music: Reid Nibley
THY HOLY TEMPLE (Jan. 2002, 26)
    Words: Marvin K. Gardner
    Music: Vanja Y. Watkins
TO BETHLEHEM (Dec. 1991, 37)
    Words: Mabel Jones Gabbott
    Music: Michael Finlinson Moody
WE WILL FOLLOW THE LORD (Apr. 1994, 5)
    Words and music: Nita Dale Milner
WHEN I HEAR THE SCRIPTURES (Jan. 1998, 34–35)
    Words: Jan U. Pinborough
    Music: Larry W. Bastian
WHENEVER I HAVE TO CHOOSE (Jun. 1997, 38)
    Words and music: Clive J. Romney
WORTHY TO ENTER (Sept. 1995, 11)
    Words and music: Clive J. Romney

Index A

Authors, Composers, and People of Interest

A

Adams, Lonnie Dobson 131, 235
Adams, Marilyn Price 131, 235
Alexander, William 180
Allred, Virginia Byrd 22, 23
Amyot, Rebecca 143
Andersen, Dorothy S. 188, 235
Anderson, Elaine Rich 24
Anderson, May 2, 8, 9, 159
Anderson, Thelma McKinnon 87, 235
Asper, Frank W. 55
Avery, Lucy Rogers viii

B

Bach, Anna Magdalene 216
Bach, Christoph 216
Bach, Johann Sebastian 212, 216–19, 235
Bach, Maria Barbara 216
Back, Heather 31, 139
Ballantyne, Dawn Hughes 165
Ballantyne, Joseph 76, 80–81, 187–88
Bassford, William Kipp 47, 235
Bates, Elizabeth Fetzer 117–18, 168, 236
Battishill, Jonathan 53
Beesley, Alvin A. 52, 236
Beesley, Wilford A., Jr. 47, 48, 236

Beethoven, Ludwig van 179, 213, 218
Bello, Georgia W. 186, 236
Bennett, Jenny Runswick 24
Bennett, Wallace F. 24, 111–12, 159–60, 236
Benson, Ezra Taft 14, 121, 143
Berg, Richard C. 191, 236
Berlioz, Hector 215
Black, Carol Baker 114, 150, 236
Bourgeous, Polly 64, 236
Boyle, Dessie Grant 12
Bradbury, William B. 183–84
Bradshaw, Merrill 112–13, 236
Brady, Janeen Jacobs 43, 44, 95, 236
Bray, Jo Marie Borgeson 123, 256
Brown, Newel Kay 143–44, 174–75, 236
Brown, Olga Carlson 206, 237
Bucher, Lester 54, 237
Bunker, Wilma Boyle 63, 192, 237

C

Cahoon, Matilda 63, 181, 237
Callis, Charles A. ix
Cameron, John C. 126
Campbell, Hal K. 101–3, 237
Campbell, Joan D. 101–3
Cannon, Tracy Y. 111–12, 237
Cannon, Virginia B. 22, 25

INDEX A

Careless, George 45
Carter, Daniel Lyman 24, 71, 142
Carter, Nancy K. Daines 118
Chadwick, Ruth H. 60
Chaffin, Rose Walker viii
Challinor, F. A. 81, 238
Chopin, Frederic 215
Christensen, Mads viii
Clark, Amasa Lyman xii
Clark, J. Reuben 41
Cleator, Alice Jean 198
Clinger, Richard 155
Coleman, Satis N. 195
Conant, Grace Wilbur 107, 189
Coombs, Lucy Robinson viii
Cooney, Betty Lou 186–87
Cope, Gordon viii, ix
Cornwall, J. Spencer 55, 100
Crosby, Fanny J. 183
Cundick, Robert 68, 89–90, 135, 209

D

Darley, Roy M. 129–30
Davidson, Marcia 170
Davis, D. Evan 92
Davis, Mary Jane McAllister 172, 184
Davis, Pat 92
Dayley, K. Newell 92–93, 126, 132, 154–55, 182–83
Dayton, Lynn 228
DeMille, Cecil B. 13
Dodge, Mary Mapes 47
Doxey, Joanne Bushman 113–14, 123–24

E

Elliott, Lynn 115
Eriksson, Carolee 228
Excell, Edwin O. 83–84

F

Fausett, Lynn vii, ix, 11
Felt, Louie Bouton 2, 7, 9–10
Ferguson, Mrs. Doctor 6
Fisher, Aileen 205
Fisher, Doris F. 173
Fisher, William R. 173
Fox, Luacine Clark 122–23
Fox, Ruth May 168
Franklin, Benjamin 207
Friberg, Arnold 13
Fugal, Sandy 77

G

Gabbott, Mabel Jones 56–57, 61, 65–67, 70–71, 74–75, 78, 85–86, 89–91, 96–97, 109, 140, 155–56, 174–75, 209–10
Gardner, Lyall 130
Gardner, Marvin K. 93, 95, 253, 255–57
Gardner, Ruth Muir 24, 130, 142, 152–53, 170–71, 193–94
Gates, B. Cecil 55
Gates, Crawford xiv, 102–4, 109–10, 209
Geibel, Adam 146
Giles, DeAnn Hickman 144
Gluck, Christoph W. von 219
Gordon, Glenn 196, 240
Gordon, Grace 146

INDEX A

Gordon, Ingrid Sawatzki 191
Gottschalk, Louis 215, 240
Gourley, Mary Curtis 23
Graham, Patricia Kelsey vi, 77, 79, 104–5, 139–40, 147, 196–97, 229, 232–33, 249, 272
Graham, Rose Thomas 100, 241
Grant, Heber J. 7, 9, 11–12, 111, 160, 202
Grassli, Michaelene Packer 2, 18–20, 24, 141, 229, 256
Gunn, Carol Graff 156–57, 166–67

H

Haight, David B. 4
Haight, Louisa Leavitt viii, 4
Hansen, Bill N., Jr. 118–19
Hansen, Lisa Tennsmeyer 118–19
Hanson, William Frederick 202
Harris, Jerolde 24
Harrison, Thelma J. 158, 241
Haydn, Franz Joseph 53, 54
Hess, David C. ix
Hess, John W. vii, 4, 5
Hiatt, Duane E. 115
Hill, Chester W. 89, 157, 241
Hill, Mildred 72, 241
Hill, Patty Smith 72, 241
Hill, William Wallace 72
Hinckley, Gordon Bitner 10, 22, 115–16, 121, 181, 227, 254
Hinckley, May Green vii, 2, 10–14, 159
Hirano, Akiko 42
Hoffman, Roger 151, 174
Hogan, Nora 209, 255

Holbrook, Glenna Tate 185, 206, 241
Hoole, Daryl Van Dam 43
Howells, Adele Cannon 2, 11–13
Huffman, Laurie 92–93, 241
Hughes, David viii
Hull, Richard 32, 207
Hunter, Donnell 132, 241

J

Jack, Mary R. 44
Jackson, Beatrice Goff 106, 241
Jensen, Joyce Mills 165–66, 242
Jepson, Betty Jo Nelson 24
Johns, Cecilia 192
Johnson, Anna 58, 82, 99–100, 175, 179–80, 198–99, 242, 255
Jolley, Mary Ellen Jex 160

K

Kaelin, Anne 173
Kaillmark, George 116, 242
Kammeyer, Virigina Maughan 102–3, 169, 242
Keeler, J. J. 55
Kelsey, Mae Feinauer xi
Kenney, Susan Clark 23
Kimball, Maud Belnap 163–64, 242
Kimball, Spencer W. 14, 42, 61, 121, 184, 225
Kirk, Diane 24
Kirkell, Miriam H. 170
Kirkpatrick, William 73
Kjar, Margorie Casteton 126–24, 185, 196–94, 206, 242
Kleinman, Bertha A. 202
Kodaly, Zoltan 145

INDEX A

L

Lamb, Charles 191
Lamb, Mary 191
LaMontaine, John 68
Lawler, Jeanne P. 105–6, 110, 112, 162, 205–6
LeeMaster, Vernon J. 164
Lehenbauer, Ruth Benson 130
Leonard, Amy viii
Likes, L. Claire 144
Liszt, Franz 213
Lloyd, Sylvia Knight 60, 81, 108
Lowden, C. Harold 147
Luch, Phyllis 31, 41, 46, 65, 99, 162
Luke, Jemima 81
Lundberg, Joy Saunders 48
Luther, Martin 72, 212
Lyon, A. Laurence xiv, 61, 62, 79–80, 99–100, 150–51, 173–74

M

M. E. P. 147
MacDowell, Edward 213–14, 221
Maeser, Georgia 200
Major, Marian 161
Malin, Annie Pinnock 215
Mangum, Marzelle 194
Mann, Margaret 127, 137
Manookin, Robert P. 55, 108, 122, 209
Matthews, Daphne 118
Maughan, Patricia Critchlow 169, 193
Maxwell, Neal A. 177
McAllister, John Daniel Thompson 171–73, 184
McConochie, Barbara 127–28, 210–11
McKay, David O. 15, 123, 202
McKellar, Hugh D. 230
McMaster, Clara Watkins 60, 127, 134, 136–37, 148, 177–78
McNees, Mildred E. Millett 209
Mendelssohn, Felix 50–51, 104, 212, 217–19
Meredith, Joleen Grant 182
Metz, Lois Lunt 190
Millard, William Joseph viii
Miller, Gertrude Stayner viii
Miller, Helen Mar Cheney viii, 4
Milne, Jaclyn Thomas 114, 150
Miner, Caroline Eyring 154
Moesinger, Suzanne Sessions 23
Moody, Michael Finlinson 23, 65, 70, 74–75, 78, 106, 149, 209
Mozart, Wolfgang Amadeus 137–38, 214, 220–21
Murray, James R. 80

N

Newell, Charlene Anderson 69–70, 87, 116, 208
Newell, Mark 70
Nibley, Reid N. xiv, 44, 125
Nicola, Randy 24, 37
Nielsen, Patricia Haglund 76, 158–59

O

Oaks, Dallin H. 84, 165
Obray, Barbara Boyer 201

Ogelvee, Louise M. 63
Okazaki, Chieko 197
Olauson, Maggie 64
Olsen, Rita Mae 188–89
Oman, Susan Staker 20
Ovard, John xiii
Ozment, Maurine Benson 195–96, 207

P

Pace, Cynthia Lord 120–21
Packer, Boyd K. vii
Parker, Judith Wirthlin 15, 52
Parker, W. H. 81
Parmley, LaVerne L. 2, 12, 14, 15, 16, 47, 129–30, 142, 170, 173
Payne, I. Reed 69
Pearson, Carol Lynn xiv, 124–25
Perry, Janice Kapp 48, 49, 50, 95–96, 106, 133, 145–46, 154, 163
Petersen, Faye Glover 135, 184
Peterson, DeVota Mifflin 153
Pettit, Mildred Tanner 15, 41, 43, 63–64, 181
Pheatt, Fanny Giralda 184
Phelps, William Wines 3, 117
Pinborough, Jan Underwood 73–74
Pingree, Carmen 125
Pinnock, Hugh 30
Pitcher, Gladys 155
Plato xi
Poorman, Nellie 178
Provost, Della Dalby 173

R

Rack, Mary Louise Oglevee 63
Randall, Naomi Ward 15, 41, 42, 43, 129–30
Randolph, Richard 173
Read, Dorothy Little 134
Reading, Lucile Cardon 88, 171–73
Remsen, F. 57
Renstrom, K. Moiselle 10, 56, 59, 82–84, 131, 157–59, 181–82, 185–87, 190, 199–200, 204
Reynolds, Becky-Lee Hill 57, 162
Richards, LeGrand 67, 70, 74, 86, 91, 109, 156
Richards, Rhoda H. viii, 4
Riley, James Whitcomb 57, 168
Robertson, Leroy J. 68, 156, 166
Robinson, James Henry viii
Robinson, Rita S. 87–88, 157
Robinson, Sarah Richards viii
Rodgers, Ralph, Jr. 92–93
Rogers, Aurelia Spencer vii-ix, 16, 4–6, 193
Rogers, George viii
Rohlfing, Laurel Parker 23
Romney, Marion G. 40
Rorem, Ned 68
Rowley, Greitje Terburg 23, 46, 47, 66–68, 143, 198–99, 203–4, 207, 212, 214, 221
Ryser, Thelma Johnson 89
Ryskamp, Peggy Hill 51

INDEX A

S

Sargent, Virginia 32, 177
Schreiner, Alexander 55, 58–59, 68, 82, 99–100, 175–76, 179–80
Schubert, Franz 178–79, 212–13, 217–18
Schubring, Julius 50
Scott, Louise B. 201–3
Scott, Richard G. xiv
Seeley, Gladys Ericksen 91
Shakespeare, William 178, 212, 217–18
Shipp, Trudy Swenson 23
Shumway, Naomi Maxfield 2, 16–18, 119
Shurtleff, Lynn R. 169
Sleeth, Natalie W. 150
Smith, Emma Hale 3, 117
Smith, Joseph F. 7
Smith, Joseph Fielding 15, 138
Smith, Joseph, Jr. 102, 115–16, 119, 121
Smith, Norma B. 123–24
Smyth, A. C. 135
Snow, Eliza Roxey viii, 3–8
Snow, Lorenzo 7
Sorensen, Nonie Nelson 161
Sorenson, Michael 153
Spencer, Bessie Saunders 69
Spencer, Beverly Searle 182
Sprunt, Lois Coombs 193–94
Steed, Sharon 127
Stevens, Mayre Beth 22, 23
Stevens, Rebecca 192
Stevenson, Robert Louis 53
Stewart, Debbie 139
Stewart, Leone Rogers viii, ix

Stewart, Linda Call 23
Stratton, Beth Groberg 51
Stravinsky, Igor 41

T

Talbot, Nellie 83
Taylor, Daniel 198
Taylor, Elizabeth Cushing 107
Taylor, John 4, 7
Taylor, Frances K. 108–9, 165–66
Tchaikovsky, Peter Ilich 212, 215
Thayne, Mirla Greenwood 98
Thomas, Norma Madsen 201
Thurman, Stan 24, 32
Tudor, Tasha 31
Turkle, Brinton 31
Turner, Nancy Byrd 68
Twitchell, Royce Campbell 86
Tyler, Walter G. 146–47

W

Watkins, Vanja Yorgason 24, 28, 47–48, 51, 54–55, 62, 88–91, 93–94, 104, 119–21, 127, 134, 136, 138, 140–41, 144–45, 148, 152–53, 170–71, 177, 188–89
Watters, Lorrain E. 161
Welling, Job viii
Weston, Rebecca 46
Wheelwright, Lorin F. 84–85, 164
White, Marilyn Curtis 69
Whittaker, Beth Maryon 20, 31, 42, 139, 168
Wilton, Arthur 198
Winder, Barbara 114

INDEX A

Wirthlin, Joseph B. 15, 52
Wolford, Darwin 24, 41–45,
　51, 64, 68, 73–74, 84–85,
　96–97, 127–28, 132–33,
　148–49, 160, 209, 212,
　214–15, 219–20
Wood, Anne Aylett 23
Wood, Lucille F. 201–3
Woodruff, Wilford 7

Woodworth, Samuel 117
Woolley, Rachel 139
Woolsey, Maryhale 57, 162
Wordsworth, William 14
Wright, Ruth Broadbent 24

Y

Young, Dwan 2, 17, 18, 22, 24,
　130, 142, 170

Index B

Alphabetical Song Titles

A

A Child's Prayer 49
A Happy Family 161
A Happy Helper 160
A Prayer 56
A Prayer Song 55
A Smile Is Like the Sunshine 201
A Song of Thanks 53
A Special Gift Is Kindness 128
A Young Man Prepared 143
Air from Orpheus 222
All Things Bright and Beautiful 182
Andante 220
An Angel Came to Joseph Smith 100
Autumn Day 191
Away in a Manger 74

B

Baptism 110
Beautiful Savior 85
Beauty Everywhere 183
Because God Loves Me 184
Because It's Spring 187
Before I Take the Sacrament 92
Be Happy! 201
Birds in the Tree 187
Book of Mormon Stories 119

C

Called to Serve 148
Can a Little Child like Me? 47
Children All Over the World 52
Choose the Right Way 138
Christmas Bells 81
Come with Me to Primary 196
Covered Wagons 175

D

Daddy's Homecoming 168
Dare to Do Right 137
Dearest Mother, I Love You 166
Did Jesus Really Live Again? 87
Distant Bells 224
Do As I'm Doing 208

E

Each Sunday Morning 217
Easter Hosanna 89
Every Star Is Different 127

F

Faith 108
Falling Snow 192
Families Can Be Together Forever 154
Family History—I Am Doing It 106
Family Night 158

INDEX B

Family Prayer 155
Father, I Will Reverent Be 63
Fathers 167
Father Up Above 57
Father We Thank Thee for the Night 46
Follow the Prophet 116
For Health and Strength 54
For Thy Bounteous Blessings 54
Friends Are Fun 199
Fun to Do 195

G

"Give," Said the Little Stream 185
God's Daily Care 231
God's Love 108
God Is Watching Over All 180
Go the Second Mile 144
Grandmother 163

H

Had I Been a Child 97
Happy, Happy Birthday 212
Happy Song 200
Have a Very Happy Birthday! 212
Have a Very Merry Christmas! 79
Head, Shoulders, Knees and Toes 207
Healthy, Wealthy, and Wise 210
Heavenly Father, Now I Pray 53
Heavenly Father, While I Pray 57
Hello, Friends! 195
Hello Song 198
Help Me, Dear Father 110
Help Us, O God, to Understand 93
Here We Are Together 199
He Died That We Might Live Again 88

He Sent His Son 66
Hinges 208
Home 157
Hosanna 88
How Dear to God Are Little Children 151
How Will They Know? 152
Hum Your Favorite Hymn 133

I

I'll Walk with You 126
I'm Glad to Pay a Tithing 132
I'm Thankful to Be Me 48
I'm Trying to Be Like Jesus 97
If with all Your Hearts 51
If You're Happy, 201
Impromptu 215
In Our Lovely Deseret 232
In Quietude 217
In the Leafy Treetops 187
It's Autumntime 191
I Am a Child of God 41
I Am Glad for Many Things 132
I Am Like a Star 140
I Believe in Being Honest 131
I Feel My Savior's Love 93
I Have a Family Tree 162
I Have Two Ears 203
I Have Two Little Hands 205
I Hope They Call Me on a Mission 145
I Know My Father Lives 44
I Like My Birthdays 112
I Lived in Heaven 43
I Love to Pray 59
I Love to See the Temple 107
I Need My Heavenly Father 52
I Often Go Walking 164

INDEX B

I Pledge Myself to Love the Right 138
I Pray in Faith 50
I Thank Thee, Dear Father 46
I Think the World Is Glorious 181
I Think When I Read that Sweet Story 82
I Want to Be a Missionary Now 144
I Want to Be Reverent 62
I Want to Give the Lord My Tenth 132
I Want to Live the Gospel 130
I Wiggle 204
I Will Be Valiant 139
I Will Follow God's Plan for Me 142
I Will Try to Be Reverent 63

J

Jesus Has Risen 90
Jesus Is Our Loving Friend 83
Jesus Loved the Little Children 84
Jesus Once Was a Little Child 81
Jesus Said Love Everyone 85
Jesus Wants Me for a Sunbeam 84

K

Keep the Commandments 129
Kindness Begins with Me 128

L

Latter-day Prophets 122
Lift Up Your Voice and Sing 194

Listen, Listen 114
Little Jesus 71
Little Lambs so White and Fair 83
Little Pioneer Children 171
Little Purple Pansies 190
Little Seeds Lie Fast Asleep 189
Love Is Spoken Here 156
Love One Another 124
Loving Shepherd 218

M

Mary's Lullaby 74
Morning Prayer 219
Mother, I Love You 167
Mother, Tell Me the Story 165
Mother Dear 166
My Country 176
My Dad 169
My Flag, My Flag 177
My Hands 205
My Heart Ever Faithful 219
My Heavenly Father Loves Me 179
My Mother Dear 165

N

Nephi's Courage 120

O

Oh, How We Love to Stand 209
Oh, Hush Thee, My Baby 77
Oh, What Do You Do in the Summertime? 190
Once There Was a Snowman 192
Once Within a Lowly Stable 73
On a Golden Springtime 103
Our Bishop 123
Our Chapel Is a Sacred Place 64
Our Door Is Always Open 196
Our Primary Colors 198

INDEX B

O Rest in the Lord 221

P

Picture a Christmas 78
Pioneer Children Sang As They Walked, 170
Pioneer Children Were Quick to Obey 171
Popcorn Popping 188
Prelude In F 223

Q

Quickly I'll Obey 160

R

Rain Is Falling All Around 188
Remember the Sabbath Day 135
Repentance 109
Reverence 61
Reverence Is Love 65
Reverently, Quietly 60
Roll Your Hands 206

S

Samuel Tells of the Baby Jesus 68
Saturday 159
Search, Ponder and Pray 115
Seek the Lord Early 114
Shine On 128
Sing a Song 195
Sing Your Way Home 157
Sleep, Little Jesus 76
Smiles 201
Springtime Is Coming 186
Stand for the Right 137
Stand Up 209
Stars Were Gleaming 69
Supplication 223

T

Teacher, Do You Love Me? 150
Teach Me to Walk in the Light 149
Tell Me, Dear Lord 149
Tell Me the Stories of Jesus 82
Thanks to Our Father 53
Thanks to Thee 45
Thank Thee, Father 58
Thank Thee for Everything 47
There Was Starlight on the Hillside 71
The Articles of Faith 120
The Books in the Book of Mormon 119
The Books in the New Testament 118
The Books in the Old Testament 118
The Chapel Doors 136
The Church of Jesus Christ 96
The Commandments 117
The Dearest Names 167
The Family 158
The Golden Plates 102
The Handcart Song 174
The Hearts of the Children, 105
The Holy Ghost 113
The Light Divine 233
The Lord Gave Me a Temple 134
The Nativity Song 80
The Oxcart 173
The Priesthood Is Restored 104
The Prophet Said to Plant a Garden 186
The Sacrament 91
The Sacred Grove 103
The Shepherd's Carol 72

INDEX B

The Still, Small Voice 113
The Things I Do 146
The Wise Man and the Foolish Man 210
The Word of Wisdom 134
The World Is So Big 184
The World Is So Lovely 184
This Is God's House 63
This Is My Beloved Son 95
To a Wild Rose 216
To Be a Pioneer 172
To Get Quiet 207
To Think about Jesus 90
Truth from Elijah 105
Two Happy Feet 204
Two Little Eyes, 202

W

We'll Bring the World His Truth 147
We're All Together Again 198
Westward Ho! 172

We Are Different 199
We Are Reverent 61
We Bow Our Heads 58
We Welcome You 196
Whenever I Think about Pioneers 175
When Grandpa Comes 164
When He Comes Again 99
When I Am Baptized 112
When I Go to Church 136
When Jesus Christ Was Baptized 111
When Joseph Went to Bethlehem 70
When We're Helping 162
Where Love Is 125
Who Is the Child? 75

Y

You've Had a Birthday 213
Your Happy Birthday 211

Bibliography

In addition to personal experiences and interviews, I have used the following sources:

Cannon, Virginia B. *Our Children's Songs: Teaching the Gospel with the Children's Songbook.* Salt Lake City: Deseret Book, 1992.
Children's Songbook. Salt Lake City: The Church of Jesus Christ of Latter-day Saints, 1995.
Davidson, Karen Lynn. *Our Latter-day Hymns: The Stories and the Messages.* Salt Lake City: Deseret Book, 1988.
Deseret Sunday School Songs. Salt Lake City: Deseret Book, 1909.
Ensign. Salt Lake City: The Church of Jesus Christ of Latter-day Saints.
Friend. Salt Lake City: The Church of Jesus Christ of Latter-day Saints.
Graham, Patricia Kelsey. *A Children's Songbook Companion.* Salt Lake City: Aspen Books, 1994; now published Springville, UT: Cedar Fort, 2005.
Hess, Margaret Steed. *My Farmington: A History of Farmington, Utah, 1847–1976.* Farmington, UT: Helen Mar Miller Camp, 1976.
Kavanaugh, Patrick. *The Spiritual Lives of Great Composers.* Nashville, TN: Sparrow Press, 1992.
Kenney, Scott G., ed. *Wilford Woodruff's Journal, 1833–1898 Typescript.* Midvale, UT: Signature Books, 1984.
LDS Church News, section of *Deseret Morning News.* Salt Lake City: Deseret News Publishing Co.
Madsen, Carol Cornwall, and Susan Staker Oman. *Sisters and Little Saints: One Hundred Years of Primary.* Salt Lake City: Deseret Book, 1979.
Montgomery, June and Maurice Hinson. *Stories of the Great Composers: Short Session on the Lives and Music of the Great Composers with*

BIBLIOGRAPHY

Imaginary Stories Based on Fact. Van Nuys, CA: Alfred Publishing Co., Inc., 2000.

Perry, Janice Kapp. *Songs From My Heart: The Stories Behind the Songs.* Sandy, UT: Sounds of Zion, 2000.

Peterson, Janet and LaRene Gaunt. *The Children's Friends: Primary Presidents and Their Lives of Service.* Salt Lake City: Deseret Book, 1996.

Rogers, Aurelia S. *Life Sketches of Orson Spencer and Others, and History of Primary Work.* Salt Lake City: Geo. Q. Cannon & Sons Company, 1898. Reprinted 1978 for the 100th birthday celebration of Primary. Family Press, Andrew Locy Rogers Family Organization.

Smith, Jane Stuart and Betty Carlson. *The Gift of Music, Great Composers and Their Influence.* Wheaton, Illinois: Good News Publishers, 1995.

The Hymn. Hymn Society of America, vol. 40 no. 4, 38: 1989.

Whitcomb, James Riley. *Complete Poetical Works of James Whitcomb Riley.* Peattie, New York: Garden City Publishing Co., Inc., 1941.

About the Author

Pat Kelsey Graham loves children, music, and the gospel. She studied education, music, and commercial art, earning a bachelor's degree from Brigham Young University and a master's of education from the University of Utah. Experience as a music teacher in the Church, at the University of Utah, and as a piano teacher since 1962 helped prepare her for the assignment as chairman of the *Children's Songbook* committee. Sister Graham composed five songs included in the *Children's Songbook*: "I Am Like a Star," "Picture a Christmas," "The Nativity Song," "The Hearts of the Children," and "We Are Different."

In 1980, she was called to the Primary general board and was asked to create a monthly sharing time page for the *Friend* magazine, which she wrote until her release in 1988. Her other published works include *Sing Out!, Sing Out About Families, Helping Children Compose, The Power of Music,* and *A Children's Songbook Companion.*

With her husband, G. Robert Graham, she served a welfare mission to the Detroit, Michigan area. They are the parents of six wonderful children and twenty-two grandchildren who call her "Grandma Music."

Additional stories about the songs would be welcomed and considered for future printings. Please email grandmamusic@juno.com.